THE KHARIAS

THE KHARIAS

SARAT C. ROY
&
RAMESH C. ROY

GYAN

Published by

Gyan Publishing House
5, Ansari Road
Daryaganj, New Delhi-110002
Phone: 011-47034999, 9811692060
E-mail: books@gyanbooks.com

Distribution Network
gyanbooks.com
India, USA, Canada, UK, Australia

ISBN: 978-93-7225-518-8 (HB)

First Published, 1937

2nd Impression 2025

Printed at: Gyan Press, Delhi.

THE KHARIAS

Author: SARAT C. ROY & RAMESH C. ROY

THE KHĀṚIĀS

Map of the Kharia Country. (*The Kharia area is shaded.*)

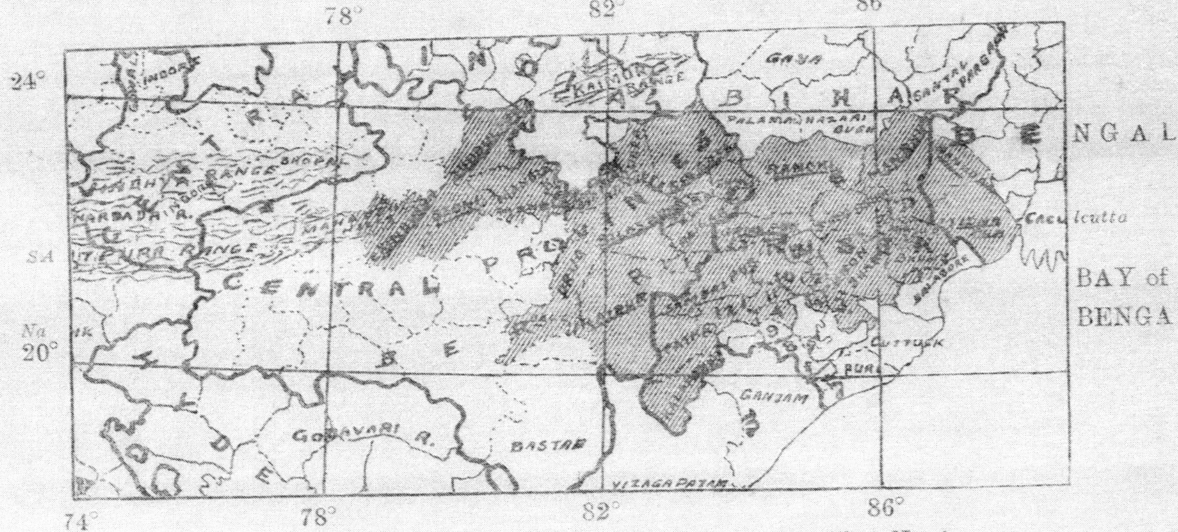

Index to the Map:—1. Nilgiri. 2. Pal-Lahara. 3. Ḍhenkenal. 4. Aṭhmalik 5. Narsingpur. 6. Nayāgaṛh. 7. Ranpur. 8. Daspālla. 9. Baud. 10. Bāmṛā. 11. Rairakhol. 12. Sonepur. 13. Bonai. 14. Talcher.

THE KHĀRIĀS.

By

Sarat Chandra Roy, M. A.

Honorary Member, Folk-Lore Society, London; Foundation Fellow of the National Institute of Sciences of India; Editor, "Man in India"; Author of "The Orāons of Chotā Nāgpūr"; "The Mūndās and Their Country;" and other works.

and

Ramesh Chandra Roy, M. Sc.

With numerous illustrations and a Map;

&

A Foreword

By

Dr. R. R. Marett, M. A., D. Sc., LL. D., F. B. A.

Rector, Exeter College, Oxford; Author of "The Threshold of Religion", "Faith, Hope, and Charity", "Sacraments of Simple Folk", "Anthropology", "Tylor", etc., etc.

"*Man in India*" Office, Ranchi.

1937.

Special Acknowledgements.

We desire to acknowledge our debt of gratitude to Maharaja Sir Pratap Chandra Bhañja Deo, K. C I. E, of Mayurbhañj and his former Dewan Dr. P. K. Sen, Bar-at-law, and to Khan Bahadur A. G. Khan and Mr. H. D. Christian, the then Superintendents respectively of the Jashpur and the Gangpur States, for affording us kind hospitality and requisite facilities for research among the Khāṛiās of their respective States. We also owe our thanks to various officers of those States, particularly to Mr. P. Achārya, Archæological officer of the Mayurbhañj State, for their kind services during our tours in those States. Our thanks are also due to Mr. H. Chakravarti, Manager of the Dhalbhūm Estate, for similar kind help.

S. C. Roy.

R. C. Roy.

Preface.

The present work is the outcome of twelve years' study of the life and customs of the Khāṛiā tribe. During the latter part of this period my son Ramesh Chandra Roy was associated with me in the investigations.

The Khāṛiā tribe, in their three divisions, is spread over such a wide area that local variations of the customs recorded in this volume necessarily occur. As the Dūdh section of the tribe has its stronghold in the Rāñchi District of Chōṭā-Nāgpur, the Ḍhelki section in the Jāshpur State of the Central Provinces, and the Hill or Pāhāṛi section in the Mayurbhañj State of Ōṛissā, we have taken the customs and institutions of the three sections of the tribe in those three areas respectively as the standard, and described them with comparative fullness, noting only certain important variations among the Khāṛiās settled elsewhere. The three sections of the tribe represent three successive levels of primitive culture, and thus furnish fruitful material to the beginner in the study of social anthropology for a comparative study and clear comprehension of the earlier stages in the evolution of human culture. Such studies might advantageously precede the study of text-books dealing with the principles of social Anthropology.

My most grateful thanks are due to Dr. R. R. Marett, one of the greatest living authorities in Anthropology, for the illuminating Foreword that he has so kindly written for this work. I desire to take this opportunity of expressing my cordial thanks to our numerous Khāṛiā friends who most readily helped us in our investigations. Although the number of our Khāṛiā informants have been too numerous to mention individually special indebtedness to the Rev. Samuel Bāgē—a Khāṛiā Protestant Missionary, and three Khāṛiā teachers, Babus Pātrās Ḍūngḍūng, Nuas Kerkeṭṭā and Ignace Soreng, and to Babu Prem Prakas Kerkeṭṭā—a College student, for supplying us with certain items of information and throwing light on a few doubtful points of interpretation. To the Rev. Father Marcus Ṭeṭeṭehoiñ, so far the only Khāṛiā Catholic Missionary, we are indebted for the Khāṛiā names of some medicinal roots and herbs and the method of using them. To the Rev. Father L. Cardon, S. J., and the Rev. Father H. Gallagher, S. J., who have lived and worked among the Khāṛiās for several years, we are indebted not only for kindly showing us their short notes (published for private circulation among Catholic Missionaries) regarding certain customs of the Dūdh and Ḍhelki Khāṛiās respectively, but also for helpful discussions regarding certain items of Khāṛiā custom and belief. Finally, our grateful thanks are due to Prof. P.C. Mahalanobis, M.A. (Cantab), I.E.S., of the Presidency College, Calcutta, for the trouble he kindly took in helping my son Ramesh Chandra Roy, in the calculation of the anthropometric data and generally helping him in his anthropometric analysis.

The system of transliteration of Indian names and words followed in this work has been the same as that used in my book entitled "*Orāon Religion and Customs*", and explained in the Preface to that work.

Ranchi (India) S. C. Roy.

CONTENTS.

Foreword by Dr. R. R. Marett... vii

Chap. I. Habitat and Population... ... 1

Chap. II. Origin and Migrations... ... 21

Chap. III. Previous Accounts of the Khāṛiās... 49

Chap. IV. Physical Anthropology of the Khāṛiās...57

Chap. V. Material Culture... 70

Chap. VI. Social Organisation... 116

Chap. VII. Tribal Government... 163

Chap. VIII. Birth, Childhood and Puberty Rites...198

Chap. IX. Marriage, Pregnancy and Divorce... 223

Chap. X. Death and its Attendant Ceremonies...282

Chap. XI. Religious Beliefs; Deities and Spirits...307

Chap. XII. Religious Feasts and Festivals... 333

Chap. XIII. Magic and Witchcraft... ... 387

Chap. XIV. Folklore and Myths, Amusements and Games... 414

Chap. XV. Khāṛiā Art, Dances and Songs... 473

Chap. XVI. Conclusion: General View of Khāṛiā Life and Manners... ... 512

Appendix I. Physical Measurements... ... i

" II. Averages of " " xxx

" III. Local Distribution of Clans... xxxii

" IV. Source of Hill Khāṛiā Origin-myth... xxxvi

FOREWORD

By

R. R. MARETT, M. A., D. Sc. (Oxon.),
LL. D., F. B. A.

There is a saying that 'the world knows little of its greatest men', and I am inclined to apply it to the case of Mr. Roy and India. Nay, I dare say that in this country too his books, printed as they are in India, are not often seen in the windows of our booksellers; though over here few of my anthropological brethren, to do them justice, would seem to be unfamiliar with his writings. But, as regards India, I have a strong suspicion that there still prevails a general lack of interest among the cultured classes in respect to the diversified customs of their ancient land, teeming as it is with folk who have worked out the problem of life for themselves in a thousand different patterns, all alike worthy of intensive study on the part of one who would understand the laws of human life in order to improve it. Now I doubt if there is any part of the world that can compete with India in the sheer number of those who are anxious to frame a philosophy of life, and to do their best to live up to it. Quite rightly, however, they associate this philosophy as intimately as possible with their religion; for, since philosophy and religion are in common concerned with ultimate questions, this is undoubtedly the attitude of mind most likely to unify and harmonize the sadly distracted energies and aspirations of the human spirit.

But, if on the whole of inferior status, science, as the study of the actual conditions that have hitherto attended and in some sense determined the development of all life, and of our own life in particular, deserves its fair share of attention from the seeker after the highest and most comprehensive truth. Idealism makes sickly food unless a pinch of realism be added by way of salt. Just as a healthy soul involves a healthy body, so the quest of spiritual good entails a reasonable acquaintance with the art of retaining our precarious hold on the surface of this planet. As earth-bound creatures we owe it to our higher selves not to neglect those lower things which happen to be essential to our continued existence. Nor is it simply a matter of keeping on good terms with matter. As members of society we condition one another from without no less than, so far as real sympathy is established, we can do so from within. Hence history and such historical disciplines as sociology and social psychology can well afford to aim at an objective treatment analogous to, if distinct from, the empiricism of the physical sciences. Before spiritual contact can be made between one people and another, they must have come to realize in a more or less disinterested manner the nature of the differences that keep them apart. An engineer would be a fool if he tried to throw a bridge across a river without having previously explored the further bank. Thus, though I believe that Kipling's jingle about East being East and West West involves no more than a half-truth, the most well-meaning efforts of Europe to promote a mutual understanding of our several needs, so that we may the more usefully give and take, must have little result unless India is willing to take an equal hand in the game. And it must begin with acquiring an adequate self-knowledge. At present, I think, we at this end know our Europe for all the good and the bad that it contains far better than the educated Indian knows his India; nor indeed does he often know his own part of India as thoroughly as objective methods would help him very easily to do.

Now it would be an impertinence were I to touch on those difficulties caused by caste which may be partly responsible for that slight air of self-righteousness with which some of my Indian students—though by no means all—are wont to profess entire ignorance of the habits of certain of their more backward folk, almost as if the latter belonged to another order of Nature. But this at least may be said for science that it recognizes no taboos. For the pure man of science all things are pure. Unfortunately the 'man in the street' —who is to be found wherever there are streets, and often too where there are none—indulges in his 'colour-prejudice' and what not, and thus accentuates those superficial peculiarities that form the chief excuse for all kinds of sectional selfishness. I can testify that in my own case anthropology has convinced me, once for all, of the utter narrowness of such an outlook. May I then venture to recommend to India—and I speak more especially to young India, with which I am in closest touch—to master and to help forward the anthropological study of their own country? Again and again I have noted in the examination papers of some Indian student a real gift for the subject; though sometimes one cannot but suspect that he is exploiting that gift for what profit it may yield at the moment. I would, then, that Mr. Roy might convert a host—I observe with pleasure that he has converted his son—to follow in his footsteps; for this way, I am sure, lies not only present enlightenment but the future moral welfare of India.

By way of postscript I might perhaps be allowed to make a few suggestions, directly arising out of my experience as a teacher of Anthropology, that may serve to guide a beginner through the veritable jungle with which the student of primitive life is faced—a prospect so alarming that too often he withdraws in cowardly despair. Such trouble, I think, comes from starting from the wrong end of the subject, and filling the head with long words and sweeping theories derived from text-books of the epitomizing type. But anthropology is a science that thrives on induction—in other words, proceeds from the particular to the general, and throughout adapts its architecture to the nature of its material. I recommend, then, that by way of a start our student should read some monograph—or, better still, several of them, so that he should be led to draw comparisons on his own account—wherein is set forth what I might call the biography of some social group of simple habits in all its wealth of detail. Moreover, for the Indian student—since, like charity, anthropology should begin at home—I recommend that he acquaint himself with some of the simple folk who dwell near at hand. In and about Chōṭā-Nāgpur, for instance, he will find plenty of suitable specimens, with the additional advantage that Mr. Roy will be at his elbow to show him exactly how such facts need to be treated.

Now there are technical matters, such as the anthropometry or the linguistics, that provide tough meat calling for a matured power of digestion; but this objection does not apply to most of the social anthropology, which consequently can be assimilated by any mind that comes to it with that appetite for fresh experience which so often deserts a sophisticated palate. After all, there is an elemental quality in the simple life that ought to appeal to the young, more especially if we believe with the psychologists that a certain recapitulation of rudimentary tendencies is implicit in mental development. Let it be noted, too, that the simple life ought to be, and, as Mr. Roy proves, can be, described in simple language; all that parade of terminological grandiloquence being singularly inappropriate in regard to peoples possessed of no more than a vocabulary expressive of their very limited outlook. Science at its best is the enemy of all cant, and what it asks of its devotee is only that he should try to be objective in his attitude towards nature, including human nature—that, as it were, he should forget himself in the object. This principle applied to the empirical study of Man means that, above all else, it is necessary to seek to put oneself in the other fellow's place.

Translated, then, into terms of method, the principle in question bids us begin by forming a picture of the habitat, and of its demands on folk who for the most part depend on it directly, and, owing to the feebleness of their arts, are not in a position to modify it greatly; but, on the contrary, are largely at the mercy of a Nature untamed and correspondingly harsh.

outside the little world of the Khāṛiās, we have a sharp economic contrast as between the hillmen who mostly depend on hunting and the gathering of the spontaneous produce of the jungle ; the Ḍhelkis, who, though on the right side of the line that divides the food-raiser from the mere food-collector, are still addicted to the wasteful method of *jhūm* cultivation ; and, finally, the Dūdh section of the population who understand terracing, and, in general, have a better command over their food-supply. Here, then, are all the makings of an intensive study of human ecology within a single and manageable area.

Passing from environmental control to social orgaiza-tion, we need not be accused of overdoing the economic interpretation of history if we detect a close correlation between the conditions of the food-quest and the forms of social grouping respectively associated therewith. A demographic survey will immediately reveal differences in sheer density of population that cannot fail to affect the degree of co-operation possible in each set of circumstances. Thus we find every grade of social cohesion from the collectivism of a rude family system to a nascent individualism involving distinctions of rank—one that, however, does not interfere with intermarriage and freedom of intercourse. At the same time there develops a centralized authority, so that the community through its acknowledged representatives has a far better chance of holding its own in the face of all those modern tendencies that threaten to rob the lesser peoples of that individuality which is their birthright and the source of their spiritual strength.

This last consideration leads us on to the subject of the moral life which it must be the supreme task of

Social Anthropology to endeavour to view as it were from the inside. But a primitive community does not 'wear its heart on its sleeve'. It is comparatively easy to provide it with an exterior history; but, however thorough and replete with statistics, this can never suffice as a true account until supplemented with a portrayal, as intimate as it can be made, of the 'soul' of the people concerned. Needless to say, one must be able to commune with them in their own tongue, and must have acquired the social tact that will alone persuade them to impart the 'lore'—the songs, proverbs and so forth—that is the key to their inner life.

It is, however, needless to explain to an inhabitant of India that the final clue to the whole character of a people is provided by the religion,-a term, however, that must be understood in a liberal sense, so as to include a great deal that, to an educated mind, might seem to verge on superstition or even magic. Here let the student start from exterior facts open to direct observation, such as the whole system of rites, both occasional and periodic, and especially from the latter which will yield a complete guide to the 'calendar customs', or, as one may call it, the religious year. Then comes the more delicate task of interpreting all this ritual, one that needs not only knowledge of the language, but sympathy and an open mind; for a very crude symbolism will often be found to co-exist with feelings, thoughts and actions worthy of admiration as a credit to our common humanity.

So much, then, for what I deem to be the only fruitful method of that insight into human conduct and character which Social Anthropology is able to bestow on every friend of mankind, and I am sure that Mr. Roy's work is a model of how such research should be conducted. So my advice to India is, briefly, this: LEARN TO KNOW THYSELF.

Exeter College, Oxford. } R. R. Marett.

THE KHĀṚIĀS

CHAPTER I.

HABITAT AND POPULATION.

(i) *Habitat.*

The succession of hill-ranges in the Ōṛissā Feudatory States and Chōṭā Nāgpur, rolls back towards Central India. In various parts on the tops and slopes and at the foot of these hills and in the valleys between them and on the plateaux formed by them, different aboriginal tribes have their home. Of these tribes the Khāṛiās are one of the most interesting and widely scattered.

Local Distribution.

There is a considerable but fluctuating immigrant Khāṛiā population in Assam and its neighbouring Bengal District of Jalpāiguṛi. Offshoots of the tribe strayed generations ago into the highlands of the Bānkuṛā District in West Bengal and the southern borders of the Bengal District of Midnāpore, and became Hinduized. The principal habitat of the Khāṛiās, however, extends from the central hill-ranges of the Mayurbhanj State of Ōṛissā in the south-east and the hills of Singbhūm and Manbhūm districts to the north of Mayurbhanj, through the hills and plateaux of the Rānchi District now in Bihār and the Sambalpur District in Ōṛissa, and fourteen out of the twenty-four Feudatory States of Ōṛissā and the adjoining Central Provinces States of Jāshpur, Udaipur, Rāigaṛh, Sakti and Sarangaṛh in the middle, to as far west as the Bilāspur, Rāipur, Drug and Chhindwārā Districts of the Central Provinces.

Natural features.

This wide area forms part of the "Central Belt" of India, and lies roughly between 20° and 23° North Latitude and 79° and 87° East Longitude. In the extreme east of this belt dwell the Erengā or Hill Khāṛiās, in the middle the Dūdh Khāṛiās, and in the west the Ḍelki or Ḍhelki Khāṛiās with a sprinkling of Dūdh Khāṛiās . Roughly speaking, this extensive habitat of the Khāṛiās presents the appearance of an ill-shapen uneven trough flanked on the east by the Simlipāl hill-ranges of Mayurbhanj and the Dalmā range of Manbhūm which rise to an elevation of about 3,000 feet above the sea-level and on the west by the plateau formed by the Sātpurā Hills in the Chhindwārā District of the Central Provinces at an elevation of more than 2,000 feet above the level of the sea, and with its lowest depression nearer the western end in the plains districts of Bilāspur and Drūg than in the middle. With the exception of these comparatively low-lying plains areas, the Khāṛiā country consists mainly of a rugged mass of wooded hills and comparatively open elevated plateaux intersected by hill-streams and interspersed here and there with comparatively fertile river-valleys .

Habitat of the Hill Kharias.

The Hill Khāṛiās have their stronghold in the wildest parts of this area, in the Simlipāl range of the Mayurbhanj State, and have spread further to the north in the hills of the Singbhūm (Dhalbhūm Parganā) and Mānbhūm Districts of Chōṭa Nāgpur. Scattered offshoots of this branch of the Khāṛiās have strayed further to the east and north-east into the adjoining areas of the Midnāpore and Bānkuṛā Districts of Bengal, and south and south-west into the adjoining Ōṛissā Feudatory States of Nilgiri on the south, and

1. A Hill Khāṛiā's hut and his *jhūm* cultivation

2. Hill Khāṛiās before their hut.

(To face p. 2)

Mayurbhanj, Keoñjhar, Bonāi, Pāl Lahara and Dhenkānāl on the west and south-west. Of the hill-ranges which afford shelter to the Hill Khāṛiās, the Simlipāl Range in Mayurbhanj rises to an elevation of from 2,013 to 3,823 feet[1] and the Dalmā range, which forms part of the boundary between the Singbhūm and the Mānbhūm Districts, rises to 3,407 feet . On the tops and slopes and at the feet of these hills as also on and about some smaller hill-ranges of the Dhalbhūm Parganā of the Singbhūm District and the Barābhūm Parganā of the Mānbhūm District and the hills of the Feudatory States of Ōṛissā named above, the Hill Khāṛiās lead a hand-to-mouth existence by collecting honey and silk-cocoon, lac and some other jungle produce, by gathering edible herbs and wild fruits and digging out edible yams and tubers with their primitive digging-sticks and rude hoes called *khantās*, and occasionally by hunting deer or some smaller game. Shifting agriculture by the wasteful process variously known as *Dāhi* or *Kōmān* or *Jhūm*, which they used to practise up till recently, is now being mostly stopped by the State authorities in Mayurbhanj and a few other States and by the Zemindars in British Districts. Some Hill Khāṛiā families have recently been induced to come down from the hills and take to plough cultivation .

Climate. The climate in Mayurbhanj is more or less humid but in Dhalbhūm and Mānbhūm and in most of the Ōṛissā Feudatory States inhabited by the Khāṛiās it is dry. In summer the heat in the lower

1. The various peaks of the Simlipal Range are Meghasani, 3824 feet; Simlipal peak, 2559 feet; Gurguria, 2013 feet; Khijuri, 2414 feet; Chahal, 2521 feet; Makabir, 2604 feet; Bhangbura 2576 feet; and Barakamra, 2726 feet.

levels is fairly intense, the temperature sometimes rising as high as 110° or more but in the higher ranges the temperature is somewhat cooler. The winter months are fairly cold and invigorating on these hills. But the hill-tracts are more or less malarious, particularly in the rainy season and in autumn and in the earlier part of the cold weather.

Fauna. The tiger, the leopard, the panther, and the bear roam in the bigger forests of the Hill-Khāṛiā country. The *Sambar* deer (*Cervus unicolor*), though now getting rare, haunt the high and inaccessible hills, and the spotted deer roam in small herds in low-lying lands near some pools or streams. The wild pig, the wild dog, the jackal, the monkey and the squirrel haunt the forests. The pea-fowl and jungle-fowls of various kinds are met with in the jungle areas. Elephants are numerous in the Simlipāl hills of Mayurbhanj and in a few of the other Feudatory States of Ōṛissā.

Flora. The *Śāl* or *Śakhua* (*Shorea robusta*) and the *Mahuā* (*Bassia latifolia*) are the most important trees of this region. Clumps of old *śāl* trees serve as the sacred groves or temples of the Khāṛiās; *śāl* wood is used for building and repairing their houses and cattle-sheds and for fencings and enclosures and for making agricultural and other implements; *śāl* branches and twigs are used for fuel; *śāl* flowers are needed for their religious worship and festivals; and *śāl* leaves are utilised for making cups and platters. The yellow flowers of the *mahuā* (*Bassia latifolia*) are used as an important article of food and also for the manufacture of a kind of spirituous liquor. The *Karam* (*Nauclea Cordifolia*) tree,

3. Hill Khāṛiā Type (front)

4. Profile of 3.

(To face p. 4)

besides its use for the rearing of lac, is also valued for its ceremonial uses. The *Simli* (*Bombax Malabaricum*) or the cotton tree which gives its name to the Similipāl Hills attains in the hills to a large size. Among the creepers of his native jungles the one which is valued most by the Khāṛiā is the *Chihor* or *Gungu* (*Bauhinia scandens*), of which the leaves are used by him for manufacturing rude umbrellas and rain-hats and water-proof capes and also cups and flat platters, the fibrous bark is used by him in making into strings and ropes and the pods are fried and the seeds eaten. In the uplands of parganās Dhalbhūm (in the Singbhūm district) and Barābhūm (in the Mānbhum District) lac-bearing *Kusum* (*Schleichera trijuga*) and the *Palās* (*Butea frondosa*) are indigenous. Among the fruit-bearing trees of these jungles, the *Bair* (*Zizyphus jujuba*), the *Āorā* (*Phyllanthus emlica*), the *Piār* (*Buchania latifolia*), and the *Bael* (*Aegle marmelos*) may be mentioned.

The Dudh Kharia Country.

Leaving the Hill Khāṛiā country on the east of the "Central Belt" and crossing over to the Rānchi plateaux we come to the main centre of the Dūdh Khāṛiā section. Their stronghold lies along both sides of the rivers Sankh and South-Koel in the Gūmlā and Simdegā Sub-Divisions of the Rānchi District and extends further south to the Gāngpur State in the Central Provinces along the valleys of the Sankh and the Ib, with an overflow still further south along the valley of the Ib to that part of the District of Sambalpur in Ōṛissā which lies to the west of the river Mahānadī.

The Dhelki Kharia—Country.

In the Gāngpur State of Ōṛissa as we proceed along the valley of the Ib further north-west towards the Jāshpur State of the Central Provinces, we find the proportion of Ḍelki or Ḍhelki Khāṛiās to Dūdh Khāṛiās increasing till in the north-western Thānā of Talserā in Gāngpur, the Ḍhelkis are found to predominate. Passing over into the Jāshpur State of the Central Provinces we find that out of 64 villages which the Khāṛiās inhabit, only in three villages there are a few families of Dūdh Khāṛiās (namely, 8 families consisting of 39 members in village Baluabāhār, 6 families consisting of 30 members in village Sigjore and one family of 3 members only in village Kansābel). All the Khāṛiās of the remaining 62 villages, numbering 429 families and 2,864 individuals, belong to the Ḍelki or Ḍhelki branch.

Natural feature of the habitat of the Dudh and Dhelki Kharias.

In the western Feudatory States of Ōṛissā, namely, Bāmra, Riārkhōl, Sōnepur, Āṭhmalik, Paṭnā, and Kālāhāṇḍi,—as in the British Districts of Sambalpur—we find both Dūdh Khāṛiās and Ḍhelki Khāṛiās with a sprinkling of Hill Khāṛiās who are generally known in those parts as Erengā-Khāṛiās. Except the open parts of the valleys of the Sankh and of the Koel, much of the Dūdh Khāṛiā area in the Rānchi District is partly covered with jungles intersected by ranges of hills. Of the hills of the Biru Parganā of the Rānchi district, which is the principal centre of the Dūdh Khāṛiās, the highest peaks are Bhounr Pāhāṛ (2,492 feet) and the isolated peak of Ālu Pāhāṛ (2,172 feet) in the valley of the Sankh. The elevation of the valleys of the Sankh and the Ib in the Gāngpur

5. Hill Khāṛiā type

6. Hill Khāṛiās going to jungle.

(To face p. 6)

State and the Sambalpur District where Dūdh Khāṛiās and Ḍhelki Khāṛiās live together, and also that of the Heṭhghāṭ or lowland areas of the Jāshpur State (mostly in thānā Tapkarā) which are inhabited by the Ḍhelki Khāṛiās, is only 700 feet above the sea level and thus about a thousand feet lower than the Dūdh Khāṛiā area of the Rānchi District. These tracts are more or less open and are only dotted here and there with hill ranges and isolated peaks, some of which rise to a height of over 2,000 feet above sea-level. The tree-clad hills and mountain ranges of the Ōṛissā Feudatory States form three watersheds, towering one above the other, and running from south to north with fine valleys in between and magnificently wooded hill-ranges with peaks from 2,500 to over 3,500 feet high, culminating in Malaygiri, 3,895 feet high, in the Pāl Laharā State. Down these watersheds pour the three great rivers of the inner tablelands, namely, the Mahānadī in the south and south-west, the Brāhmaṇī in the middle, and the Baitaraṇī in the east and north-east. From the eastern bank of the Baitaraṇī rise the lofty hill-ranges of Mayurbhanj. The physical aspects of the Khāṛiā areas in the Surguja and Udaipur States and the plateau districts of Seoni and Chhindwārā in the Central Provinces bear a general resemblance to those of the Gāngpur and Sambalpur areas of Ōṛissā. The districts of Bilāspur and Drūg which lie in the Chhatisgaṛh Plains Division form a land-locked plains-area which is more flat and has a lower level than the other Khāṛiā areas but are bounded on every side by more or less rugged country. The parts of the Rāipur district where some Khāṛiās are found lie beyond the confines of the Plains and are very wild and broken.

Fauna and Flora. The fauna and flora of these areas inhabited by the Dūdh and Ḍhelki Khaṛiās bear a general resemblance to those of the Hill Khāṛiā country. But in some Dūdh Khāṛiā and Ḍhelki Khāṛiā villages, particularly in the Rānchi District, groves are planted, and round the village sites the jackfruit (*Autocarpus integrifolia*), the *Pipal* (*Ficus riligiosa*), the *Jamūn* (*Eugenia jambolana*), the *Karanj* (*Pongamia glabra*), and the *Tetar* (*Tamarindua indica*) trees are generally met with. Elephants are found in a few only of the Khāṛiā areas, such as in the Gāngpur and Jāshpur States. Other wild animals and birds that we meet with in the hills and jungles of the Hill Khāṛiā country are also mostly found in the land of the Dūdh and Ḍhelki Khāṛiās as well.

Climate. The climate of the habitat of the Dūdh and Ḍhelki Khāṛiās may be said to be generally healthy. The period from August to November is ordinarily the season for malaria in the jungly parts of the country. The cold is temperate, but on the higher levels comparatively more severe, while in the hot weather the heat is at times trying, particularly on the lower levels. In the rains the heat is much less intense, though on the lower levels the dampness of the atmosphere is rather discomforting.

(ii) *Social Environment.*

The culture of the Khāṛiās, as of other peoples, is influenced to some extent not only by their natural environment but also more or less by their human environment. Even the Hill Khāṛiās, who are most shy and conservative and keep themselves as much aloof as

7. Type of Hill Khāṛiā Woman (Front and Profile)

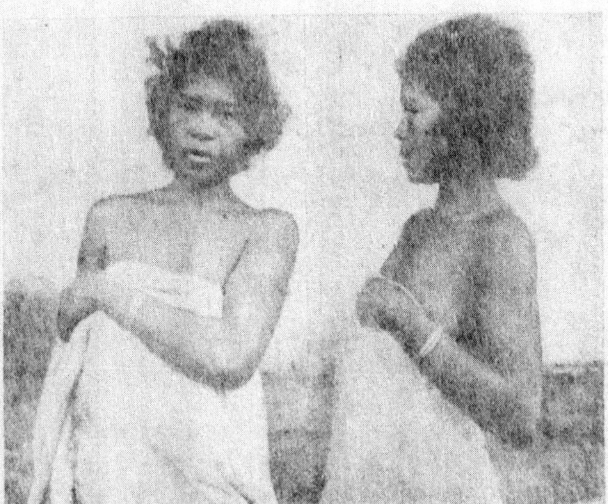

8. Another Hill Khāṛiā Woman (Front and Profile)

(To face p. 8)

they can from contact with other tribes and castes, have not altogether escaped the influence of their neighbours of other culture. The fact that they have adopted the speech of their Hindu neighbours is evidence of their intimate contact with the Hindus for a considerably long period in the past. Among their present-day neighbours, the Hill Khāṛiās have, on and below the Mayurbhanj hills, such tribes as the Bāthuḍi (probably a backward branch of the Bhūiyās), the Hō (called *Kōl* in these States), the Sāntāl, the Hindu or Hinduised caste of Gouṛs or Ahīrs (milkmen and cattle-herds), Tāṅtis (weavers), Kumhārs (potters) and Kāmārs (black-smiths),—all on a somewhat higher level of culture than themselves. In Singbhūm (Dhalbhūm parganā) and Mānbhūm (Barābhūm parganā) too, they have for their neighbours such tribes as the animistic Sāntāls and Hōs, the Hinduised Bhūmij, the Kūṛmi, the Goālā, the Kūmhār and the Lohār, all on a higher level of culture than the Hill Khāṛiā, and all more or less influenced by Hindu ideas. The Hinduizing influence of the Mayurbhanj Rāj, which prohibits cow-killing within the State, also reaches the remotest corners of the State. In spite of their aloofness and exclusive habits, their contacts with their neighbours of other castes and tribes are not infrequent nor negligible.

As for the Dūdh Khāṛiās and the Ḍhelki Khāṛiās, who live in settled villages, they have for their neighbours various Hindu castes, from Brāhmaṇs and Chhatris down to the lowest castes of Ghāsis and Chāmārs, besides aboriginal tribes such as the Mūṇḍās and the Orāons,—with all of whom they come in daily contact. Even in the past the Dūdh Khāṛiās, at any rate, must have come under the influence of Hindu ideas as is evidenced by the taboo on cow-killing and beef-eating observed by at least one section of them known as the *Bargohoñṛi* or the 'higher section'. Their religious ideas, too, have to a small extent been influenced by popular Hinduism. A number of local Hindi words in Chōṭā Nāgpur and the Central Provinces, and Ōṛiyā words in Sambalpur and the Ōṛissā Feudatory States, have been adopted in the Khāṛiā vocabulary. Even certain relationship-terms for which the Khāṛiās have no distinctive terms in their native tongue (except only general classificatory nomenclature) have been adopted from their Hindu neighbours. The Hill Khāṛiās have even lost their own language and adopted the language of their dominant neighbours, namely, Bengali in Mānbhūm and Singbhūm and Ōṛiyā in Mayurbhanj. In this and other ways their neighbours have slowly influenced, more or less, the speech and thought, ideas and customs of the Khāṛiās.

Influence of Christian Missions.

Besides the influence of neighbouring aboriginal tribes and Hindu castes, the European Christian Missionary has also, within the last fifty years, affected the culture of the Dūdh and Ḍhelki sections of the Khāṛiās to some extent. Out of the 146,037 Khāṛiās in Chōṭā Nāgpur and Ōṛissā, as many as 63,725 now profess Christianity. In the neighbouring C.P. State of Jashpur only 335 Khāṛiās out of a total Khāṛiā population of 4,148 have accepted Christianity. Christian influence has indirectly affected even non-Christian Khāṛiās in some respects, although to a very small extent. It was principally their economic troubles and the oppression and persecution of their Hindu landlords and money-lenders that drove the bulk of these Khāṛiā

9. Hill Khāṛiā Couple.

10. A Hill Khāṛiā Type.

(To face p. 10)

converts to the Christian fold. A few families accepted Christianity to protect themselves from the persecution of their fellow-tribesmen who suspected them of witchcraft and sorcery. Under European Christian influence there has been among the converts an appreciable improvement in cleanliness in their persons and clothes and in their houses and surroundings. The Christian Co-operative Banks and other institutions have to some extent stimulated a spirit of thrift in them. Under Christian influence, too, they have now come to disregard the old tribal taboos on such useful occupations as weaving, pottery-making and smith's work. In general, the Christian Missions have given an impetus to the intellectual and industrial progress of the people through the spread of education. At the same time, however, the spread of Christianity has introduced a certain amount of complexity and artificiality in the Khāṛiā convert's life, and tended to destroy the old tribal solidarity and to impair the old exuberance of spirits and enjoyment of life among their youth. "In place of natural flowers their young women now deck their hair with gay ribbons ; in place of their old home-spun *sāṛis* embroidered with patterns of flowers and leaves in coloured thread many of their women now dress themselves in slim white or coloured *sāṛis* of either Indian or foreign mill manufacture, particularly on Sundays and feast days, and blouses and chemises of European style". [2] The Christian Missions have, however, infused new hopes in them and given them a better appreciation of their rights as men and as

2. S. C. Roy in the *Journal of the Bihar & Orissa Research Society*, Vol XVII, p. 387.

tenants and a somewhat wider outlook on life, and have enabled them to improve socially, economically and intellectually. In some instances, however, the life of the converts has become more complex and artificial and somewhat out of touch with their non-Christian tribe-fellows. Their native simplicity, zest in life, and love of Nature would appear to have been impaired to some extent. There is also a tendency to develop a superiority complex. But the introduction of new economic, intellectual and religious interests by the Missions has provided a compensating stimulus to make up in part for the loss of their old primitive simplicity and exuberance of spirits. Christian Missions among the Khāṛiās have indirectly affected the non-Christians as well. "A desire for improving their material condition through education and remedying their social evils has been stimulated among non-Christian aboriginals by the example of their Christian fellows. Associations and societies of their own have been started by non-Christian aborigines to discuss ways and means and to raise funds and adopt other measures to improve the economic and social condition of their communities. The old faith in spirits has been considerably shaken and the religious reform movements that are now and again started amongst them appear also to have been stimulated partly by contact with Christian ideas". It may be noted that the non-Christian Khāṛiās of the Rānchi District have joined with their Christian brethren in starting a "Khāṛia Improvement Society" to devise ways and means for their social uplift. [3]

3. Ibid Vol. XVII, pp. 387-388

11. Dhelki Khāṛiās before their hut.

12. A Ḍhelki Khāṛiā group.

(To face p. 12)

(iii) *Population.*

In the Census of 1931, the Khāṛiā population in Oṛissā and Chōṭā-Nāgpur was returned as 1,46,037 and in the Central Provinces as 13,266. No separate figures for the large population of Khāṛiā immigrants in Assam and the small Khāṛiā population in Bengal could be obtained because "in the interests of economy they were not sorted for separately on this occasion", as we were informed by the Census authorities. In the Census of 1921, the non-Christian Khāṛiās in Assam numbered 14,257 of whom 11,840 were returned as speaking the Khāṛiā language. Besides these, the Christian Khāṛiās of Assam who were included within the large Indian Christian population of 44,259 in the Assam Valley Division, must have included a large proportion of the Khāṛiā population of Assam.[4] And in 1931, the Khāṛiā population in Assam may be presumed to have been larger or, at any rate, not smaller than in 1921, for the annual emigration of aboriginals from Chōṭā-Nāgpur to Assam has been larger in the last few years than in previous years, as is only natural on account of the present economic distress. If to the Census figures for the Khāṛiās in Chōṭa-Nāgpur and the Central Provinces we add 20,000 as the approximate Khāṛiā population in Assam and Bengal, (on the basis of the Census of 1921), the total Khāṛiā population in India will come up to

4 *Census of India*, 1921, Vol. III. Assam Pt. II. Tables. pp. 101-& 63 The author of the wild *Kharias of Dhalbhum* appears to be mistaken in his statement that the total Kharia population in Assam in 1921 was 14,257 (*The Wild Kharias of Dhalbhum*, p. I). He is also mistaken in thinking that the Kharia speakers of the Central Provinces are confined to the Raigarh and Jashpur States. (*Ibid.*)

1,79,303 (one lakh seventy-nine thousand three hundred and three), or, in round numbers, to one lakh and eighty-thousand.

It is unfortunate that the population of each of the three sections of the tribe was not separately enumerated at the last or any previous Census. But there can be no question that the Dūdh Khāṛiās far out-number the Ḍhelki Khāṛiās and the Pāhāri Khāṛiās together. Almost all the Khāṛiā population of the Rānchi District, numbering 75,083 at the last Census, belong to the Dūdh section and so do the majority of the Khāṛiās in the Gangpur State numbering 36,656. The Hill Khāṛiās are found almost entirely in the Mayurbhanj State and in a few other Feudatory States of Ōṛissā and in the Singbhūm and Mānbhūm Districts of Chōṭā-Nāgpur, besides a negligible number in the Bānkuṛā and Midnāpore Districts of Bengal. The Khāṛiā population of the Mayurbhanj State numbers 11,573, that of the Singbhūm District 5,879, and of the Mānbhūm District 4,398, thus making a total of 21,850. Besides these the small Khāṛiā population of the Nilgiri state numbering 89, Keōñjhar numbering 347, Bonāi 227, Tālchar 87, Dheñkānāl 1,049, are mostly Hill Khāṛiās. The Khāṛiā population of the Jāshpur State of the Central Provinces, numbering 3,806, almost wholly consists of Ḍhelki Khāṛiās and so does a fairly large proportion of the rest of the Khāṛiā population of the Central Provinces. The following table will show the respective population of the Khāṛiās in the different British Districts and Feudatory States of Bihār and Ōṛissā and the Central Provinces in 1931 :—

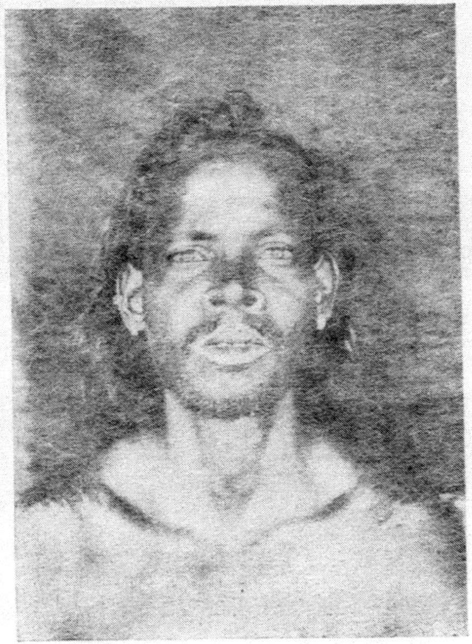

13. Dhelki Khāṛiā Type.

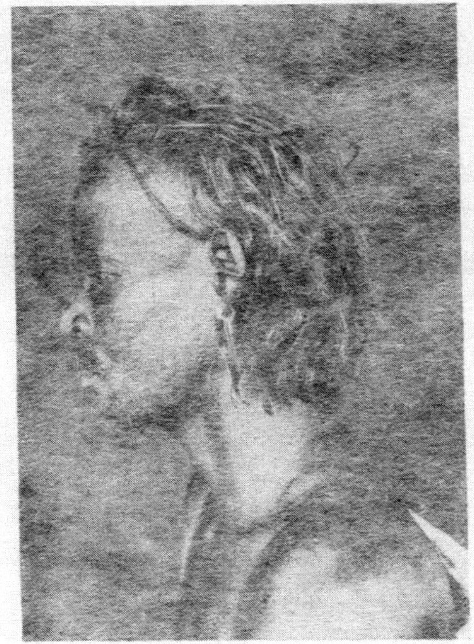

14. Profile of 13

(To face p. 14)

Chōtā-Nāgpur. (85,360).

Rānchi District—75,083 (Males 37,200; Females 37,883)
Mānbhūm „ — 4,398 (M. 2,310; F. 2,088)
Singbhūm „ — 5,879 (M. 3,144; F. 2,735)

Orissa. (51,806).

Sambalpur „ — 1,884 (Males 894; Females 990)
Mayurbhanj State —11,573 (M. 5,732; F. 5,841)
Gāngpur „ —36,656 (M. 17,966; F. 18,690)
Dhenkānāl „ — 1,349 (M. 601; F. 748)
Bāmṛā „ — 1,996 (M. 978; F. 1,018)
Other States — 1,793 (M. 924; F. 869)

Central Provinces. (13,266).

Jubbalpur District— 1 (Male).
Seoni „ — 3 (M. 2; Females 1)
Chhindwārā „ — 648 (M. 307; F. 341)
Rāipur „ — 1,026 (M. 522; F. 504)
Bilaspur „ — 1,444 (M. 687; F. 757)
Drug „ — 124 (M. 54; F. 70)
Jashpur State — 4,148 (M. 2,046; F. 2,102)
Sakti „ — 109 (M. 60; F. 49)
Raigarh „ — 4,192 (M. 2,011; F. 2,181)
Sarangarh „ — 856 (M. 374; F. 482)
Surguja „ — 241 (M. 122; F. 119)
Udaipur „ — 471 (M. 231; F. 240)
Korea „ — 3 (M. 1; F. 2)

Kharia Population by Religion

Of this total of 1,59,303 Khaṛiās in Chōṭā-Nāgpur and Ōṛissā and the Central Provinces, 78,794 are males and 80,608 are females. As many as 64,060 have been recorded as Christians, 63,907 as Hindus, and only 31,336 as adhering to their tribal religion. In this connection it should be noted that Census records of the religion of the aboriginal tribes as Hindus are to be taken with a large grain of salt. The delimitation between Animists and Hindus in many cases depends on the idiosyncracies of individual Census enumerators, and the indifference or ignorance of the unconverted aborigines. Most aborigines who themselves claim to be Hindus are essentially 'animists', and Christianity, in most cases, still supplies only a thin veneer over deep-seated 'animistic' ideas, beliefs and practices.

Variation in Population.

The Khāṛiā population in Chōṭā-Nāgpur and Ōṛissā was 1,02,071 in 1901,-133,657 in 1911,-1,24,531 in 1921, and 1,46,037 in 1931. In the Central Provinces, the Khāṛiā population was 13,266 in 1931, but for previous Censuses, exact figures are not available. In Russel's *Tribes and Castes of the Central Provinces* [5] the total Khāṛiā population in the Central Provinces in the year 1911 is given as "about 900 persons". But this is obviously either a misprint for "about 9000" or a gross under-estimate. Russel appears to have been under the wrong impression that the Khāṛiās in the Central Provinces exclusively "belonged to the Bilaspur District and the Jashpur and Raigarh States". [6] If he had looked into Table X (Language) of the Central Provinces Census for the year 1911, he would have found that as many as 8,238 persons were returned as speaking the Khāṛiā language; and these Khāṛiā-speakers were found in Districts Rāipur and Bilāspur,

5. Vol. III, p. 445
6. *Ibid*

15. Dhelki Woman suckling her babe in front of her hut.

16. Dhelki Women husking and winnowing rice.

(To face p. 16)

and in six Feudatory States, viz., Sakti, Rāigaṛh, Saran-gaṛh, Surgūjā, Udaipur, and Jāshpur.[7] And it must be remembered that there were in all probability then, as there are now, a number of Khāṛiās no longer speaking the Khāṛia language. Similarly, in the Census of 1921, although the Khāṛiās were not included in Table XIII (*Caste, Tribe*, and *Race*), the number of Khāṛiā speakers in the Central Provinces is returned as only 5,926, distributed among the five Feudatory States of Sakti, Raigaṛh, Sarangaṛh, Udaipur and Jāshpur.[8] It is not understood why the moderately large population of Khāṛiās speaking their native tongue in the Bilāspur District, if not elsewhere, in the Central Provinces were not shown as such in 1921.

(iv) *Linguistic and Racial Affinities.*

According to Sir George Grierson the Khāṛiā language is a branch of the Mūṇḍā languages which, together with certain other languages, form the "Austro-Asiatic sub-family" of the great "Austric family" of languages, the other sub-family being the "Austronesian." Of the Mūṇḍā languages, according to Grierson, Kherwāri is the principal language and has eleven principal dialects, namely, (i) Santāli, (ii) Mūṇḍāri, (iii) Hō, (iv) Bhūmij, (v) Kōṛwā, (vi) Bīrhaṛ (or Bīrhōṛ), (vii) Agāriā, (viii) Asūri, (ix) Birjiā, (x) Tūrī, and (xi) Kōḍā, besides some unspecified dialect or dialects. Five other languages besides Kherwāri are included in the Mūṇḍā family.

7. *Census of India*, 1911, Vol. X, Central Provinces and Berar, Part II. *Tables*. p. 81

8. *Census of India*. 1921 Vol. XI, Central Provinces and Berar, Part 11. *Tables* p. 89.

These are :–(1) Kōṛkū, (2) Khāṛiā, (3) Juāng, (4) Savara and (5) Gadava. The Kōṛwā language, spoken principally in the Jāshpur and Surgūjā States of the Central Provinces is said to connect Kherwāri with the remaining Mūṇḍā languages. The Kōṛwā language is more closely related to the Kuṛku language of the Koṛku tribe of the Mahadeo Hills of the Central Provinces. Kuṛku, in its turn, is found to agree in important points with the Khāṛiā language of Chōṭā Nāgpur and the Central Provinces and with the Juāng language of the Kēoñjhar and Pāl Laharā States of Ōṛissā; and Khāṛiā leads over to Savara and Gadava in the Ōṛiyā districts of Vizāgāpaṭam and Ganjām in the north-east of the Madras Presidency.

All these kindred Mūṇḍā languages, according to Grierson, as said above, form branches of a sub-family called by him the Austro-Asiatic, which includes Nicobarese besides the Mūṇḍā languages and Mon or Talaing, Palaung-Wa, Khāsi, Khmer and the languages spoken by the Sakai and the Semang. The other sub-family of the Austric family includes Indonesian, Malagasy (the language of Madagascar), Melanesian, Polynesian and other dialects of the Pacific Islands including Saloñ or Selung of the Mergui Archipelago. It may be noted that the Khāṛiā language is spoken by practically all Khāṛiās of the Rānchi District and the adjoining States of Gāngpur and Jāshpur, and by a number of Khāṛiās in Udaipur, Rāigaṛh, Sarangaṛh and Bilāspur. In Mayurbhanj the Khāṛiās speak a corrupt dialect of Ōṛiyā and in districts Singbhūm, Mānbhūm, Bānkuṛā and Midnāpur they speak a corrupt patois of Bengali. In Surgūjā and some other parts of the Central Provinces,

17. Type of Dūdh Khāṛiā youth.

18. Profile of 17.

(To face p. 18)

most Khāṛiās speak the local Hindi. In other areas the Khāṛiās have, generally speaking, adopted the language of their nearest neighbours, so that in the Ōṛissā Tributary-States, some Khāṛiās speak Orāon, some speak Mūṇḍāri, and some Ōṛiyā.

We have already noted that the Hill Khāṛiās have forgotten their native tongue and speak a corrupt form of Ōṛiyā in the Ōṛissā States and a corrupt Bengali in Singbhūm (Dhalbhūm) and Mānbhūm. The following specimen of a conversation in the Khāṛiā patois of Bengali will show how the Bengali language has been corrupted by its Khāṛiā speakers of Mānbhūm:—

Q. *Tui Kuthi?*—(From what place are you?)
A. *Jhunjka.*—([I am of village] Jhunjka.)
Q. *Kis āinē?*—(What have you brought [for sale to the market]?)
A. *Nā.*—(Lac).
Q. *Katta āinē?*—(How much have you brought?)
A. *Ek ser?*—(One seer.)
Q. *Bandhnā Rab-bārē hithnā-kai?* (Does not the Bandhnā [festival] come off on Sunday?)
A. *Haw.* (Yes.)
Q. *Bandhnā hebak je se din Pāhāṛ pūjā hai nā?*—(Is not Pāhāṛpūjā held on the same day on which the Bandhnā festival is celebrated?)
A. *Nā.*—(No.)

It is interesting to note that this corrupt patois of Bengali is always used by the Singbhūm and Mānbhūm Khāṛiās when they talk among themselves; but when speaking to persons of other castes and tribes they generally use the common Bengali of the locality so far as they can.

The small population of Khāṛiās in the Bankuṛā District also use a corrupt patois of Bengali of which the following specimen is given in Grierson's *Linguistic Survey of India*, vol IV, page 207 :-

Ek nōkar rahinā duiṭi buā. ('One man-of were two sons', i. e., A certain man had two sons).

Dui janar mahā saru buā bunitanā-gayā. ('Two men-of among small son said, i. e., The younger of the two sons said :)

Je mui bhāg pāma mohor hai dē. ('Which I share get mine that give', i. e., Give me my due share.)

Ihālē ōhar bābā bhāg kari dinā. ('Then his father shares having-made gave', i. e., Thereupon his father gave him his share after partition.)

Although language is by itself no test of race, the physical features, the social structure, and certain common religious ideas and usages point to the racial affinity of the Khāṛiās with the other Mūṇḍā-speaking tribes.

19. Dūdh Khāṛiā type.

20. Ḍhelki Khāṛiā type.

(To face p. 20)

CHAPTER II.

Origin and Migrations.

(i) *Divisions of the Tribe*.

Khāṛiās - a branch of the Mūṇḍā stock.

The Khāṛiās have been classed on racial and cultural—particularly linguistic—grounds among the Mūṇḍā group of the aborigines of India. Of this group, still sometimes called the 'Kolarian' group, the Mūṇḍās, the Sāntāls, the Hōs and the Savaras are generally better known than the Khāṛiās and other tribes such as the Gadavas, the Asurs, the Birhōṛs, the Juāngs, the Koṛkus and the Kōṛwās. Though in point of numerical strength the Khāṛiās are inferior to the better-known Mūṇḍā tribes named above, in point of ethnological interest they do not yield to any of those allied tribes.

Point of special interest.

In fact, a special interest would appear to attach to the Khāṛiā tribe. The three distinctive divisions of the tribe, known respectively as the *Pāhāṛi Khāṛiā* or Hill Khāṛiā (sometimes called the *Erengā Khāṛiā* or the Wild Khāṛiā), the Ḍhelki Khāṛiā and the Dūdh Khāṛiā represent different grades of primitive culture. The Hill Khāṛiās are still found mostly in the food-gathering and hunting stage of economic culture, with occasional practice of a rude system of shifting cultivation. Their social system and religious ideas and practices are also about as primitive as their economic life. The next division of the tribe, the Ḍelki or Ḍhelki Khāṛiās, as they are called, though they have long been food-producers and have taken to regular plough cultivation and evolved a more advanced social and religious system than the Hill Khāṛiās, are still in a somewhat lower level of material culture than the Dūdh Khāṛiās. The Dūdh Khāṛiā section of the tribe is in point of culture more progressive than the other sections, and ranks with the Mūṇḍā the Hō and the Santāl among the most advanced of the Mūṇḍā-speaking tribes of India. In physical features, too, the Ḍhelki Khāṛiās stand midway between the Pāhāṛi Khāṛiās with their coarse features and the Dūdh Khāṛiās with their comparatively finer features.

Risley in his *Tribes and Castes of Bengal*, [9] mentions six "sub-castes" of the Khāṛiās, namely, *Bergā Khāṛiā, Ḍhelki Khāṛiā, Dūdh Khāṛiā, Erengā-Khāṛiā, Mūṇḍā-Khāṛiā, Orāon-Khāṛiā*. But his 'Bergā Khāṛiās', 'Mūṇḍā Khāṛiās' and 'Orāon Khāṛiās' may be left out of account as they are not definite and distinctive sections of the tribe. The term 'Bergā' is probably a corruption of the Hindi word 'Bigṛā' meaning 'spoilt' or 'degraded' or 'mongrel,' applied to Khāṛiā families who are believed to have originated in intermixture of a Khāṛiā with a partner of some other tribe or caste, and the names 'Mūṇḍā Khāṛiā' and 'Orāon-Khāṛiā' are applied specifically to families who had their origin in intermixture between Khāṛiās and Muṇḍās, and Khāṛiās and Orāons, respectively. These sections have no distinctive organisations

9 Vol. II, *Appendix*, p. 77

21. Type of Dūdh Khāṛiā woman.

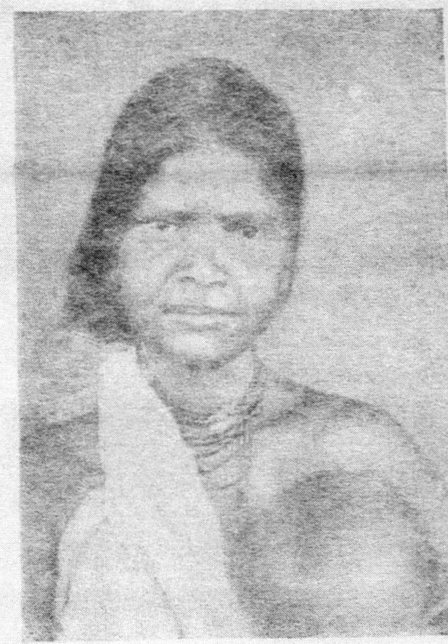

22. Profile of 21

(To face p. 23)

or special cultural characteristics of their own and need not therefore be separately dealt with.

The traditions of the Dūḍh Khāṛāis and the Ḍhelki Khāṛiās still retain memories of the time when they together formed one compact tribe and their migrations from their former home in the Vindhya and Kaimūr ranges to Chōṭā-Nāgpur lay along practically the same route. The Ḍhelki Khāṛiās also recount traditions of their former home in Chōṭā Nāgpur on the banks of rivers Koel and Sankh in what are now the Gūmlā and Simḍegā Sub-divisions of the Rānchi District, and their subsequent displacement by the Dūdh Khāṛiās and migration to the west and south into what are now the adjoining territories of the Jāshpur State of the Central Provinces and the Gāngpur State of Ōṛissā. A large number of Dūdh Khāṛiās, too, migrated southwards to the Gāngpur State and pushed the main body of the Ḍhelki Khāṛiās further north-north-west into the Jāshpur State. The name 'Ḍelki' or 'Ḍhelki' (from the Khāṛiā root 'Ḍel' to come) is said to have been bestowed by the Dūdh Khāṛiās on the 'Ḍhelki' Khāṛiās to denote that the Ḍhelkis preceded them ("*seng ḍelki*", meaning "came first") from their original home. As these later immigrants were more strict in the matter of food, and would neither eat beef nor take cooked rice at the hands of people of other tribes, they, it is said, adopted the name of 'Dūdh Khāṛiās' (i. e., Khāṛiās pure as 'dūdh' or milk) by way of distinction.

It may, however, be noted that the more conservative among the Ḍhelki branch, would deny the name of 'Khāṛiā' to their Dūdh brethren and confine the name to themselves alone as genuine full-blooded Khāṛiās, designating the Dūdh section as *Mūṇḍās*'.

As, however, both the Dūdh and the Ḍhelki sections of the Khāṛiās are now settled agriculturists and have many customs in common we shall give a joint account of their customs and institutions, noting such differences in customs as exist between the two sections. But as the Pāhaṛi or Hill Khāṛiās do not retain any traditions of common descent with either the Ḍhelki or the Dūdh Khāṛiās, and still remain on a distinctly lower stage of culture, we shall give, where necessary, first an account of the life, customs and usages in which this section of the tribe differs from the others. The Hill Khāṛiās may be taken to represent an earlier stage of culture which the Ḍhelki and Dūdh sections have long outgrown.

(ii) *Traditional Origin and Tribal Name.*

As for the origin of the tribal name 'Khāṛiā', nothing can be said for certain. Mr. Russel's collaborator Rai Bahadur Hirālāl suggested its derivation from *Khar-Khar*, a planquin or litter. He stated that in the Ōṛiyā country, Orāons, who carry litters, are also called *Khāṛiās*—a contraction of *Kharkhariā*. This derivation is "in accordance with the tradition of the Khāṛiās that their first ancestors carried a bānghy, and with the fact that the Kols are the best professional *dhooli-bearers*." [10] This derivation appears to be rather far-fetched and not very probable. In Chōṭā Nāgpur which is the principal centre of the Dūdh Khāṛiās, these people hold a fairly

10 *Tribes and Castes of the Central Provinces.* Vol, III, p. 446.

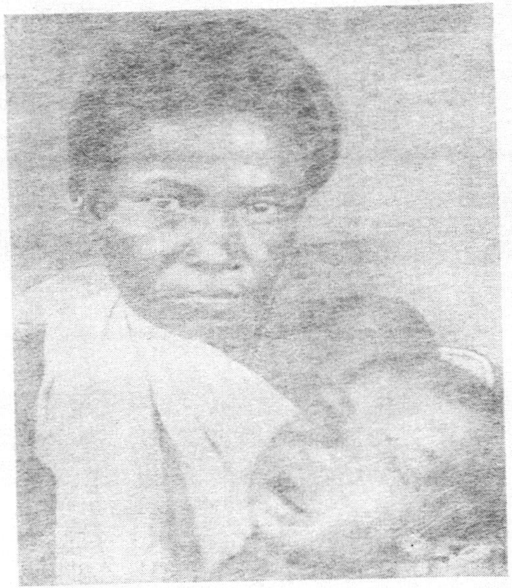

23. Dūdh Khāṛiā Woman with her baby

24. Dūdh Khāṛiā bowing (*johār*) to his superior.

(To face p. 24)

high position and are not generally employed as palanquin-bearers. In Ōṛissā, the Bāuris and the Kōṛās or Kōṛā Matiās have the 'bānghy' (carrying-pole) for their *santak* or emblem but the Khāṛiās of Mayurbhañj have the sword (*khaṇḍā*) for their *santak* or emblem. It appears more probable that the name 'Khāṛiā' is a variant of the tribal names—'Hōṛō' (man) adopted by the Mūṇḍās, 'Hō' or 'Hoṛ' adopted by the Hōs, 'Kōṛ-Ku' adopted by the Kōṛkus or Kurkus, and Kōṛwā' adopted by another branch of the Muṇḍā race. Against this derivation it may be said that in the Khāṛiā language the word for 'man' is not a derivative of the same root from which the words 'Hōṛ', 'Kōṛwā' and 'Kōṛku' are derived. It may, however, be pointed out that although the general Khāṛiā term for man is '*lebu*', yet when 'man' as distinguished from 'woman' (*Konselḍu*) is meant, the Khāṛiā uses the term *Koḍpoṛu.*[11]

As for the original habitat of the Khāṛiās, their division into three main sections, and the past migrations of their different sections, we have to depend only on vague tribal traditions. But so far as the Hill Khāṛiās are concerned even the dubious and obscure light of tradition with regard to their former migrations is lacking. For, their only tradition of origin represents them as autochthones of the Mayurbhañj Hills. The Ḍelki or Ḍhelki Khāṛiās and the Dūdh Khāṛiās possess traditions somewhat more definite, though rather of a general nature, regarding their past wanderings. From these traditions, interpreted in the light of the present distribution of the tribe and other available evidence, we may from a more or less probable conjecture of the

11 G. C. Banerji, *Introduction to the Khāṛiā Language*, p. 24.

alternative courses, one or other of which their former migrations might have taken.

Dalton in his *Ethnology of Bengal* (p. 160, *foot-note*) records the following tradition of origin:—"There is a tradition that the Khāṛiās with another tribe called Purāns were the aborigines of Mohurbhañj, one of the Katak Tributary Mahals. They aver that they and the family of the chief (Bhañj), were all produced from a pea-fowl's egg, the Bhañj from the yoke, the Purāṇs from the white, the Kharias from the shell". The tradition which was recounted to us by several Hill Khāṛiās of

Hill Khāṛiā Tradition of Origin.

the Mayurbhañj State (such as Kāri Charan Dihuri of Kānchhiṇḍā, and Pañchu Dehuri of Kusumbandhā) is as follows :—God created first the sky and the earth and then a pea-fowl. The bird laid an egg. The egg burst. And from the shell of the egg issued the first Khāṛiā, from the white of the egg the first Purāṇa (now a Hinduised caste of Mayurbhañj, probably a section of the Bhūiñyās with whom Risley [12] identifies them), and from the yellow of the egg the ancestor of the ruling Bhañja family of Mayurbhañj. This is said to have happened at a place called Ādipur in the present Pānchpiṛ Subdivision of the State; and the first ancestor of the Khāṛiās is said to have been named Ādi Khāṛiā. It is interesting to note that, according to the tradition of the Mayurbhañj Rāj family, Ādi Singh (Bhañja) was the name of the first Bhañja Rājā of the Mayurbhañj State. [13] Some Hinduised Khāṛiās add that,—of the

12 *The Tribes and Castes of Bengal*, Vol. 11 p. 180.

13 *District Gazetter of the Feudatory State of Orissā.* (1910), p. 239. See also *History of Orissa*, Vol. II by *R. D.* Banerjee, p. 454.

25. A group of Dūdh Khāṛiā Women.

26. Dūdh Khāṛiā Women camping under a tree.

(To face p. 26)

descendants of Ādi Khāṛiā, Gandharb-Khāṛiā settled at Rāirāngpur (present headquarters of the Bāmanghāṭi sub-division of the Mayurbhañj State), Bidu Khāṛiā settled at Lohāgaṛh, Hari Khāṛiā at Haripur-gaṛh, and Bāsu Khāṛiā at Jashipur (formerly known as Dāspur). The Khāṛiās of the Simlipāl Hills, they said, are the descendants of Bāsu Savara. This Bāsu Savara is represented in Hindu traditions as a devotee of the God Srī Krishṇa. The tradition goes that a Brāhmaṇ named Vidyāpati whom Rājā Indra-Dyumna, King of Mālwa, had sent out in search of the God Vishnu or Srī Krishṇa, found Bāsu Savara secretly worshipping the deity in the jungle of Nilāchala (on the site on which the present temple of Jagannātha at Puri stands) in the form of an image made of some blue-stone. This Brāhmaṇa, who won the confidence of Bāsu Savara, became enamoured of the daughter of this Savara and married her. The name *Bāsu* has been since further Āryanized into Visva-Vasu. [14]

Some Khāṛiā families of Mayurbhañj who have acquired the title of *Pāṭa-bandhā* because they possess the privilege of placing a silk cloth (*pāṭa*) over the *Ratha* or wooden car of the God Srīkrishna or Jagannātha on the occasion of the Ratha Yātrā or Car festival celebrated bp the Ruler of Mayurbhañj at this capital, also call themselves Brāhmṇa Khāṛiās. Some have further improved npon this legend. One Kāshinath Pāṭabāndhā of village Darkhuli (a village about 5 miles to the north-west of the capital at Bāripadā) gave the following improved version of the legend: "The first Bhañja Rājā came out of the yolk of the egg of a peahen; from its white came out the ancestor of the

14 *District Gazetter of Puri* p. 97

Purāṇas; from the membrane (*uri*) sprang the ancestor of the Ōrāoñs and from the shell sprang the first ancestor of the Khāṛiās. This is why the Khāṛiās do not kill the pea-fowl nor eat its meat. We Pāṭa-bāndhā Khāṛiās are really Brāhmaṇa Khāṛiās. There are only twenty families of Brāhmaṇa Khāṛiās in the Mayurbhañj State and twenty families in Dhalbhūm." We could not however trace out these Pāṭabāndhā Khāṛiās in Dhalbhūm. It may be mentioned that during the Car Festival (Rath-Yātrā) and the bathing festival (Snān-Yātrā) of the deity Jagar-nātha at Puri, the reputed descendants of Bāsu, the Savara, have still the privilege of touchingthe image and, in fact, they act as the custodians of the Deity and His car for the occasion. These Savaras who are attached to the Puri Temple are called—"*Daitas*". [15] This term 'Daita', it need hardly be noted, is an abbreviation of 'Daitya' which is an appellation applied to certain pre-Āryan inhabitants of India in ancient Sanskrit writings.

It appears likely that in this Khāṛiā tradition of origin from an egg, an ancient origin-myth of the Mūṇḍā stock has been mixed up with later Hindu traditions about Srī Krishṇa and Bāsu Savara and the Bhañja myth of their egg-born first ancestor. The myth about the origin of a tribe from one or more eggs is also found among the allied tribe of the Sāntāls. According to Sāntāl traditions a goose and a gander were the first living beings created by God (*Ṭhākur Jiu*); the goose laid two eggs, out of which were hatched the first human pair who became the progenitors of the Sāntāls. [16]

15 *Puri District Gazetter* (*1929*) p. 120.

16 Dalton, *Ethnology of Bengal*, (1872), p. 209; O'Mally, *District Gazetteer of the Santal Parganas*, p. 117.

The way in which accretions are gradually made to the original nucleus of an ancient tradition will be seen from the following legend given by a man of the Hindu-ised caste of *Purāṇs* named Gāṭeyā Nāyak of village Kādapāni in the Sadar Sub-division of Mayurbhañj. His account was as follows:—

"The semen of Bhagwān (God) fell on earth and it took the form of a pea-fowl's egg. By Bhagwān's command the egg was taken care of by the ancient Hindu Rishi (holy sage) Vaśiṣṭha. In due time ths ancestor of the Bhañja kings issued from the yolk, the ancestor of the Purāṇ tribe from its white, the ancestor of the *Jārā* Savara from the *jāl* or membraneous coating of the egg, and from the shell sprang the ancestor of the Brāhmaṇa Khāṛiās. The present descendants of Jārā Savara [17] are the Brāhmaṇa Khāṛiās, whose descendants have the privilege of placing the silken cloth or net over the sacred car (Ratha) of Jagannātha at the Ratha-Yātrā festival at the capital of Mayurbhañj; and so too are the 'Daitās' or 'Daita-patis' of Puri who take a principal part in the Ratha-Yātrā festival there". It may be noted in this connection that, according to Sir George Grierson, the Khāṛiā dialect is more closely allied to Savara than to any other Mūṇḍā dialect, and bears some similarity to Kuṛku and Juāng. [18]

The legend of the autochthonous origin of the Hill Khāṛiās of Mayurbhañj would thus appear to have been probably developed out of an origin-myth of the Mūṇḍā

17 It may be noted that the Mahābhārata (Book XVI) states that an old wild huntsman of the woods named Jarā, through mistake, shot Vāsudeva or Srikrishṇa to death in the forest.

18 *Linguistic of India* Vol IV., *Mūṇḍā and Draviḍian Languages* page 22.

stock which, owing to its chance similarity with the origin myth of the ruling Bhañj family, has since been embellished and given a local value by this section of the Khāṛiās. This question will be further discussed in Appendix IV, *post.*

Some old Hill Khāṛiās living on the Dhalbhūm hills gave us the names of their first ancestor and ancestress as *Sabbar-Buṛhā* and *Sabbar-Buṛhi.* This would appear to indicate that the Khāṛiās originally formed a branch of the great Savara people. The tradition of the Mayurbhañj Khāṛiās that they are the descendants of Bāsu Savara lends further support to this conjecture. General Cunningham [19] points out that the Mūṇḍā-speaking Sāntāls are called Savaras by their neighbours, the Māl Pāhāṛias, and he concludes a long chapter on the Savaras as follows:—"My conclusion is that, in early times where the name of the Savara is used, it probably covers all the different divisions of the '*Kols*', (that is to say, all the Mūṇḍā tribes as they are now called), who, in early Aryan times, spread far and wide over the Central Hill Belt of India".

In *The Mūṇḍās and their Country* [20] and in Mr. B. C. Mazumdar's book on the *Aborigines of the Highlands of Central India,* [21] the same view has also been adopted. Mr. Tarak Nath Das at p. 23 of his small monograph entitled *The Wild Kharias of Dhalbhum* (Calcutta University, 1931), describes the tribe as—"The Kharias or Chhabbars as they call themselves".

19 *Report of the Archaeological Society of India, Vol. XVII, p. 125* *Ibid* page 139.

20 *Ibid* p. 52 foot-note.

21 pp. 15, 26.

Evidently it did not strike Mr. Das that the name that he heard mispronounced as "Chhabbars" was really "Sabbara" or "Savara".

The Hill Khāṛiās, like the present Savara tribe of Ōṛissā, have at the present day no language of their own but have adopted the language of their neighbours—namely, *Ōṛiyā* in Mayurbhañj and other Ōṛissā States, and *Bengali* in Singhbhūm (Dhalbhūm), Bankurā and Manbhūm. But even these Hill Khāṛiās in Bengali-speaking areas still retain some Ōṛiyā words in their vocabulary, thereby indicating their migration from Oṛissā and supporting the tradition of Mayurbhañj having been their centre of dispersion. Thus, we found such Ōṛiyā words as 'Māipa' for a female 'Niāñ' for fire, 'Peja' for gruel, still used by the Khāṛiās in the Dhalbhūm and Manbhūm hills.

From the facts that the Hill Khāṛiās have forgotten their own language and that their social customs and institutions are far more primitive than those of the other sections of the Khāṛiās, it may be inferred that the former separated from the latter long—long—ago. It must have taken the other sections of the Khāṛiās several long centuries to rise to their present level of culture from the much lower level of primitive culture in which the Hill Khāṛiās are still found. Even if we suppose the Hill Khāṛiās to be a degenerate branch of the Khāṛiās it must have taken a very long time to produce the very wide gulf that now separates two levels of culture.

In one of the legends of origin cited above, Jārā Savara is said to be the ancestor of the Hinduised section of the Hill Khāṛiās who are assigned a part in the ceremonies connected with the Ratha-Yātrā celebrations in Mayurbhañj and who therefore style themselves as Brāhmaṇa Khāṛiās. Now the Savaras of the Ganjām district in Madras are divided into six sections (*Sudda*, *Sannapania*, *Mela*, *Lodoro*, *Jārā*, and *Lombo-Lānjiā* or long-tailed), of which one is *Jārā or Jārā* Savara. [22] Jārā is not given as the name of any of the sections of the Savaras in Bihār or Ōṛissā. (There are, it may be noted, no Savaras in Bengal). Risley, tells us that "the Savaras of Ōṛissā Tributary States are divided into four sub-tribes—*Bendkar*, *Parira*, *Jhāṛuā*, and *Palli*. The name of 'Jhāṛuā' which resembles 'Jārā' means 'pertaining to jungles" (and therefore, presumably, 'wild'). [23] Thurston in his *Castes and Tribes of Southern India* [24] gives the names of the six sub-divisions among the Hill Savaras of Southern India (Ganjam and Vizagapatam districts) as follows;—"*Jati Savara* or *Maliah* (Jungle) *Savara; Arsi, Arisi* (monkey), or *Lombo Lānjiā* (long-tailed); *Luara* or *Muli* (workers in iron); *Kindal* (basket-makers); *Jabu* (lining in the hill country beyond *Kallakota* and *Puttaguja*); and *Kumbi* (potters)." Neither does any section of the Savaras of Bundelkhaṇḍ nor do the Savaras of the United Provinces nor those of the Central Provinces, known as the Chhatisgaṛhi Savaras (*Laṛiā Savara*), nor do the Savaras of Oṛissā appear to possess the name of *Jārā* or some similar name.[25] It is probable

22 *The Ganjam District Manual*, by T. J, Maltby (1918), p. 70.

23 *The Tribe and Castes of Bengal*, Vol. II, p. 243

24 Volume VI p. 301

25 *Tribes and Castes of the Central Provinces*, by Russel 1916 Part II, 504

that *Jārā, Jhāṛuā* and *Jādu* or *Jāṛu* may be variants of the same name. If this be so, it will not be unreasonable to infer that the Hill Khāṛiās who claim to have been intimately associated or connected with the Jārā-Savars may have found their way from their original home in some part of the Central Hill Belt of India by the same route as the Savaras of the Ganjām district, and thus reached the Mayurbhanj hills which became the centre of their subsequent dispersion. The fact that the Hill Khāṛiās have forgotten their tribal tongue and differ widely in their traditions and customs from the main body of the tribe except on some fundamental ideas and beliefs may be accounted for, as we have already suggested, by their separation from the main body of Khāṛiās by a wide intervening territory for a considerably long period.

(iii) *Early Migrations.*

Whereas the Hill Khāṛiās regard themselves as the autochthones of the Mayurbhanj hills, both the Dūdh Khāṛiās and the Ḍhelki Khāṛiās possess traditions of their ancient migrations from the Kaimur Plateau which, at Rōhṭāsgaṛh, rises to an elevation of 1,490 feet above the sea-level. All the elders of the Dūdh Khāṛiās and Ḍhelki Khāṛiās whom we questioned recounted the tradition of their ancestors having once lived in "Ruidās-Paṭnā", and thence come down what they called "Khāṛiā Ghāṭ" to Chōṭā Nāgpur. The Ḍhelki section migrated from their ancient home on the Rohṭās plateau sometime before the Dūdh Khāṛiās, and made settlements along the banks of River Sankh in the south-western parts of the Rānchi district. Tapkarā (now in Parganā Bhōuṅrpāhāṛ, thānā

Kōlēbirā), and Tāmṛā (now in Parganā Biru, thānā Simḍegā) are named among their earliest settlements and principal centres in those days in what is now the Rānchi District. Later the Dūdh Khāṛiās came to the country where the Ḍhelkis had preceded them. These later immigrants, who had developed stricter notions of purity in food, called themselves the Dūdh Khāṛiās (*lit.*, Milk Khāṛiās, probably meaning—Khāṛiās ceremonially clean or pure as milk), and regarded as outcastes the earlier Khāṛiā settlers in the land whom they called *Ḍhelki* (or Ḍella-ki) or *Seng Ḍelki* (lit., he came first). The ground assigned for this "outcasting" is that the Khāṛiās took food cooked by the Mūṇḍās who were already in occupation of the country when the Ḍhelkis arrived there. On being "outcasted", the Ḍhelki Khāṛiās crossed over to the other side of the hills which separate the Simḍegā, Ṭhiṭhāiṭāngar, Kurḍeg and Bolbā thānās of the Rānchi district from the present Feudatory States of Gāngpur and the western part of Jāshpur.

Dūdh Khāṛiā migration-traditions go into greater details. Thus, Māhto (*alias* Suleman) Kerkeṭṭā and some other Dūdh Khāṛiās of Simḍegā, and Rām Induār of Tābādih (*Thānā* Simḍegā) gave us the following version :—"The ancestors of the Dūdh Khāṛiās and the Ḍhelki Khāṛiās lived as one people under their own king in Ruidās-Pātnā.[26] Their Khāṛiā Rājā named Moreng was very rich and had large herds of cattle. He was attacked by an Āhīr Chief and his people, and was

26 *Ruidās* or *Rohidās* is the correct name for Rohṭās or the Rohṭās plateau. Paṭnā is named along with Ruidās probably to indicate the direction (north) in which Ruidās lies. 'Paṭnā', it may also be noted, is a corruption of the Sanskrit term 'Paṭṭan' meaning 'settlement'.

worsted. The Khāṛiā Chief left Ruidās-Paṭnā with his elder sons and followers leaving his wife and younger sons and some tribe-fellows in the old home, because the younger sons were too young to undertake the hardships of the journey. The Gohār Pūjā (Cattle-shed festival) of our tribe is really the propitiation of the spirit of the Ahīr-Āhīrin with whom our ancestors fought at Ruidās-Paṭnā. The Khāṛiā Chief and his sons and followers moved on to this country (Chōṭā-Nāgpur) and settled in Parganā Biru [27] and its neighbourhood (in the south-western part of the present Rānchi District). Later on, when the younger sons of the Khāṛiā Chief became old enough to undertake long journeys, they and their companions too left Ruidās-Paṭnā and passed through the Chōṭā Nāgpur plateau along the valley of the [South] Koel through Pālkōṭ, Basiā, and Kolēbirā to parganā Biru. On the way many families settled down all along the banks of the Koel. Their first halt on the Chōṭā Nāgpur plateau was at a place called Murgu. And one of their main centres and halting-places which tradition remembers is village Pōrā in thānā Basiā. In Parganā Biru they met the Ḍhelki Khāṛiās who had preceded them. As the later immigrants were led by those younger sons of the Khāṛiā Rājā who had been left behind with their mother as sucklings they came to be called "Dūdh" Kharias (*lit.*, Milk-Khāṛiās). Later, at one of their tribal dances, twelve Dūdh Khāṛiā young men eloped with Mūṇḍā girls, and their offspring came to be known as Mūṇḍā Khāṛiās or Penṛāi-Khāṛiās.

27 *Biru* is a Khāṛiā word meaning 'hill'. It is the name of a Parganā or fiscal division in the Simḍegā subdivision of the present Rānchi District.

These latter now live in villages Bhāounr-Pāni, Kilgā and some other places in Simḍegā Thānā, and at Kinderḍegā and a few other villages in Kolebirā Thānā. The Ḍhelki Khāṛiās and Mūṇḍā-Khāṛiās kill cows and oxen and eat beef whereas we Dūdh Khāṛiās do not. Mūṇḍā Khāṛiā girls and women have their arms and chests and sometimes their legs and even feet tattooed as among Mūṇḍā and Orāon women, and the same is the case with the Ḍhelki Khāṛiās, but our (Dūdh Khāṛiā) girls and women have only three short vertical lines [28] (the outer lines terminating in a crook) tattooed on their foreheads but no tattoo marks on the rest of the body."

Some Dūdh Khāṛiā elders, such as Tingul Kerkeṭṭā of Sālḍegā (thānā Simḍegā) and Abhirām *alias* Somā Ḍūngḍūng of village Birkerā in thānā Simḍegā, gave us the following variant of the tradition of the migrations of their ancestors :—"Our ancestors went from Ruidās Patnā to Khāṛiā-ghāṭ, thence to Murgu, thence through some other places whose names I do not remember to Nāgpur (Chōṭā-Nāgpur) where the ancestors of my clan (Ḍūngḍūng) and those of the Kerkeṭṭā clan halted at a place named Kumhāriā and the ancestors of the Kulu clan settled at Patura Kinirkelā, those of Torpa clan at Sālēguṭu and those of the Ba' clan at Banāguṭu, those of Soreng (rock) clan at Barwē,—all in thānā Basiā, and cleared the jungles and settled down in those parts. Others moved on to Barwāḍi in thānā Kolēbirā and settled there. My ancestors leading a pack-bullock loaded with the

28 Among the small Dūdh Khāṛiā population of Jāshpur, the women have three vertical lines on the forehead and three on each temple, and a few have even tattoo-marks on the chests and legs, apparently in imitation of their Ḍhelki sisters.

wealth they had brought with them proceeded further forward on their journey. Arriving at a place now known as Siru Kōn̄ṛēkerā in thānā Kolēbirā the pack-bullock refused to move. My ancestors purchased Siru Kōn̄ṛēkerā with the wealth they had brought with them. Some of the ancestors of the Kerkeṭṭā clan moved on and settled down at Aghormā and at Barwāḍi in thānā Kolēbirā; the ancestors of the Bilūng (Salt) clan settled at Bilūngbirā, those of the Kirō (tiger) clan at Bāgēserā, both in thana Pālkōṭ, and so forth. When their population increased, the descendants of the original Dūdh Khāṛiā settlers dispersed to different places all around. The Ḍhelki Khāṛiās had preceded them into the Biru Parganā where they had cleared jungles and established villages. Our ancestors named these pioneers as 'Ḍhelki' or 'Seng Ḍhelki', that is to say, those who 'came first'. 'Seng' in our language means 'first'. When our ancestors found that these pioneers of the tribe had no scruples in eating at the hands of other castes and tribes, they outcasted them; and as the number of Dūdh Khāṛiās increased, the Ḍhelki Khāṛiās crossed the hills that separate the Biru parganā of the Rānchi District from the Gāngpur and Jāshpur States and settled in those States."

A number of Ḍhelki Khāṛiās of the Gāngpur and Jāshpur States (such as Lalhu Khāṛiā of Jambāhār in Jāshpur, and Bhuṇḍā Khāṛiā of Liploe in Gāngpur) gave us the bare tradition of their former home in Ruidās-Paṭnā, their migration through Khāṛiā-ghāṭ to Biru Parganā in the Rānchi District and the subsequent arrival of the Dūdh Khāṛiās. With regard to the name, 'Ḍelki' or 'Ḍhelki' Khāṛiā', they told us,—"To indicate 'going' the Dūdh Khāṛiās use the word 'Chol', but we use the term 'san'; but both the Dūdh Khāṛiās and ourselves use the word 'Del' meaning 'to come'. But whereas the Dūdh Khāṛiās say "[Ārki] *Ḍellā-ki*" (they went), we Ḍhelki Khāṛiās say 'Ḍelki'; and whereas the Dūdh Khāṛiās say "[Ārki] Cholla-ki" (they come), we say 'sanning'. Hence, the Dūdh Khāṛiās call us *Seng-Ḍelki* (he came first) and, we, in our turn, call them 'Cholkoi-Khāṛiās'. The Cholkoi Khāṛiās, however, call themselves 'Dūdh Khāṛiās' and claim to be 'pure' Khāṛiās, and that is the name by which they are now generally known. They, however, regard us as their elder brothers; and so we are also known as 'Baṛ or Baṛkā Khāṛiās', whereas they are known as the 'Chhōṭ' Khāṛiās". Many Dūdh Khāṛiās agreed in saying that the Ḍhelki Khāṛiās are known as 'Baṛ or Baṛkā - Khāṛiās' and themselves as the 'Chhoṭkā Khāṛiās,' and accounted for this by saying that the former are descendants of the elder brother and the latter of the younger brothers. Dalton [29] also mentions another tradition, which, however, we have not yet come across. That tradition is that "they had come from the south, and that, driven from the country they had originally occupied, they had ascended the valley of the Koel till they found themselves in their present location". Dalton [29] opines that both the traditions, namely migration from the north and immigration into Chōtā Nagpur from the south, may be true. "They may have fallen back south from the Gangetic Provinces, pass through the Vindhyan range, and come gradually round to the south-eastern watershed of Chutia Nagpur." This appears

29 *Ethnology of Bengal*, p. 159

indeed very probable. Dalton does not, however, mention the source of his information regarding this tradition of migration from the south.

Another tradition recorded by Russel [30] traces the descent of the Khāṛiās from the elder of two brothers of whom the younger by reason of his superior intelligence and taste was made king and became the ancestor of the Nāg Vaṁśī Rājās of Chōṭā Nāgpur who, Russel adds, "are really Mūṇḍās; and this story is exactly like that of the Parjas in connection with the Rajas of Bastar".

It may be noted that this story also appears to be a reproduction with slight variations of the legend of the Mūṇḍās as to their own relations with the Mahārājā of Chōṭā Nāgpur. Mr. Russel does not state where he or his informant came across this tradition. Mr. Russel further says that the theory that the Khāṛiās stand in the relationship of younger brothers to the Mūṇḍās derives some support from the fact that, according to Sir Herbert Risley [31], the Mūṇḍās will take daughters in marriage from the Khāṛiās but will not give daughters to them, and the Khāṛiās speak of the Mūṇḍās as their elder brothers. But our enquiries show that Risley was misinformed that Mūṇḍās ordinarily take Khāṛiā wives. Whereever a Mūṇḍā takes a Khāṛiā wife he is outcasted and his children become "Khāṛiā-Mūṇḍās", a hybrid section, which Risley includes as one of the sub-tribes of the Mūṇḍās. So this tradition of respective descent of the Mūṇḍās and the Khāṛiās from two uterine brothers may be left out of account as suppositive.

30 *Tribes and Castes of the Central Provinces* Vol. 111, p. p. 445-6

31 *Castes and Tribes of Bengal*, Vol. 11, Appendix, p. 102

The tradition which calls the Mūṇḍās the elder brothers of the Khāṛiās is, however, true in the sense that both belong to the same 'Kolarian' stock, and that the Mūṇḍās preceded the Khāṛiās to Chōṭā Nāgpur.

Although the exact route followed by the different branches of the Khāṛiā tribe in the migrations that brought them to their present habitat is shrouded in obscurity, such traditions as are still remembered by them and other cognate tribes as well as the present distribution of this tribe and some other cognate tribes point to the probability of their having once occupied the fertile river-valleys north of the Vindhya and the Kaimur ranges. With the advent probably of the Āryans they, like most of the existing Mūṇḍā tribes, would appear to have gradually moved up the hill ranges on their south and taken shelter on the wooded plateaus of the Vindhya and Kaimur ranges. One section of the Khāṛiās, in course of time, probably pushed forward under the pressure of other tribes, made their way further to the south and south-east into what are now the Ōṛissā States and found a suitable stronghold in the hill-ranges of what is now the Mayurbhanj State, and from that centre of dispersion, in time, some spread further north and east to the hills of what are now the Singbhum and Manbhum districts. These were the ancestors of the present-day Pāhāṛiā Khāṛiās or Hill Khāṛiās. It would be futile to seek to trace the exact route by which they reached their present habitat, as they retain no traditions of their past migrations. The Dūdh Khāṛiās of the Simḍegā sub-division of the Rānchi District still sing a song which is said to be reminiscent of their defeat at the hands of a powerful enemy who captured many of their men and repulsed the tribe from the valley of the Ganges. There is perhaps some basis for the conjecture that from the Vindhyan hills they came down the valley of the Mahānadī to the Ōṛissā Feudatory States and finally ensconced themselves in the Mayurbhanj hills. The Mahānadī has its source in the wild mountains of the Bastār State in the Central Provinces and, flowing eastwards along the southern borders of the Bilāspur District and Rāigaṛh State and the northern borders of the Rāipur District and the Sarangaṛh State, enters the Ōṛissān district of Sambalpur and thence proceeding in a south-easterly direction through the highlands of Sōnpur, Āṭhmalik, and a few other Feudatory States of Ōṛissā, emerges upon the Ōṛissan delta about seven miles west of Cuṭṭack. The Savaras whom Hill Khāṛiā traditions represent as having been one with, or most closely related to, themselves would also appear to have proceeded along the valley of the Mahānadī and thence entered what are now the Ganjām and the Vizāgāpaṭam Districts. Having separated from the main body of the tribe and isolated themselves in the hill fastnesses of Mayurbhanj and some other Feudatory States of Ōṛissā and in the hills of Dhalbhūm (in Singbhum) and Barābhum (in Manbhūm) long enough to lose their native tongue and having been cut off from intimate intercourse with more advanced communities and cultures and having had to spend all their energies in a strenuous struggle for existence, they have remained well-nigh stagnant during all these long centuries and have perhaps slipped down one or two rungs in the ladder of civilisation and have been far outstripped in the race of life by the other two main divisions of the tribe—the Ḍhelki and the Dūdh.

The next division of the Khāṛiās to leave the Rohṭṇsl 'plateau was probably the Ḍhelki. Their traditions only speak of their own settlement in Chōṭā Nāgpur on the banks of the river Sankh. They make no mention of the River Koel (South Koel) nor are there any traces of ancient settlements of Ḍhelki Khāṛiās in the valley of the South Koel. But even to this day some remnants of the Ḍhelkis are found in the valley of the Sankh. The Sankh rises in the north-west of Rānchi district, debouches from the Rājāḍerā plateau of that District southwards across the lower plateau of the Barwē Parganā of the same District, and forms the boundary line between the Rānchi district and the Jāshpur State of the Central Provinces on its west, and finally turns westward and enters the Gāngpur State of Ōṛissā on the south-west of the Rānchi District, where after a course of several miles it joins the South Koel to form the Brāmhaṇī river. The North Koel rises not far from the source of the Sankh and flows northward through the valley of Bishunpur in Rānchi and the district of Pālamau where, after a course of 186 miles, it falls into the Sōn below the Rohṭās plateau. It is not unlikely that the Ḍhelki Khāṛiās may have followed the upward course of the North Koel from below Rohṭās as far as to its source in the north-west of the Rānchi district, and from there followed the course of the Sankh from its source to their traditional centres further down on its banks. For the greater part of its course the North Koel flows through parallel ranges of hills which run from east to west and form a covered way by which the Ḍhelki immigrants could march with comparative safety through areas already occupied by other primitive tribes. The Koel, it may be noted, is the sacred river of both the Ḍhelki and the Dūdh Khāṛiās just as the Dāmodar is the sacred river of their congeners the Santāls.

Another possible route of Khāṛiā immigration into Chōṭā Nāgpur, would be from the Rohtās Plateau in what is now the Shāhābād District through the Vindhyan hills in the Mirzāpur District of the United Provinces and the Sirgujā State across the Khuṛia Plateau ("by the Khāṛiāghāṭ") in the Jāshpur State and thence across the Sankh which is fordable on foot except during the rains, to their former homes in the south-west of the Rānchi district. The Vindhyan and Kaimur ranges are connected by a continuous chain of hills with the extensive plateau of Central India which extends on the west as far as the highlands of Amarkanṭak—the source of the river Narbadā; and their connection with the Upper-ghāt or highlands of the Surgujā and Jāshpur States extends through Central India and the Central Provinces as far to the east as the plateaus of Chōṭā Nāgpur which form the source of the Dāmōdar, the Subarnarekhā, the Koel and the Sankh.

The third division or the Dūdh Khāṛiās who migrated last from the Rohṭās Plateau and are said to have dislodged the Ḍhelki Khāṛiās from the banks of the Sankh in the Rānchi district, generally cherish the tradition that their first settlements in Chōṭā Nāgpur lay on the banks of the South Koel in thānās Basiā and Pālkōṭ towards the centre of the Rānchi District whence they gradually spread south and west along the valley of the Sankh. If this tradition is correct, the Dūdh Khāṛiās, on their arrival on the Chōṭā Nāgpur plateau, probably by following the upward course of the North Koel, did not, like the Ḍhelki Khāṛiās, follow the course of the Sankh but turned westwards and then descended southwards along the valley of the South Koel, dropping colonies in what are now thānās Ghāgrā, Gumlā and Sisāi, till they reached what are now the Pālkōṭ, Basiā and Bāno thānās which provided a suitable home and sufficient arable lands for a large number of them, though not for all. And so a fairly large number of Dūdh Khāṛiā families migrated further south to what are now the Kolebirā, Simḍegā and Kūrḍeg thānās of the Rānchi district in the valley of the Sankh. There they found the Ḍhelki Khāṛiās already in occupation of the more fertile lands. The tradition of both these sections of the tribe agree in asserting that owing to disagreement between the two sections, the Ḍhelkis crossed over to the Gāngpur and Jāshpur States across the Sankh, leaving the Dūdh section in occupation of their former settlements in the Rānchi District. As their population increased, a number of Dūdh Khāṛias moved further up the Sankh to the north and north-east and settled in thānās Rāiḍih and Chainpur. The Khāṛia population (almost wholly Dūdh Khāṛiā) in these thānās of the Rānchi District is, according to the last Census, distributed as follows: Ghāghrā, 506; Gumlā, 4,207; Sisāi 2,611; Pālkōṭ, 8,903; Bāno, 1,085; Kōlēbirā, 9,280; Simḍegā, 24,727; Kūrḍeg, 9,727; Rāiḍih, 2,741; and Chainpur, 107. Only 130 Khāṛiās in all were recorded in the remaining parts of the Rānchi district (Rānchi Sadar and Khūnṭi Subdivisions).

A second likely route for the Dūdh Khāṛiās would be the first alternative route up the North Koel and down the Sankh which we have suggested as a possible route of migration of the Ḍhelki section. In following this route, the Dūdh Khāṛiās would, on entering the Rānchi district, pass first through Chainpur thānā where 127 Khāṛiās were enumerated at the last Census, then through Rāidih thānā where 2,741 Khāṛiās were enumerated, then to Kūrḍeg and Simḍegā thānās where 24,727 and 9,727 Khāṛiās respectively have been enumerated. Here they would find the Ḍhelki Khāṛiās already established; and the traditions of both the Ḍhelki anh Dūdh Khāṛiās agree in saying that the former left these parts in possession of the latter and crossed over to the Jāshpur State on the west and the Gāngpur State on the south.

Another probable route both for the Dūdh and the Ḍhelki Khāṛiās would be partly the same as that suggested in the case of the Hill Khāṛiās. The Khāṛiās might have proceeded from the Kaimur hills to the Central Provinces where a portion of them are found and thence eastwards through what are now the Sambalpūr District and Gangpur State. From Gangpur instead of going further down the valley of the Mahānadī they might have turned northwards to what is now the Rānchi District. The South Koel and the Sankh rivers unite their waters at Pānposh in the Gāngpur State to form the Brāmhaṇī. From there the Ḍhelkis who came first might have followed the upward course of the Sankh and found themselves in what are now the Simḍegā and Kurḍeg thānās of the Rānchi district and settled there. The Dūdh section might have followed the upward course of the South Koel and found themselves in what are now the Bāno, Basiā, Pālkōṭ, Gumlā, and Sisāi thānās of the Rānchi district, and many families of them would settle down in those parts. But as there was already a large population of Orāoṅs and Mūṇḍās in those areas, they would not afford sufficient room and particularly suitable arable lands for all the Khāṛiā immigrants. Finding their further progress up the Koel useless on account of the previous occupation by the Mūṇḍās and Orāoṅs, a considerable number of Dūdh Khāṛiā families would proceed south and south-west to the comparatively wilder and more spacious and sparsely occupied areas in what are now the Kolēbirā, Simḍegā and Kurḍeg thānās. In the Simḍegā and Kurḍeg thānās in the valley of the Sankh they would find the Ḍhelki Khāṛiās already in occupation of the more open and fertile tracts. The tradition of both the Dūdh and the Ḍhelki sections agree in asserting that the former pushed the latter from these parts across the Sankh into the adjoining Gāngpur State of Oṛissā and Jāshpur State of the Central Provinces. As the Dūdh Khāṛiās increased in population, a number of them, too, would cross over to the Gāngpur State, and in time some of their overflow might have passed on further westwards to the Central Provinces again where perhaps they found some remnants of their own tribe.

This last supposed route would accord with the tradition which Dalton records of the Dūdh Khāṛiās having come from the south, and ascended the valley of the Koel. It would also fit in more or less with the other traditions of all sections of the Khāṛiās and harmonise them to some extent, and would account more satisfactorily for the present distribution of the Khāṛiā population. The only tradition which would militate against this view is that recorded by Russel according to which some Central Provinces Khāṛiās refer to their relations with the Nāg-Vaṁśī Rājās of Chōṭā Nagpur. It is not improbable that the Chōtā Nāgpur Khāṛiās may originally have passed through the Central Provinces on their way to Chōṭā Nāgpur, and some Khāṛiās from Chōtā Nāgpur may at a later period have been pushed back again to the Central Provinces under pressure of population, and they might have carried back with them the tradition of their relations with the Nāg-Vaṁśī Rāj family of Chōṭā Nāgpur. It may also be noted that a few branches of the Nāg-Vaṁśī family are still found in the Central Provinces.[32]

Philological evidence would also appear to lend support to this supposition of the Khāṛiās having migrated through the Central Provinces to their present habitat in Chōṭā Nāgpur and Ōṛissā. We have it on the authority of Sir George Grierson[33] that the Khāṛiā language in important points agrees with the Korkū language of the Mahādeo Hills in the Central Provinces on the one hand, and the Juāng dialect of the Kēonjhar and Pāl Laharā States of Ōṛissā and the Savara and Gadava languages of the north-eastern districts (Ganjām now in the new Province of Ōṛissā and Vizāgāpatam in the Madras Presidency) on the other. Āryan principles, however, now "pervade its grammatical structure and vocabulary", so that "it is no longer a typical Muṇḍā language". "It has been compared to a palimpset, the

32 As, for example, the ruling family of the Kalāhāṇḍi State.

original writing on which can only with difficulty be recognised".

Whatever the route the different sections of the Khāṛiās may have followed in their past migrations, it is clear that they have not always been what they are to-day. They have travelled from one region to another, they have come in more or less contact with various communities and cultures, they have changed, however slowly and imperceptibly, their manners, habits, and speech; one section of them—the most backward—has changed its Austric language altogether for Āryān dialects, and the other two have considerably modified their speech under the influence of the Āryan languages of their neighbours. One section—the most primitive—is slowly exchanging its older nomadic life of food-gatherers for a comparatively settled life of more or less shifting agriculture, another—the Ḍhelki—has experienced prosperity and then misfortune and dispersion, and the third and most successful of the three main sections shows a remarkable vitality and power of expansion. But although the Khāṛiās no longer represent the actual primitive culture of prehistoric times, their backward sections still give us some idea of the low economic and social condition and the crude religious and moral ideas of relatively primitive culture.

CHAPTER III.

Previous Accounts of the Khāṛiās.

The earliest account of the Khāṛiā tribe appeared in an article headed "*The Kols of Chota Nāgpur*" by Colonel Dalton in the pages of the *Journal of the Asiatic Society of Bengal* [34] for the year 1866. The portion dealing with the Khāṛiās covers two pages only. The next account appeared in a paper headed "*Notes of the Kherriahs, an Aboriginal Race living in the hill tracts of Manbhum*" by V. Ball, M. A., of the Geological Survey of India, published in the *Proceedings of the Asiatic Society of Bengal* for the year 1868. This is really a reproduction of the account recorded in V. Ball's personal Diary or *Journal* under date January 28th, 1867. That Diary appeared *in extenso* in his volume entitled *Jungle Life in India* [35] published in 1888. It deals with the Hill Khāṛiā section of the tribe, and covers five pages only.

The third account of the tribe is that given by Dalton in his *Ethnology of Bengal* [36] published in 1872. In four pages Dalton gave a short account of the distribution of the Khāṛiā population as known to him, their Traditions, Religion, Marriage customs, Disposal of the dead, and Tattooing.

34 Vol. XXXV, part I, pp. 155 ff.

35 V. Ball, *Jungle Life in India or the Journeys and Journals of an Indian Geologist*, (London, 1880), pp. 88-92.

36 Pages 158-161.

The fourth account, compiled by H. H. (afterwards Sir Herbert) Risley and edited by W. W. (afterwards Sir William) Hunter, was published in 1877 in Volume XI (Lohardaga) of the *Statistical Account of Bengal*.[37] It merely reproduced the account given by Dalton in his *Ethnology of Bengal*. In Vol. XVII (Manbhum) of the *Statistical Account of Bengal*,[37] also edited by Hunter and compiled by Risley, was reproduced V. Ball's account given in the *Proceedings of the Asiatic Society of Bengal for 1868* and referred to above. Quotations from Ball's account were prefaced by the following introductory note: "The Kharias of Manbhum are a wilder and less civilised branch of the Kolarian tribe of the same name which has been already described in the STATISTICAL ACCOUNT OF LOHARDAGA. As their mode of life is peculiar and the tribe is probably dying out like the Birhors in the Hazaribagh and Palamau districts, I extract the following paragraphs from a note by V. Ball, published in the *Proceedings of the Asiatic Society of Bengal* for 1868."

The fifth account of the tribe is that contained in an article headed "Notes on some Kolarian Tribes", published by the late A. P. Driver of Rānchi, in the *Journal of the Asiatic Society of Bengal* [38] in two instalments, the first instalment appearing in 1888 and the second in 1891, and the two covering altogether some ten pages only. The first instalment gives a brief account of the Plains Khāṛiās, and the second a similar brief account of the Hill Khāṛias.

---

37 Pages 263—266.

38 Vol. LVII, pp. 1-6, and Vol LX, part I, pages 28-32.

The next account is contained in Risley's *Tribes and Castes of Bengal* [39] also published in 1891. It covers about seven pages of volume I of that work. In volume II of the same work a list of the divisions and clans of the tribe as known to Risley is given in an Appendix.

In one or two *District Gazetteers* and *Census Reports* very brief notices of the tribe occur but do not add much to our knowledge of the tribe.

In 1916 appeared a nine-page account of the tribe in Russel's *Tribes and Castes of the Central Provinces of India*.[40] Russel refers to previous accounts of the tribe and says, "The previous accounts noted above are defective on many points, but this may be explained by the fact that there was no attempt at a complete survey of the tribe before". It is unfortunate, however, that even Russel's own account (based, as he says, on notes taken by Rai Bahadur Hira Lal at Raigarh with extracts from Colonel Dalton's and Sir H. Risley's accounts), was also rather fragmentary and in certain matters inaccurate. For one thing, Russel and his collaborator do not appear to have carefully inquired as to what different Districts and States, in the Central provinces and beyond, the Khāṛiās inhabited.

The latest account of the tribe is contained in a short monograph of 38 pages by Mr. Tarak Chandra Das on the *Wild Khāṛiās of Dhalbhum* and published by the Calcutta University in 1931. The author admits in his Preface that "It is incomplete in many respects, being the result of enquiry conducted for a very short period of

39 Vol I, pages 466-472, and Vol II, pp 77-78.

40 Vol III, pp. 445-453.

about ten days only". The value of the essay is further discounted by the fact that the author collected his facts from only a few Hill Khāṛiās of an outlying part of the Hill Khāṛiā area. The essay is divided into four chapters. In Chapter I, headed 'The People and Its Habitat', the author begins with an account of the distribution of the tribe. He is mistaken in supposing that "the Khāṛiā speakers of the Central Provinces come from Raigarh and Jashpur States only", and that "the Khāṛiās of Assam all hail from Chota Nāgpur and Orissa". Mr. Das gives individual measurements of only five men, and from a comparison of his "averages" with Risley's data, concludes that "the wild Khāṛiā presents all the characteristic features of a typical pre-Dravidian". Then he quotes from Dalton the tradition of origin from a pea-fowl's egg, and from Russel the tradition which connects the Khāṛiās with the Nag-Vaṁśi Rajas of Chōṭā Nāgpur, and from Driver the supposed division ot the Khāṛiās into, among other sub-tribes, 'Khāṛiā Muṇḍā' and 'Khāṛiā Orāoṅ', and goes on to say 'Risley also refers to the Khāṛiā-Muṇḍā section of the tribe and derives them from unions between Khāṛiā women and Muṇḍā men. The Muṇḍās allow their men to marry Khāṛiā women, but prohibit the marriage of their daughters with the Khāṛiā men". If Mr. Das had made personal enquiries from the very few Khāṛiās whom he met and measured he would have found that they would resent the suggestion that Khāṛiā tribal custom would, at least at the present day, allow any union of a person of their tribes with a person of the opposite sex belonging to the Muṇḍā or Orāoṅ or any other tribe or caste. Such unions do occasionally (though now-a-days very rarely) take place, but are not sanctioned either by Khāṛiā tribal custom or by Mūṇḍā or Ōrāoṅ tribal custom and the parties to such an union are outcasted and come to be described as 'Mūṇḍā–Khāṛiā' or Ōrāoṅ–Khāṛiā', as the case may be, if the male partner is a Khāṛiā. They pass under the general name of 'Bergā Khāṛiā' meaning 'Hybrid Khāṛiā'. The word 'Bergā' would appear to be a corruption by metathesis of the word 'Bigṛāo' (gone wrong). From the Appendix of Risley's *Castes and Tribes* it will be seen that among the sub-tribes of the Khāṛiās, Risley [41] mentions 'Mūṇḍā-Khāṛiā' and 'Orāoṅ-Khāṛiā' and not 'Khāṛiā Mūṇḍā' and 'Khāṛiā Orāoṅ' (as Driver puts down by mistake). It is with reference to the sub-tribes of Mūṇḍās that the name 'Khāṛiā-Mūṇḍā' [42] and with reference to the sub-tribes of Orāons that the term "Khāṛiā-Orāoṅ" [43] occur.

Mr. Das concludes his first chapter with his view of the charactor of the people. He notes that "a morose disposition and an extremely sad outlook on life, timidity and improvidence are the main features of the Khāṛiās". This is, in the main, true, only of the Hill Khāṛiās as it would be of most other tribes on a similar level of culture living under similar extremely unfavourable conditions. But Mr. Das is not correct in saying that "Music and dancing * * do not break the monotony of their ordinary evenings". A visit to a real Hill Khāṛiā settlement and a single night spent in or near such a Settlement and an examination of the contents of their

41 *Tribes & Castes of Bengal*, Vol II, p. 77.

42 *Ibid*, p. 102.

43 *Ibid*, p. 113.

huts, will show that the drum is one of their extremely few valued possessions, and the *tuhilā* or rude guitar and one or more bamboo flutes, are also treasured in some houses; and the seemingly morose Hill Khāṛiā has as keen an appreciation of the melody of song and the rhythm of dance, as his more advanced neighbours and congeners like the Plains Khāṛiās, the Mūṇḍās, the Hōs, and the Sāntāls. Not only do Khāṛiā young men and women dance in moon-lit nights in their settlements but, occasionally, parties of Khāṛiā boys or girls go to other Khāṛiā settlements to join in dances with the boys or girls of those villages, and hold dancing contests or matches, so to say. The party who is worsted has to pay a fine to the winning party. Story-telling and riddle-solving furnish other diversions which give them zest in life. The annual round of feasts and festivities also relieve the monotony of their daily routine and afford occasions of mirth and merriment to these simple folk.

In the second chapter Mr. Das deals with the "Domestic Life" of the people. In twelve short pages he gives all that he has to say of the 'Occupations', 'Food and Drink', 'Village sites, Huts and their construction', 'Domestic Utensils', 'Domestic Animals', 'Dress and Ornaments', and 'Weapons.' The account is necessarily meagre and the author's information is not always accurate. Thus, at p. 9, he mentions the absence of organised hunting among the Khāṛiās. He obviously did not find out that annually in the month of Chait on an appointed day there is an organised hunting excursion in which all the adult members of one or more settlements take part, and which has a great social value and religious importance to the people.

Mr. Das gives the names of six exogamous clans but does not give their meanings nor states whether they are totemstic or not. He says that he visited some more wild Khāṛiā settlements in the Mayurbhanj State. If he had made enquiries on this point from those Khāṛiās he would have found out that the Mayurbhanj Khāṛiās of the present day practically know no clan names and even those sophisticated Khāṛiās who, in imitation of their neighbours of other tribes and castes, have retained or rather re-adopted some clan name or other (generally the Nāg or cobra), have no observances or customs connected with the clan-totem and recognise no bar whatsoever to intermarriage between families bearing the same clan name. The Hill Khāṛiās of Singbhūm and Mānbhūm Districts have indeed either adopted or retained some clan names and now practise exogamy as between those clans. It is worth noting that these few clan names (except one, namely, *Hembrom* which Mr. Das does not mention) are not among those known to the Dūdh and Ḍhelki sections among whom the totemic clan system is still in full force, though these names are common to some other tribes of the Mūṇḍā family such as the Santāl neighbours of the Hill Khāṛiās. Mr. Das's brief account of the huts, domestic utensils, dress, ornaments, and weapons of the Hill Khāṛiās is, so far as it goes, on the whole, correct. But his account of their social customs and religious beliefs and practices is not only very meagre, but does not appear to be always accurate.

Rev. Father L. Cardon published, a few years ago, a pamphlet of about a dozen pages regarding the

Manners and Customs of the Dūdh Khāṛiās. So far as it went, it gave a correct account of the people. Four or five years ago, another Catholic Missionary, the Rev. Father H. Gallaghar, published in a Missionary journal, meant only for private circulation among Roman Catholic Missionies, a few short articles on the Birth, Death and Marriage Customs and religious feasts of the Ḍhelki section of the Khāṛiās. Through the courtesy of the author we had the advantage of reading his manuscripts in 22 type-written pages. From personal investigations we found that the accounts of these two sections of the Khāṛiās as contained in these two Missionary publications meant only for private circulation were accurate so far as they went; and we owe our thanks to their authors for their kindness and courtesy in allowing us to read them.

This is practically all the extant literature on this very interesting-tribe. No systematic attempt appears to have been hitherto made to make an exhaustive survey of the physical and cultural anthropology of the different divisions of the tribe. The present monograph embodies the results of the beginnings of such a systematic attempt.

CHAPTER IV.

Physical Anthropology Of The Khāṛiās.

Observations on the physical features of the Khāṛiās occur in some of the previous notices of the tribe, but they are imperfect and of little scientific value. The only anthropometric measurements of any value were those made for Risley's *Castes and Tribes*, but they were confined to the Khāṛiās of the Rānchi District who are mostly Dūdh Khāṛiās though it is not unlikely that some Ḍhelki Khāṛiās might have been included among the persons whose measurements have been recorded by Risley. The very few measurements taken by Mr. Tarak Chandra Das were from an outlying area and too meagre to be of much value. So far as we are aware, the present Chapter and its appendices contain the first comparative study of the physical characteristics of the three main divisions of the tribe.

(i) *Method.*

During May 1930 and November 1931, we took measurements of 270 individual Khāṛiās belonging to different sections resident in the central areas of the regions occupied by them. We purposely avoided collecting materials from the outlying or borderland areas in order to exclude as far as possible the effects of infiltration from outside. The sections and the respective localities from where the measurements were taken are given below :—

Dudh Khāṛiā,—Ranchi district (Chōtā Nāgpur), and Gangpur State (Ōṛissā)

Dhelki Khāṛiā,—Gangpur State (Ōṛissā) and Jashpur State (Central Provinces).

Hill or Erenga Khāṛiā,—Mayurbhanj State (Ōṛissā)

Methods of Mesurements :—Martin's anthropometric instruments have been used and the instructions given by him generally followed: The individuals measured were all adult males between the ages of thirty to forty-five. The measurements of all such adults without selection or discrimination available in a few of the villages we visited were taken, only such individuals as were suffering from some serious disease or showed obvious signs of deformity were omitted. The following measurements were taken by the standard method, as described below for the information of lay readers :—

1. *Stature* :—The subject was made to stand erect on the ground (horizontal as far as possible) with heels in contact, axis of vision horizontal, upper limbs pendant and palm of hands turned inward with fingers pointing downwards, (that is, in what is known as military position). The height of the vertex (highest point on the head) above the ground was measured by the Anthropometer in the vertical position.
2. *Head height* :—This was found out by subtracting height of the tragion above the ground from the stature.
3. *Maximum Head length* :—The maximum distance between the Glabella (median point of the brow-ridge) and opisthocranion was found by Martin's calipers. A moderate pressure was applied.

4. *Maximum Head breadth* :—The greatest horizontal transverse diameter of the vault of the head above the supermastoid and zigomatic crests was measured by Martin's calipers.

5. *Minimum Frontal breadth* :—The shortest distance between the two fronto-temporalia (the two inner-most points on the frontal crest on each side) was measured by Martin's calipers.

6. *Bi-zigomatic diameter* :—The distance between the most widely separated points on the lateral surface of the zygomatic arches was measured by Martin's calipers.

7. *Bi-gonial breadth* :—The distance between the outer points of the angles of the lower jaw (that is, between two gonions) was measured.

8. *Nasal length* :—The distance between the Nasion (the meeting point of the fronto-nasal and internasal sutures as felt by the fingers) and the sub-nasal (the apex of the angle formed by the lower margin of the nasal septum and the philtrum) was measured by Martin's sliding compasses.

9. *Nasal breadth* :—The maximum breadth between the external surface of the alae of the nose was found by Martin's slide compasses.

10. *Superior Facial length* :—The distance from Nasion to Stomion (the median point in the oral fissure where the lips are in natural position) was measured by Martin's slide compasses.

11. *Morphological Facial length* :—The distance betwen Nasion and Gnathion (the lowest point in the middle

line on the lower margin in the mandible) was measured by Martin's slide compass.

12. *Horizontal circumference of the head* :The maximum circumference was taken above the supra-orbital ridges and above the opisthocranion by the tape.

(ii) *General Appearance.*

The Khāṛiās are of medium stature and their skin-colour varies from brown to light black ; but the skin-colour of the females is lighter than that of the males. They are of robust health with well-proportioned body and limbs, but their body is not so thick-set as that of the Mūṅḍās and the Orāons among whom they live.

The Khāṛiās generally have long, plentiful, black or dark-brown (among the Hill section mostly due to non-use of oil and exposure to the sun) hair on the head. But now-a-days many Dūdh Khāṛiās cut their hair short ; and the Ḍhelkis cut their hair short only in front but wear it long at the back. Very few men have hair on the face and on the rest of the body ; even those who possess such hair have a very scanty moustache, beard, or chest-hair.

The forehead is often slightly or even moderately retreating though it is not uncommon to find a slight bulbous forehead ; but a complete vertical forehead is rarely seen. The supraorbital ridges are moderately developed in the majority.

The nasal root is usually very depressed and nasal bridge often concave. The eyeslits are small and are either straight or slightly oblique inwards and, in a very few cases, the tendency to form the epicanthic fold is also found. The lips are thick and, though not always everted, have in some cases a tendency to be everted.

In the majority, the malars are moderately developed and the zygomatic arches prominent. These together with the mandibular angle and square or oval chin give a squareness to the face (found more among the Ḍhelkis). Though the face is often oval, pentagonal faces are not uncommon. The females have generally oval faces and their malars, eyebrow ridges and zygomatic arches are not so marked as those of the males. The prognathous face in both the sexes is not uncommon (more common among females) and this prognathism is due generally to the alveolar region.

A collection of photographs was taken in the field out of which some are reproduced in this volume.

(iii) *Analysis of Physical Measurements.*

The actual measurements are given in Appendix I, Tables 1 to 111. The mean values and the standard deviations are given with probable errors (which are directly calculated by the moment method); and the cofficient of variation for each item is also given in the Appendix.

From the analysis of the metric data we get the following results [44] :—

In their cephalic Index the number of dolichocephals and mesocephals are as follows :—

44 For standard of classifications, see Haddon, *Races of Man* p. 10.

	Dūdh.	Ḍhelki.	Hill.
Dolichocephalic (77)	93	97	60 or 85.7 %
Mesocephalic (77–82)	7	3	10 or 14.3 %
Total:	100	100	70

There is a complete absence of brachycephals. The respective average cephalic indices are:—Hill, 74.77 ± 17; Ḍhelki, 73.16 ± 14; Dūdh, 73.67 ± 55.

As regards the Length-Height Index the numbers for the different indices are:—

	Dūdh.	Ḍhelki.	Hill.
Hypsicephalic (63+)	53	45	33 or 47.15 %
Orthocephalic (58–64)	41	47	33 or 47.15 %
Chamaecephalic (-58)	6	8	4 or 5.7 %
Total	100	100	70

The average Length-Height Index of the Hill is 64.44 ± 25; of the Ḍhelki 62.33 ± 24; Dūdh 62.86 ± 25.

The numbers for the different Nasal Indices are:—

	Dūdh.	Ḍhelki.	Hill.
Mesorrhine (70–85)	39	23	19 or 27.1 %
Platyrrhine (85–100)	61	72	47 or 67.1 %
Hyper-Platyrrhine	nil	5	4 or 5.7 %
Total	100	100	70

The average nasal Index of the Hill is 88.64 ± 56; Ḍhelki 89.22 ± 4.3; Dūdh 86.81 ± .40.

The numbers for the different Morphological Facial Indices using Martin's classification [45] are :—

	Dūdh .	Ḍhelki .	Hill .
Hyper Chameprosopy (-78.9)	9	22	18 or 25.7 %
Chamaeprosopy (79.0–83.9)	30	25	23 or 32.9 %
Mesoprosopy (84.0–87.9)	41	35	15 or 21.4 %
Lepto–Prosopy (88.0–92.9)	20	16	11 or 15.7 %
Hyper–Leptoprosopy (93.0–)	nil	2	3 or 4.3 %
Total	100	100	70

The average nasal Index of the Hill is 82.78 $\pm$ .42 ; Ḍhelki 83.40 $\pm$ .31 ; Dūdh 84.61 $\pm$ .28 .

So the Khāṛiās are on the average, a dolochocephalic, hypsicephalic (orthocephalic with a tendency to be hypsicephalic), Platyrrhine and Chamaeprosopic (with a tendency to be Mesoprosopic) people .

Using Dixon's [46] classification we get the following results :—

	Dūdh .	Ḍhelki	Hill .
D.H.P.	29	35	25 or 35.7 %
D.C.P.	23	35	18 or 25.7 %
D.C.P.	4	4	4 or 5.7 %

45 See Martin's *Anthropometry* Vol. I

46 Dixon,-*Racial History of Man* - p.p. 27

Dixon's system is to be taken with reserve. See L.R. Sullvian's article in *American Anthropologist*, Vol. 23, (1923).

Dixon's notations are :—D-dolichocephalic ; M - mesocephalic ; H - hypsicephalic ; O - orthocephalic ; C - chamaecephalic ; P - platyrrhine ; M- mesorrhine. So, for example D.H.P. means "Dolichocephalic hypsicephalic platyrrhine" and so forth.

	Dūdh.	Ḍhelki.	Hill.
D.H.M.	18	9	4 or 5.7 %
D.C.M.	17	10	9 or 12.8 %
D.C.M.	2	4	nil
M.H.P.	5	1	2 or 2.9 %
M.O.P.	nil	2	2 or 2.9 %
M.H.M.	1	nil	2 or 2.9 %
M.O.M.	1	nil	4 or 5.7 %
Total	100	100	70

Dixon's fundamental types occur in the following proportion:—

	Dudh	Dhelki	Hill
D.H.P.	61.5	63.5	63.55
D.C.P.	16.5	23.5	20. 0
D.C.L.	9.5	7.0	6. 4
D.H.L.	9.0	4.5	2.85
B.H.P.	2.5	.5	1.45
B.C.P.	nil	1.5	1.45
B.C.L.	.5	nil	2.85
B.H.L.	.5	nil	1.45

Thus it would appear that the most fundamental types of Dixon's classification that have entered into the composition of the tribe are D. H. P. and D. C. P., but in actual measurements the most numerous are D. H. P. and D. O. P. (not D. C. P.).

The use of Dixon's system raises one important question. Who were the small element of brachycephalic people (now absorbed but who have produced the mesocephalic) that appear to have entered into the composition of the Khāṛiās? Or is this mesocephalic element another type, or a normal variation of the model type?

An adequate discussion of the above question cannot however be undertaken without a detailed study of the neighbouring tribes. We shall, therefore, confine ourselves to a consideration of the actual (metric) affinities between the different sections of the tribe studied by us.

We found on the cultural side that the Ḍhelki Khāṛiā stands midway between the Hill Khāṛiā living on the mountainous forests on the one hand, and the settled and well-to-do agricultural Dūdh Khāṛiā on the other. Do the physical measurements support the same conclusion? In other words, was there any parallel development in physical and cultural differentiation between the different sections of the Khāṛiā tribe?

In order to study this problem the coefficient of Caste-Distance $(D)^2$ which is a modified form (standardized for differences in size of the sample) of Pearson's coefficient of Racial Likeness $(C)^2$ has been used, [47]—

$$D^2 = \frac{1}{P} \Sigma \frac{(M_1 - M_2)^2}{\sigma_o^2} \quad \text{where} \quad \sigma_o = \frac{\sigma_1^2 n_1 + \sigma_2^2 n_2}{n_1 n_2}$$

On analysing the data and using the following notations,—M_1 = Hill Khāṛiā; M_2 = Ḍhelki Khāṛiā; M_3 = Dūdh Khāṛiā, we find the following results:—

Measurements	M_1 & M_2	M_1 & M_3	M_2 & M_3
Stature	.7270	.8176	.0004
Head Length	.5713	.3569	.0363
Head Breadth	.0294	.0395	.0002
Head Height	.0316	.0440	.0010
Least Frontal	.1572	.1792	.0021
Bi-Zygomatic	.0078	.9793	.1101

47 See P. C. Mahalanabis, "Analysis of Race Mixture in Bengal" in J. A. S. B. Vol. XXIII. 1927 No. III p. 328.

Bi-Gonial	.1563	1.2645	.4731
Superior Facial Length	.0961	.8705	.3625
Morph. Facial Length	.0106	.1599	.1172
Nasal Length	.0729	.1426	.5556
Nasal Breadth	.1909	.0680	.0184
Cephalic Index	.4855	.0258	.0074
Altitudinal Index	.8783	.2156	.0165
Morph. Nasal Index	.0074	.0828	.1459
Facial Index	.0149	.1541	.0720
Total	$D_1^2=3.4372$	$D_2^2=5.4003$	$D_3^2=1.9177$
Average	$D_1^2=.2272$	$D_2^2=.3602$	$D_3^2=.1011$

In a paper on "Tests & Measurements of Statistical Divergence" communicated to the Indian Science Congress in 1929-30, Prof. P. C. Mahalanobis showed that a small correction should be applied to the observed D^2 to compensate for the finite size of the samples. The formula for the corrected estimate is given below :—

$$D^2=\frac{1}{P}\int \frac{(Mp-Mp')^2}{\sigma_p^2}-\frac{2}{n}$$

and the variance of D^2 is given by

$$\mu_2\ (D^2)=\frac{8}{P.n}\left(D^2+\frac{1}{n}\right)$$

where P = total number of characters,

and $\frac{2}{n}=\frac{1}{n_q}+\frac{1}{n_{q'}}$, where n_q and $n_{q'}$, represent the size of the two samples under comparison (the number of characters being equal in all cases). For Hill, for $n_{q'}=70$; Dūdh and Ḍhelki $n_{q'}=100$. Therefore for Hill & Dūdh or Ḍhelki,—

$$\frac{2}{n}=\frac{1}{70}+\frac{1}{100}=\frac{17}{700}=.0243$$

and for Dūdh and Ḍhelki,—$\frac{2}{n}=\frac{1}{100}+\frac{1}{100}=\frac{2}{100}=.0200$

The correction is small and the corrected estimated values of D^2 are :—

Hill & Dūdh $=0.336 \pm .032$
Hill & Ḍhelki $=0.205 \pm .025$
Dūdh & Ḍhelki $=0.118 \pm .017$
$D^2_0 = 0 \pm .005$

So we find that the Dūdh and the Ḍhelki sections resemble one another more closely (in the characters mentioned above) than either Hill and Ḍhelki. In other words, Hill and Dūdh are more differentiated while Ḍhelki stands midway between the two. A rough sketch of the connection is given in the following figure:—

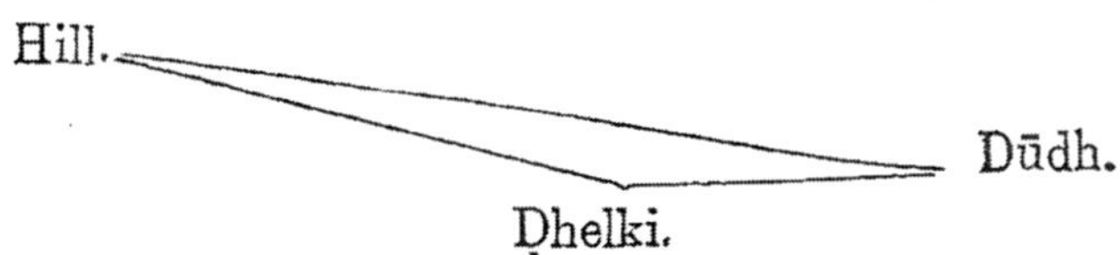

The sum of the three standardized differences (D) for each character is shown in the following table:—

Measurement	Total	Average
Bi-Gonial Breadth	1.893	.631
Stature	1.545	.515
Superior Facial Length	1.328	.443
Altitudinal Index	1.110	.370
Bi-Zygomatic Breadth	1.697	.366
Head Length	.964	.325
Nasal Length	.771	.257
Cephalic Index	.518	.173
Least Frontal Breadth	.338	.113

Morph. Facial Length	.287	.099
Nasal Breadth	.277	.092
Facial Index	.241	.080
Nasal Index	.236	.075
Head Height	.076	.025
Head Breadth	. 06	.020

The last six characters in the above table have the smallest differences, indicating that these are fairly stable among all these sections. On the other hand, the first seven show the largest differences. In other words, the physical differences between the three sections have occured mostly through these seven characters. The other two characters, Head Length and Nasal length, are less variable.

For seven characters which show pronounced differentiation the actual order in which the three samples are placed is shown below. For example, for Bi-gonial Breadth the Dūdh has the largest mean measurment, Ḍhelki comes next while Hill has the lowest value.

Measurement	*Highest*		*Middle*		*Lowest*
Bi-Gonial	Dūdh	=	Ḍhelki	←	Hill
Stature	Ḍhelki	=	Dūdh	←	Hill
Supr. Facial Length	Dūdh	←	Ḍhelki	←	Hill
Altitudinal Index	Hill	→	Dūdh	=	Ḍhelki
Bi-Zygomatic	Dūdh	←	Hill	=	Ḍhelki
Head Length	Ḍhelki	←	Dūdh	←	Hill
Nasal Length	Dūdh	←	Ḍhelki	←	Hill

(N.B.—Arrows indicate direction of development & "=" indicates "nearly equal").

It will be noticed that in no less than six out of seven characters Hill Khāṛiās occupy the extreme position.

Of these six characters, Hill Khāṛiās occupy the lowest value, viz., in Bi-Gonial, Stature, Supr. Facial Length, Head length and nasal length ; while in Altitudinal Index the Hill Khāṛiās occupy the highest extreme value, which is obvious because in all the sections head-height is a stable factor while the head-length is of least value among the Hill. In four cases Dūdh occupies the highest extreme position, and in two cases Ḍhelki occupies the highest extreme position of which, in "Stature", it is almost equal to Dūdh. Again, we find that Ḍhelki often occupies either the middle position or is nearly equal to the section occupying the middle position.

So we see that in all cases there is physical devlopment from Hill to Dūdh and often in most cases the Ḍhelki lies midway between the two.

In Appendix II, the published data collected by Mr. T. C. Das [48] and Risely [49] have been quoted for reference. The data of Mr. Das have not been used for comparison for the following reasons:—(1) Difference due to personal errors ; (2) the total number and the individual measurements are not given (only mentioned as 'very few'); (3) Mr. Das's measurements have been taken from the border region, and (4) he appears to have measured both very old men as well as young boys and thus derived the mean.[50] Risley's data have not been used for comparison owing to differences introduced by "personal errors", differences in the technique of measurement, and other reasons.[51]

48 Das, *The Wild Kharias of Dhalbhum*, p. 4

49 Risley, *Tribes and Castes of Bengal.*

50 Das, *The Wild Kharias of Dhalbhum*, Plates VII & XIII

51 *Man in India*, Vol-VIII (1928), pp. 146 ff.

CHAPTER V.

Material Culture.

(i) *General Features of the Material Culture of the Hill Khāṛiās.*

Living more or less isolated in the inhospitable hill fastnesses of the Mayurbhanj, Singbhūm (Dhalbhūm) and Mānbhūm (Barābhūm) hills, the Erengā or Hill Khāṛiās have always had to carry on a strenuous struggle for bare existence. With their mind constantly engrossed with the food problem, and with very little intimate intercourse with more civilised peoples, they could hardly possess any wider outlook than the immediate satisfaction of insistent physical needs. Almost all their activities are directed towards the solution of the food problem.

Although the Hill Khāṛiās have thus for long centuries remained stagnant in culture, yet in their own way they too have developed a primitive culture of their own: In the course of ages they too have worked out a working relation to the food-supply, though it is far from complete or satisfactory. This they have done, like other communities, by inventing, and in some cases by adopting from others, certain methods and appliances to secure such control as they may over their natural environment. These methods and appliances and the results achieved through them constitute the Khāṛiā's material culture. This culture comprises the use of fire for cooking ard burning;-the use of wood and iron for making tools and implements for digging and sowing, hunting, fishing, trapping, and cutting, spinning and weaving and for making household utensils and furniture, ornaments and combs, snuff-boxes and lime-boxes ;- the utilization of leaves and gourds and barks of trees as food- vessels and water - vessels, dishes and cups, rain- hats and umbrellas ; - the use of leaves and branches and timber of trees for constructing huts and sheds to live in and jungle grass to thatch them; – the use of jungle - creepers and tree - fibres for making ropes and strings required for the construction of huts and for other domestic purposes such as making string- beds, though rare, to sleep upon, *sikā* - nets with which to carry loads, and rope ladders with which to climb up and get down steep hills to collect honey ; - the use of leaves or bamboos for making mats and baskets ; - the use of tree - cotton for making thread ; - the use of fruit - seeds and flowers, palm - leaves and creepers for adorning the body ; - the use of stones for various purposes; and so forth .

With such rude appliances and contrivances, even the Hill Khāṛiās have succeeded to some extent in utilising the forces of nature to secure a working control of his environment, and have solved, as best as they could, the problems of food and shelter, personal adornment and clothing, self - defence and revenge, transport and barter .

Daily life of the Hill Khāṛiās .

The daily life of the Hill Khāṛiās is mainly devoted to the primary task of food - quest . Their women rise before daybreak and sweep the floors of their huts and the open spaces in their front, fetch water from the nearest spring or stream or pool, bathe themselves, and prepare the morning meal. The men, too, rise early in the morning, and after washing their faces and rinsing their mouths, they eat boiled rice, if any, left over from the preceding night's meal and kept steeped in water, or fried rice (*Mūṛi*), if available, or ripe wild figs or other fruits, and then go out either to gather edible tubers and fruits or to work on their own *jhūm* cultivation, if any, or to work on wages on the fields of some people of other tribes or castes living within easy distance, or occasionally to hunt deer, hare or other animal or bird. Sometimes men go to the jungles in batches of two or three for collecting honey or edible tubers and fruits and stay away from two to six or seven days together. On such occasions they carry with them pounded rice and salt and red pepper, and, if available, some vegetable such as *Kandri* or brinjal (*Solemen melongenw*). Adult women take a cold bath in the morning (at about 10 a.m.) and if they have any rice, boil it for food; otherwise they eat boiled rice, if any, left over from the preceding night's meal, or whatever else is available. Women do not eat with the men. If the men are likely to return home at about noon, food is prepared for them, if any food is available. When the men go to work in their *jhūm* cultivation, they return home by mid-day. If they have secured work in other people's fields or houses, within easy distance, they, too, return home at noon, with *bhujā* (fried rice or *Mūṛi*) received from their employers for *jalkhāi* or tiffin. This they bring home for their children. After attending to such household work as splitting fuel wood, they return to work after eating such food as may be available, preferably boiled rice. If they work on wages at a distance they eat the tiffin by themselves as a substitute for the mid-day meal, and return home in the evening with their wages either in kind or cash. The evening meal consists of boiled rice, if available. It may be noted that very few Hill Khāṛiās can enjoy the luxury of meals of boiled rice throughout the year. Boiled vegetables, edible leaves and tubers and *mohul* (*Bassia latifolia*) flowers often serve as their only food, besides wild fruit. In the Dhalbhūm hills, we found in the winter most Khāṛiās, men and women, going out into the forests in the morning in quest of food and returning home in the evening. In the evening, women prepare a meal with the food thus collected, and all then eat and go to sleep. It is only among those Hill Khāṛiās who have settled at the foot of the hills not far from prosperous villages of other castes or tribes that some men work on wages as day-labourers. The Hill Khāṛiās of Dhalbhūm (in Singbhūm) and Barābhūm (in Mānbhum) have very little *jhūm* or other cultivation now-a-days as this is no longer permitted by local landlords. Such of the Dhalbhūm Khāṛiās as still practise *jhūm* cultivation grow chiefly *Rama Kali* (*Phaseolus Roxburghii*).[52]

Annual round of activities. In the Mayurbhañj hills, male Khāṛiās, who have any *jhūm* or *Dāhi* cultivation, work on their fields during the agricultural season; those who have no cultivation either work as day-labourers (*Ujriās*), or go out, from May to July, to collect honey and bees'-wax or to catch birds, particularly the

52 This is the same as *Urid-Kalai* pulse. It may be noted that in *Mūṇḍāri* and *Khāṛiā* languages it is known as *Rambārā*.

species called *sar* or *mainā* which they sell or barter. They also gather wild mangoes in June and July, and silk-cocoons in August, and certain odorous resins such as frankincense throughout the year. Men and women gather the corolla of the *mahul* (*bassia latifolia*) in March and April and dig for yams with their *Khantās* and *sābars* throughout the year. They carry bows and arrows and axes while going to the jungles. A few Khāṛias are experts in killing tigers with their long bows and arrows.

In spite of this strenuous existence, young men and women among the Hill Khāṛiās, as among the Dūdh and Ḍhelki-Khāṛiās, enjoy themselves of an evening and at festive seasons with singing and dancing and playing on the *chāngu* or the *māndal* drums. Many of the songs of the Hill Khāṛiās, relate to the Hindu god Krishna or Hari, which they have obviously borrowed from their Hindu neighbours. But the Khāṛiā singers do not know who that god is. When we asked them whether it refers to their God "Boṛām" or the Sun-God, they assented, but it was obvious that they had no definite idea.

Their arduous annual round of duties is further relieved now and then by seasonal religious feasts and festivals. During respite from other work men make wooden artifacts such as pestles and mortars, bamboo sticks and bows, digging-sticks and handles of *Khantās*. They also make gourd-ladles and drinking vessels, *bahingās* or carrying-poles, and manufacture strings and ropes with *siāñṛi* creepers and chop-fibres. In the winter and spring, girls weave mats of wild date-palms and some men make leaf baskets and rain-hats, and the like. From the middle of August to the middle of November men who may have *jhūm* cultivation keep watch over the crops at night.

(ii) *General Features of the Material Culture of the Dūdh and Ḍhelki Khāṛiās.*

The Dūdh and Ḍhelki Khāṛias who have long taken to settled agriculture and have a much better organisation than the Hill Khāṛiās, have necessarily secured much better control over their food-supply. Having therefore more leisure than the Hill Khāṛiās to think of other things and feel other wants and aspirations than the mere satisfaction of immediate appetite, they have made some further headway in material culture.

They are somewhat better dressed and better housed, have more and better furniture and household utensils, weapons and implements, more and better food, more and better appliances for transport and resources and facilities for barter or trade. Short notes regarding the tools and weapons, the more important mechanical devices, household furniture, dress and ornaments and other artifacts in use among the Khāṛiās are given below. Before proceeding to describe these artifacts of material culture and their uses we shall give a short account of the daily life of the people and their annual round of duties. This is generally the same as among other settled agicultural tribes of Chōṭā Nāgpur, Ōṛissā and the Central Provinces.

Daily Routine of work of the Dūdh and Ḍhelki Khāṛiās.—The head of the family gets up early in the morning and asks the boys to un-pen the cattle. The mistress of the family similarly directs the girls to their respective duties such as fetching water from the spring or stream, and cleaning the house-floors and the yard with cowdung diluted in water. The mistress herself either spins cotton or attends to some other household duty such as fetching water. One of the girls gathers *śāg* (edible leaves or stems) or vegetables. Whether she or another girl goes to a *ṭūku* or flat rock or other place near-by where paddy is threshed, and gets rice for the day's use threshed and husked, or gets it done in the house. Either the mistress of the house or one of the girls or other women, if any, prepares the morning meal (*basi-pē*). Men and boys go out to work in their fields in the morning and return home by about noon or shortly before it, and, if they or any of them so choose, bathe at some spring or tank, and then take their meals. In summer they generally take a bath every day, but at other seasons they do so only when they feel inclined. Except very little girls, other girls and women eat after the men. The ordinary mid-day meal consists of boiled rice with either boiled pulse or, more commonly, boiled vegetables or leaves, or powdered *Mūngā S'āg*. The edible leaves generally used are *Mūngā S'āg* (*Moringa pterygosperma*), *Koinār śag* (*Bauhinia-malabarica*), *Phūṭkal śāg*, *Sarlā S'āg*, etc.

After washing their hands and mouths after breakfast, men take powdered tobacco with a bit of lime, and then may rest for a little while. They then either split fuel wood, or go to the jungles for wood-cutting or to their fields for digging. The women gather dried twigs and branches and leaves for fuel, thresh rice, or, in the summer, carry manure to their fields, or break clods of earth in the fields or weave mats with leaves of the wild date-palm. In the month of Āshār (July-August) they weed their paddy fields, and in *Bhādo* (August-September) transplant rice-seedlings on low paddy-fields, and reap upland (*Goṛā*) paddy. In *Aghān* (November-December) they reap the lowland paddy. In the evening, one of the women prepares the evening meal (*lob-lob-pē*) for the family. After each meal, the women scrub and wash the dishes and cups. After the evening meal, women spin cotton, weave mats, or do some other similar work till about midnight, after which all go to sleep.

(iii) *The Khāṛiā Villages.*

The Hill Khāṛiās have no true villages, properly speaking. Groups of from about four or five to a dozen or so families live together and form a settlement. The huts of different families are scattered sometimes a hundred yards or so apart from each other. The other sections of the Khāṛiās live in regular villages. The houses are not arranged in rows or in any other definite order. Every Dūdh or Ḍhelki Khāṛiā village has its *Ākhrā*, or dancing and meeting-place, its sacred grove or groves, and the cremation ground and clan cemeteries (*Ranabrab*). Hill Khāṛiā settlements, too, have their sacred groves but no regular *Ākhrā* nor cemetery.

The Bachelors' House. Most non-Christian Dūdh and Ḍhelki Khāṛiā settlements have each also its bachelors' house called "Giti O'". This is also used as the guest-house of the village. It is situated at one end of the village. This house is sometimes of a special type, being more pretentious and 'artistic' than the ordinary dwelling-house. But generally it is similar in construction to the average dwelling-house with this exception that there is a central post in the middle of the house to support the ridge-pole. In the larger villages, the dimensions of this house are somewhat larger than those of the ordinary dwelling-house and the central post and beams are sometimes carved. In many villages, particularly where Christianity has spread, the Bachelors' House is falling into disuse. And, in general, the Khāṛiā Bachelors' houses possess no longer the disciplinary organization and the elaborate rules and ceremonies connected with that institution among the Ōrāoñs of the Central plateau of Chōṭā Nāgpur. Among the Khāṛiās, the Giti O' is an effete institution which has long lost its utility and is fast dacaying. The Ḍhelki Khāṛiās in Rāj Gāngpur thānā call it *Gitā-chāṛi*; but among them it is only in the bigger villages where the number of bachelors and maidens is fairly large that bachelors sleep together in a separate house (*Gitā chāṛi*), and all the maidens sleep together in the house of a lone widow. There are no longer any special rites of admission nor any regulations, nor office-bearers, connected with these dormitories.

Dwelling Houses.

Even the rude Hill Khāṛiā family requires shelter from sun and rain for the two main purposes of ordinary living and cooking. The Hill Khāṛiā's dwelling-house is a small rectangular hut, with little or no plinth; but with walls made of logs of *sāl* (*Shorea robusta*) wood planted in the ground and plastered over with mud and having a roof of generally two sloping wooden frames thatched over with layers of thatching grass or paddy-straw, supported on a few *sāl* posts. Ordinarily, only one room is used by the Hill Khāṛiā for both a living or sleeping room and a kitchen. In some houses, the only room is separated into two halves, one for sleeping and the other for cooking. The cooking is generally done on an open earthen oven, made by simply digging a hole in the ground, though a raised oven on the ground is not unknown. Dry wood is used as fuel.

The dwelling houses of the Dūdh and Ḍhelki Khāṛiās are more substantial than those of the Hill Khāṛiās. They vary in construction according to the means of the family. The better-built houses, though rather few, derive their technique from the bachelors' house. A very few houses are even four-thatched. The ground-plan of their ordinary dwelling-house (see illustration) is rectangular and is about 15 to 25 feet in length and 8 to 12 feet in breadth. The plinth and the floor of the houses are generally raised by piling earth to about one to two feet above the level of the ground. The four wall-posts (B) are planted vertically at the four corners by digging holes in the ground. Larger houses may be supported upon eight posts. These wall-posts (B in the illustration) are about 7 to 10 feet in height. Similarly, the two main supporting wall-posts (A) of about 9 to 15 feet in height are planted vertically in the middle on either side of the breadth of the house. The main ridge-pole (D) is placed across the two main wall-posts (A) and is held in position within the hole made on the top of the latter and fastened with ropes made of the bark of the *chōp* (*Bauhinia scandens*). Then two more tie-beam purlins (E) are placed parallel to the ridge-pole over the wall-post (D) on either side and held in position in the same way as described above. The position of the wall-posts is determined by the condition that the first two pairs of rafters (R) on either extremity must rest on the ridge-pole, and the latter is lashed with *chōp*-bark rope within the forks formed by the crossed ends of the two rafters. The remaining five to seven pairs of rafters (R) are placed in a similar position over the tie-beam purlins (E) and the ridge pole, and the latter is again tied and fixed in a similar manner as before with the rafter. The other end of the rafter is fixed and lashed with the tie-beam purlin with *chōp*-bark rope (now-a-days iron nails are sometimes used), and the free ends of these rafters project about one to two feet from the purlin. The walls of the house are either made of bamboos or *śāl* logs or branches of trees planted vertically in the ground. These are often plastered over with mud on both sides. Many houses have also solid mud walls. Two wooden posts (C) are planted vertically, about 3 feet one from the other, at the opening left in one of the two long sides of the house for the door. Then the bamboos meant to serve as thatch purlins are placed horizontally over each side of the rafters and lashed with rope made of the bark of the *lāṇḍām* or *chōp* (*Bauhunia scandens*). Lastly, thatching-grass is laid 2 to 3 inches in thickness over the frame-work of the roof thus constructed. The finishing touch to the roof is given by placing two other thatching purlins over the roof, parallel to the ridge-pole and one on each side of it, and tied with the thatching purlins under the roof. Similarly on each side strong thatching purlins are placed over the roof, parallel to and over the tie-beam purlin and fastened to it. This is done so that the wind may not blow off the thatching grass. Windows are conspicuous by their absence.

The floors and walls are, if possible, coated over with a solution of cowdung and water to make the surface smooth. A well-to-do Khāṛiā family, as mentioned above, has more than one such hut or house.

Most of the Dūdh and Ḍhelki Khāṛiā houses have a small shed or lean-to at the back or on one side of the house. This is used as a cow-shed or a pig-sty. The more well-to-do Khāṛiā families have each more than one hut besides a separate cattle-shed and a pig-sty.

Water-Vessel Stands (garsauri). Most of the Dūdh Khāṛiā houses have, each, one or more water-vessel-stands by the side of the main house or hut.[53] Such a vessel-stand is composed of a long thick wooden plank fixed horizontally over two vertical wooden posts planted on the ground. Generally big earthen vessels or pitchers filled with drinking water are placed on it. This is said to be done in order to avoid damping the floor of the dwelling-house.

(iv) *Fire (Timsong) and Cooking*.

One side of the Khāṛiā's dwelling house is generally set apart for cooking food. Here either dug-out or raised ovens are made. Most Khāṛiās, and especially the Hill Khāṛiās, keep the fire burning day and night all the year round and even in the hot summer days. When fire goes out in any house, it is borrowed from a neighbour's. This might suggest the inference that the use and method of making fire is not their own invention. But, the Khāṛiās are, as a matter of fact, skilled in the primitive method of making fire by friction with two pieces of wood (of the kind locally known as *putri* or *desar*),– a method which they generally still employ when they go to the jungles for hunting or other business. The piece of wood placed horizontally on the ground is called the *māṛom* or *māi*

53 Similar water-vessel-stands we have also seen in front of the houses of the *Bhil* tribe in the Udaipur State of Rajputana.

(mother), and the stick perpendicularly held and twirled round on a groove in the former piece is called *ānḍrā*, *lit.*, the male [stick]. They use dry leaves as well as wood for fuel.

The Khāṛiā Forge.—It is interesting to note that the invention or use of a rude forge by the rudest section of the Khāṛiā tribe indicates the great advance in culture which they have made since the time when their prehistoric forefathers were ignorant of even any method of making fire. In order to sharpen their tools and implements the Hill Khāṛiās of Barābhūm (Mānbhūm) and Dhalbhūm (Singbhūm), who live away from villages where Lohārs or Kāmār blacksmiths live, used, until recent times, to employ, and still in rare instances employ, a primitive forge. The blast for this forge is produced by a pair of rude bellows made up of a pair of conical caps about a cubit and a half in height, made of leaves stitched together with grass and firmly planted upon hollows in the ground. The blast produced by the alternate and sudden swelling and sinking of the caps is conveyed through a pair of bamboo tubes to a heap ot ignited charcoal. The blades of the Hill Khāṛiā's implements are (or used to be) heated in this fire until they become malleable enough to be hammered with a stone into the requisite sharpness.

(v) *Food and its Preparation.*

As for the principal meals of the Khāṛiās of the different sections, we have briefly referred to them in our account of their daily life (pp. 72,76-77 *ante*). Rice, as we have seen, is the staple food of the Dūdh and Ḍhelki Khāṛiās; and the Hill Khāṛiās, too, prefer to have rice for their chief food. Most Hill Khāṛiās, however, do not grow rice themselves but procure it by barter from their neighbours whenever they can. For the rest they have to depend occasionally on the spoils of the chase, and much more frequently on edible leaves, roots, and fruits that they collect in their native jungles, and the not abundant crops of *Ramakali* (a kind of bean) and a few common green vegetables such as pumpkin gourds, sweet potatoes, brinjals, cucumbers and the like which some of them grow.

The Khāṛiās cook food by boiling, roasting or frying. They use salt in large quantities. They eat boiled rice mixed with salt without throwing out the water in which it is boiled. The Dūdh and Ḍhelki Khāṛiās prepare a sort of curry by boiling green vegetables and pulses with which they mix salt, powdered turmeric, onion and pepper. They eat fish and meat when available; but except perhaps some Ḍhelki Khāṛiās and the *Chhotgohoṇḍi* section of the Dūdh Khāṛiās, other sections of Khāṛiās strictly abjure beef. Raw meat or raw fish is not taken by any Khāṛiā. As a delicacy on certain festive occasions they prepare and eat cakes of flour made of rice or wheat or certain pulses, either boiled in water or, if possible, fried in oil. At home women do the cooking.

As for jungle produce, the Hill Khāṛiās eat almost everything that is edible. The principal jungle products used by the Khāṛiās of all sections and by the Hill Khāṛiās in particular, and the methods of their preparation for food of different jungle products and the produce of their fields are given below.

Among edible leaves (*śāg*), they eat those of *Serlā śāg* (Hacouria Romonchi), *Phuṭkal śāg* (Ficus injectoria), *Poi śāg* (Basella rubra), *Hurhuriā śāg* (Cleomene viscosa), *Oṛōl* (Hindi, *Koinār*) *śāg*, (Bauhinia malabaricum, or Bauhinia purpuria variegata), *Chākōndā śāg*, *Pechki śāg* (Arum Colacasia) and *Moongā śāg*. Except the last two, other *śāgs* or edible leaves are either boiled in water or steeped in the steaming hot starchy water drained off rice just boiled, and are mixed with a little salt and eaten as side-dishes with boiled rice. *Chākōndā śāg* and *Moongā śāg* (Moringa pterygosperma) are dried and pounded generally before being steeped in hot rice-water and are eaten with boiled rice.

Among edible roots and seeds, fruits and flowers utilised by the Khāṛiās for food may be mentioned the *Khesāri* (Scirpus Kysoor, Roxburghii) which is eaten either raw or boiled in water; *Kūndri* (Cephalandia Indica) which is either boiled or stewed or fried in oil; *Alsā* (Cephalandia spc. proculoides) called in Hindi *Ban Kūndri*, which children eat either raw or roasted in fire, and of which the seeds are also fried in oil and eaten by both the adult and the young. Tender roots of the *simri* or cotton tree (Bombax malabaricum), called in Hindi *Semar*, are eaten raw, and its seeds are also fried in oil and eaten. Certain mushrooms (*fungus*) which in Khāṛiā are called "ū'" or "ūd" are also fried in oil and eaten. *Kuril*, as the young shoots of the bamboo (Dendrocalamus strictus) are called in Khāṛiā, are boiled in water and then fried and eaten.

The seeds of the *Karkoṭā* (Dilienia Indica), called *Kerkoṭ* in Hindi, are first boiled in water, then dried and pounded, and the powder is again boiled in rice-

---

* Boiled rice is called 'Pū', unboiled rice 'Romkub', and unhusked rice or paddy 'Bā', in the Khāṛiā language.

water and eaten with boiled rice. The corolla of the flowers of the *Murun* (Bassia latifolia), called Mohuā in Hindi, is either eaten raw, or is dried and then boiled for food when required. Oil is also sometimes extracted from its seeds.

The oil generally used for preparing food by the Khāṛiā is extracted from mustard-seeds, and the oil used for burning in lamps is generally extracted from *sargujā* or the niger oil-seed (Guizotia abyssinica). Oil is also extracted from the seeds of the *Bāngru* (Sleichera trijuga) called *Kusum* in Hindi.

In the more well-to-do Khāṛiā families a sort of cake is prepared with the dried up corolla of the *Murun* and eaten as a delicacy. This is prepared by parching over a fire dried *Murun* flowers in an empty earthen pot. The parched flowers are taken out, and, while warm, pounded along with some seeds of either *sarguja* (Guizotia abyssinica) or *til* (Sesamum Indica) till they get thoroughly mixed. This is then made into small cakes and eaten.

The following jungle fruits are eaten, when ripe, by the Khāṛiās of all sections: the *Jāmun* (Eugenia jambolana); the *Tapkar*, called in Hindi *Bar* (Ficus Bengalensis); the *Konor*, called in Hindi *Jitia Pipar* (Ficus religiosa); the *Bāngru*, called in Hindi *Kusum* (sleichera trijuga), the *Tiril*, called in Hindi *Keond* (Diospyros melanoxylon); the *Luā*, called in Hindi *Dumbar* (Ficus glomerata); the *Kulap*, called in Hindi *Bael* (Aegle Marmelos); the *Char* (Buchania latifolia); the *Papra* (Gardenia Latifolia); the *Landum*, called in Hindi *Bhursā*; the *Khāksi* (Suffa sp. ?); *Irin*, called in Hindi

Bair which is the wild hog-plum ; the *Laro*, called in Hindi *Khajur*, which is the fruit of the wild date-palm (Foenix sylvestris) ; and the *Ḍāhu* or wood-apple (Artocarpus lakoocha). Of these the ripe fruit of the *Irin* or hog-plum is also dried in the sun, made into powder, and, when required, moistened in cold water and eaten as sauce with boiled rice. The seeds of the *Ḍāhu* fruit are also fried and eaten by themselves. Children, besides eating the ripe fruit of the *Tiril* (Hindi, *Keoñd*), also take the unripe fruit when very young and tender, wash it in water several times until it becomes quite white and then eat it raw. Of the *Soso* or *Bhelwā* fruit (Semicarpis Anacardium), the flower or fleshy part is eaten, but the black (seed-) portion is never eaten.

The kernel of the *Baherā* (Terminalia Bellerica) nut is eaten by children either raw or roasted. Oil is also sometimes extracted from the *Baherā* and used in cooking. The ripe fruit of the *Ḍimbu* (Cucumis spc. ?) is eaten without any preparation ; it is also cut into slices, dried in the sun, and either fried in oil or roasted in fire, aud taken as a sauce with boiled rice. The fruit of the *Kundri* is cut into slices and either fried in oil and taken with boiled rice, or is steeped in hot rice-water and eaten with boiled rice.

The Khāṛia also prepares a kind of vinegar from the ripe *Jāmun* fruit. The fruit is kept steeped in cold water for about ten days until fermentation sets in. Then the whole thing is strained and the seeds thrown out, and the liquid extract stored in bottles and used, when required, chiefly as a remedy for stomach-troubles. The pulp of the *Kulap* or the *Bael* fruit is also used in making a kind of cooling drink or *sherbat* by diluting it in cold water and sweetening it with molasses. The ripe fruit of the *Teñton* (Hindi *Imli*, Bengali *Teñtul*), or tamarind (Tamaridus Indica) is eaten as sauce with rice. The Jack-fruit and the mango (Mangifera Indica) and *Karanj* (Pongamia glabra) are grown by a few Dūdh Khāṛiās and fewer Ḍhelki Khāṛiās. The ripe jack-fruit is relished as food and its seeds are roasted and eaten by children. These seeds and also green jack-fruit are sometimes boiled and eaten as vegetable-curry.

Among pulses, the *Māso*, called in Hindi *Urid* (Phaseolus Roxburghii), is eaten raw and also by boiling in water for a side-dish with boiled rice. The Dūdh and Ḍhelki Khāṛiās grow in their fields besides *Māso*, some other pulses such as *Barai* (Phaseolus mungo), *Rahar* (Cajanus Indicus) and *Bodi* (vigna catiang); and millets such as *gondli* (Panicum miliare) and *māṛuā* (Eleusine Coracana). These are boiled in water and eaten. Besides salt, the only condiments commonly used are turmeric powder and pepper. Onion is also used. Most Dūdh and some Ḍhelki Khāṛiās now grow in or about their homestead lands certain kitchen vegetables such as brinjal, beans, cucumber, pumpkin, sweet potato, tomato, lady's - finger, and radish. Maize is also grown by some Khāṛiās.

As a delicacy, particularly at weddings and certain festivals, bread and cakes (*piṭhā*) are prepared with rice-flour. To make bread, rice is steeped in water overnight, taken out in the morning, pounded with the mortar and pestle, rolled on a stone or on a small plank of wood, made into round flat pieces and fried over a fire. To make *piṭhā*, warm water is added to rice flour to make it into dough. This dough is mixed with the flour of the *urid* pulse, and the mixture is made up into cakes. These are placed in a bamboo frame-work suspended inside an earthen vessel with boiling water; and the cakes are thus cooked by steam.

As for animal food, the Hill Khāṛiās eat almost every non-poisonous animal food except beef. They abstain also from eating pork and monkey-flesh and mutton. Certain grubs (*kalai pōk*) are caught and eaten by children with relish. A. P. Driver speaks of two sections of the Khāṛiās which he names respectively the "Pahariyas" and the "Heosas", and says that the latter "eat cows and the animals that have died of disease, and most of them wear only leaves." We have not been able to trace the "Heosas", though a few of the Mānbhum Khāṛiās, like their neighbours the small tribe of Pahiṛās (now almost extinct), have been known to wear a kind of bark-cloth in times of famine and extreme distress. But they too abstain from eating carrion. The Hill Khāṛiās of Dhalbhūm are reported by some of their neighbours to eat carrion, even of cows, if they can procure it; but the Dhalbhūm Khāṛiās themselves strongly repudiate the imputation. The Ḍhelki Khāṛiās, as we have said, have, or until recently had, no objection to eating beef which the Dūdh section religiously eschew.

V. Ball in his *Jungle Life in India* describes how during his tour in the Manbhnm District in 1865, he saw a Hill Khāṛiā matron distributing on plates of *śāl* leaves to the other members of her family for their morning meal the flesh and entrails of a small animal, and how "wrapping up her own portion between a couple of leaves, she threw it on the fire in order to give it a very primitive cooking." Although the rudest Hill Khāṛiā at the present day does not eat raw meat, the method of scorching meat for food by wrapping it up betwen leaves and throwing it on the fire is yet practised by the Hill Khāṛiās and some other neighbouring tribes on the same level of culture, some of whom (such as the Birhōṛs) still employ the primitive method of scorching meat by placing it between two red-hot stones, as we have ourselves seen.

But the Dūhh Khāṛiā and the Ḍhelki Khāṛiā, however, now usually boil meat in water and add salt, pepper and turmeric-powder to give it flavour. Meat is also roasted for food. Fish (Khāṛiā, *Kādong*) when available, is eaten with relish and cooked in the same way as meat.

Tobacco:—Most Hill Khāṛiās smoke tobacco in leaf-cigarettes (*Phikā*). Dūdh and Ḍhelki Khāṛiās chew powdered tobacco with a pinch of lime.

Domestic Animals and Fowls:—All sections of Khāṛiās keep and rear fowls. The Hill Khāṛiās rarely keep any animal except the dog. The other sections keep cattle and pigs besides dogs.

(vi) *Drink and its Preparation*.

1. *Golāng*:—The Khāṛiā, like other primitive tribes, are fond of rice-beer called *Golāng* in the Khāṛiā language. As among other Mūṇḍā tribes, it forms an essential offering to some of their deities and spirits. The method of preparation is the same as among their neighbours, the Mūṇḍās and the Orāoñs, in Chōṭā-Nāgpur. This is as follows: About eight or nine

pounds of rice, *māṛuā* (Eleusine Coracana), or *gōndli* (Panicam miliare) is half boiled in water. The water is next drained out of the boiled grains which are then spread out to dry. Rice so prepared for making beer is called in Khāṛiā "Koñsṛō pē". When quite dry and cold, the grains are rubbed between the hands and mixed with tabloids prepared of rice flour and a concoction of certain wild vegetable roots. This concoction (*rānu*) possesses intoxicating properties. This mixture of rice-grains and the tabloids is then put into an earthen jar (*Kūyū*) filled with water. The mouth of the jār is covered up with straw and its contents are stowed away to ferment for a few days, varying from three or four days in warm weather to eight or nine days in cold weather. The first drops are offered to the Ancestor-spirits. The secret of the particular roots used in the preparation of rice-beer appears to be known only to a limited number of persons who alone prepare the tabloids and sell them in the market.

2. *Phulli*:—This drink is made by stewing for twelve hours or so over a slow fire fresh *murun* (Hindi, *māhuā*) flowers mixed with beans. When the stew becomes cold it is taken as both food and drink. This is not intoxicating.

3. *Ārkhi*:—The Khāṛiās do not ordinarily distil liquor (*ārkhi*) from *murun* or *mohuā* (bassia latifolia), though they now drink such liquor with relish whenever they can obtain it.

(vii) *Household Furniture, Vessels and Implements.*

1. *Beds* (Plate V):—Most Khāṛiās sleep on a date-palm-leaf mat called *jentu pāṭiā*, spread over the

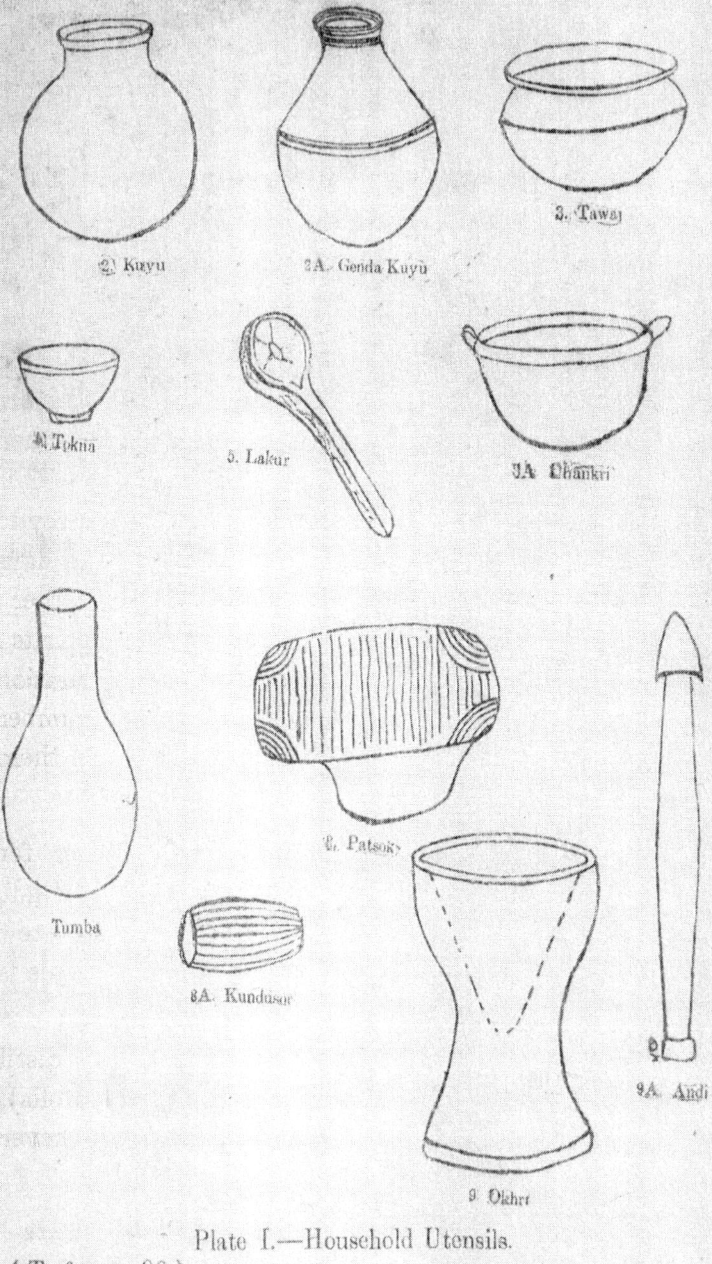

Plate I.—Household Utensils.

(To face p. 90)

bare floor. It is only in very well-to-do families that a string-bed or two may be met with. This string-bed or cot is called *Pārkōm* in Khāṛiā and *Khāṭiā* in *Hindi*. It has a wooden frame-work; and the net-work which forms the bed is made of strings of the *sabai* (*Ichaemum Augustifolium*) grass. The netting is twisted work. A rectangular plank of wood called *Soṛkōm* (Hindi, *piñṛhā*) is used by some Khāṛiās as head-rest.

2. *Gourd Vessels*:—Besides various forms of earthenware vessels described below, the Khāṛiās use gourd vessels of different shapes and sizes. The most common form of these vessels called '*Tūmbā*' (Plate II, fig. 1) is used for fetching, storing and drinking water and other liquids. Long-shaped small gourds are cut in such a way as to serve as spoons (Plate II, fig. 5). Small gourds are also used for storing seeds of different kinds.

3. *Earthen-ware Vessels*:—The Khāṛiās now use earthen vessels, though they do not themselves make them. They generally buy them in local markets either for cash or in exchange for jungle birds, deer-skins, honey, *etc*. Wheel-made pottery is made by a special caste called Kumhārs, one or two families of whom are found in the larger villages in the Khāṛiā country, living a little apart from the Khāṛiā or other aboriginal quarters (*bastis*) of the villages. Short notes on the different kinds of vessels used by the Khāṛiās with their Khāṛiā names are given below:—

Kūyū:—This is a very big baked earthen vessel for storing water (Plate II, fig. 2). A similar vessel for cooking rice is the *Goṅgḍing kūyū*.

Geṇḍā Kūyū:—This is a smaller earthen vessel for bringing water. (Plate II, fig. 2a). Still smaller ones in domestic use are the *Bhāṇḍā* and the *Chūkā*.

Tāwā:—This is an earthen vessel for cooking and frying rice, meat, *etc*. (Plate II, fig. 3).

Ḍhāñkṛi:—This is an earthen plate for eating from. *Ḍhāñkṛi Kuṇḍu* is an earthen-ware cup for holding curries.

Tōknā (Hindi):—This is an earthen cup for drinking liquids from (Plate II, fig. 4).

Due to contact with modern civilisation, these earthen vessels, plates and other utensils are now being replaced by metal vessels, especially of brass or bell-metal and aluminium, particularly among the Dūdh and Ḍhelki sections.

Lāṇḍi (Hindi, Lakur):—This is a spoon made of baked earth and also sometimes of gourd or wood. (Plate II, fig. 5).

4. *Leaf Vessels*:—Leaf-vessels and leaf-plates of different sizes are in common use among all sections of the Khāṛiās. The varieties more commonly made and used are:—

Kāṭkom (Hindi, Pātri):—This is a leaf plate made of *S'āl* or *Lamdam* or *Chihōr* (Bauhinia Vahli) leaves by stitching them with fine small stick-needles (Plate III, fig. 6). It is used for serving food upon.

Kholdā or *Kholkā* :—This is a leaf-cup made by folding one single leaf or several leaves generally of either *chihōr* or of *śāl* and then stitching them with small bamboo-splinters in the form of pins. (Plate III, fig. 6 A).

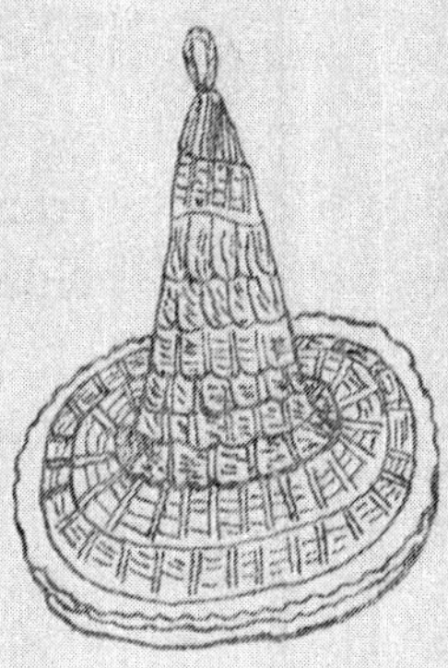

45. Korbo

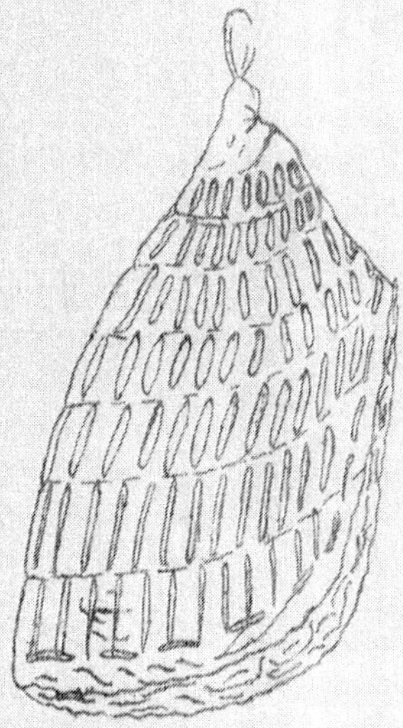

46. Gungu

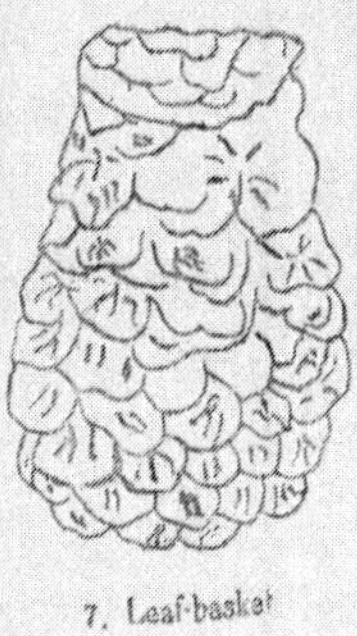

7. Leaf-basket

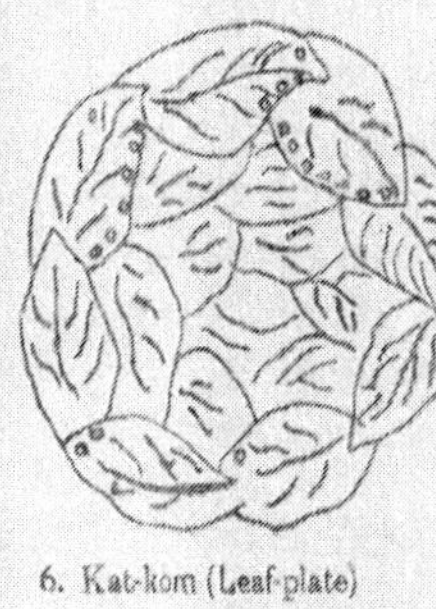

6. Kat-kom (Leaf-plate)

6A. Kholka (Leaf cup)

Plate II.—30. Industry in Leaves.
(Leaf-hat, Leaf-water proof, etc.)

(To face p. 92)

A large leaf-cup is also called *Tholi*, and a small leaf-cup is called *Sūṛū*.

Other artifacts required for preparing food are implements for husking, threshing, pounding and cutting.

5. *Implements used in husking paddy*:—It has already been said that almost every Khāṛiā woman at early morning husks paddy for the day's requirment either at holes made over rocks in or near the village or at her own house with the *Ānḍi* and *Ōkhṛi*.

Ōkhṛi :—This is the husking mortar made of a block of wood hollowed out in the form of a large inverted bell in which paddy is husked and other substances may be pounded. (Plate II, fig .9).

Ānḍi or *Enḍi*:—This is the pestle or the long piece of wood with which grain is husked in the *Ōkhṛi*. (Plate II, fig. 9 A). An iron ferule is often fitted into the bottom of the *Ānḍi* to prevent its splitting. It is held by both the hands at the butt-end (B) and wielded vertically.

6. *Implements for Pounding* :—The Khāṛiās use a flat stone (grindstone) and a rounded stone (hand-roller) for pounding turmeric and other substances as also rice and other grains besides roots and tubers.

Ri-soreng or *Pāt sōr* (grinding stone), or *Kundu Sōr* (pounding-stone).—This consists of two stones, one an ordinary piece of rectangular flat stone (grind-stone or *Pāt Sōr*), sometimes indented all over with straight notches (Pl. II, fig. 8), and the other a round handy stone-roller (*Kunḍu Sōr*) sometimes similarly indented all over (Pl. II, fig. 8 A). The thing to be powdered is placed upon the flat stone and pounded or powdered by continually rolling the stone-roller held in the hands near its two ends, forwards and backwards alternately over it.

7. *Vegetable-cutter and meat-cutter* :—

Chhūri—This is a cutting implement which consists of a piece of flat iron sharpened at one edge, like the ordinary knife blade. It is of different sizes.

8. *Basketry* :—Baskets made of strips of jungle bamboos are generally bought from the markets and not manufactured by thc Khāṛiās except by a few Hill Khāṛiā families. But baskets are made of S'āl leaves by the Khāṛiās themselves. In the weaving of baskets, work starts from the bottom. Khāṛiās also make and use bags (*Jālkhāri*) (Plate IV, fig. 16) made of a net-work of strings. The strings are made of fibres of the *Chōp*-bark.

Leaf baskets of different sizes and patterns are made by stitching the leaves, one overlapping the other, with the stalks of leaves serving as needles. The leaf-baskets are used in storing grains and carrying them in carrying-nets and poles known as *Alidargo* (*H. Sikā-bāhingā*) (Plate XI, fig. 39).

There are different kinds of baskets made in different styles and used for different purposes. The more important ones are as follows :—

Ḍhāki :—This is a very big basket made of fine rounded bamboo strips about one inch in diameter. The weaving is wicker-work. After the basket is made it is coated over with a solution of water and cow-dung so as to protect it from the attack of white ants and make the basket more durable (Pl. IV, Fig.10). It is used for carrying and measuring grains in large quantities and in

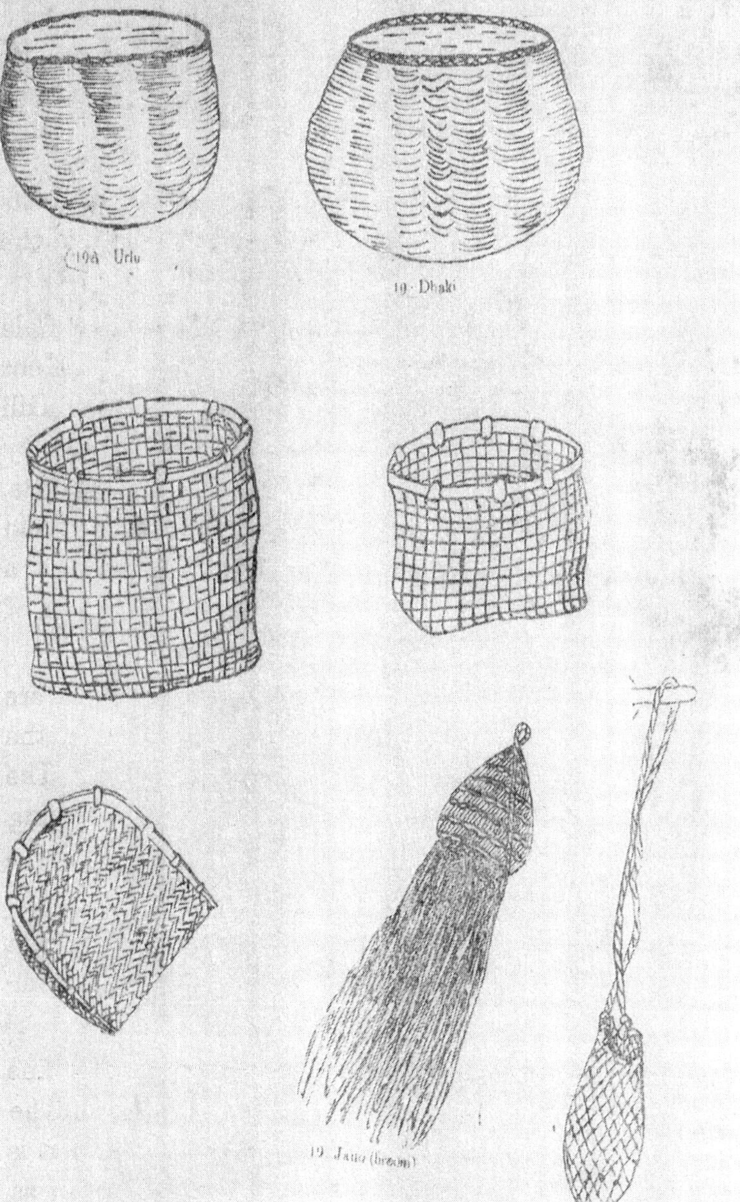

Plate III.—31. Basketry

(To face p. 94)

bringing fuel and dry leaves from the jungles.

Urlu :—This is also similar to the former but smaller in size and of a different pattern, as shown in Plate IV, fig.10 A. It is uniformly equal in diameter from top to bottom. It is used by women in carrying commodities to the markets, carrying manure to the fields, and for similar other purposes.

Daurā :—This is made of very thin bamboo strips, each of about one inch in diameter. It is a rectangular basket, though the mouth is sometimes rounded and strengthened by strong bamboo strips. The technique of the weaving is checker-work all round. It is needed for ordinary household purposes (Pl. IV, fig .11). A smaller rectangular basket of the same pattern is called *Kundui*.

Gonbid :—This is similar to the *Daurā* but round in shape.

Ḍāli :—This is a minature form of the pattern described above. It is used by boys and girls for collecting green vegetables and for keeping light household articles, e.g. eggs, *etc*. (Pl. IV, fig. 11 A).

Samu :—This is a flat winnowing-basket of twilled work made of bamboo strips, often painted. Its shape is half elliptical at the top where strong bamboo strips are used. It is used for cleaning grains and also for magical purposes. It is often coated over with a solution of water and cow-dung. (Pl. IV, fig. 12).

Jono :—This is an ordinary broom-stick either made of very thin bamboo-strips or of a kind of grass. One side, about one inch broad, of the free end is woven and then rounded up (Pl. IV,fig .13), forming a conical head at the top which is used as a handle.

(viii) *Industries.*

1. *Weaving and Spinning*:—The Khāṛiās have long been in the habit of using clothes of some sort. They do not, however, weave the clothes themselves but buy them from local weavers. Many Dūdh and Ḍhelki Khāṛiā families, however, spin thread, and possess implements for spinning threads. These have been probably borrowed from their Hindu neighbours as the names of the implements are not their own. These are:–

Charkhā:—This is the universal "Charkā" or spinning-wheel (Pl. X, fig. 35).

Rantā:—This is the common ginnning implement in use throughout India (Pl. X, fig. 36.)

Dharā:—This is also a crude instrument for preparing thread and is similar to the ordinary "ṭākli" (Pl. X, fig.37).

Kumti:—This is a rectangular frame (1½ ft. by 10 in.) consisting of small strips of bamboo with a hole on the strips through which the warp passes (Pl X, fig. 38). One end of the warp is tied to a post. The other end of the warp is tied to a stick; and the man weaves with a thin bamboo-needle called *chhuch* shown in Pl. X, fig. 38 A.

Ganjiā:—This is a small net-bag woven by the Hill Khāṛiās with *siāñṛi* fibres.

(2) *Mat–Making.*

Mats of different sizes for sleeping and sitting purposes are made by Khāṛiā women, generally with

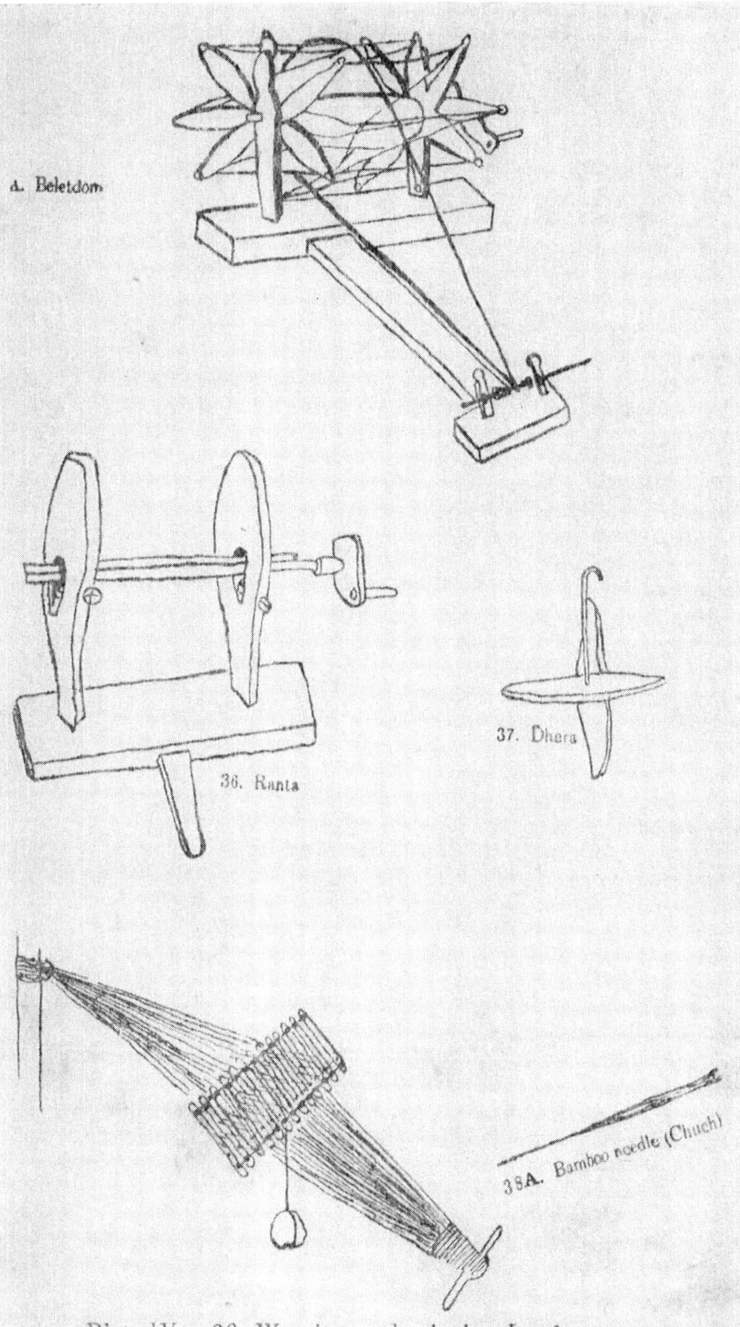

Plate IV.—32. Weaving and spinning Implements.

(To face p. 96)

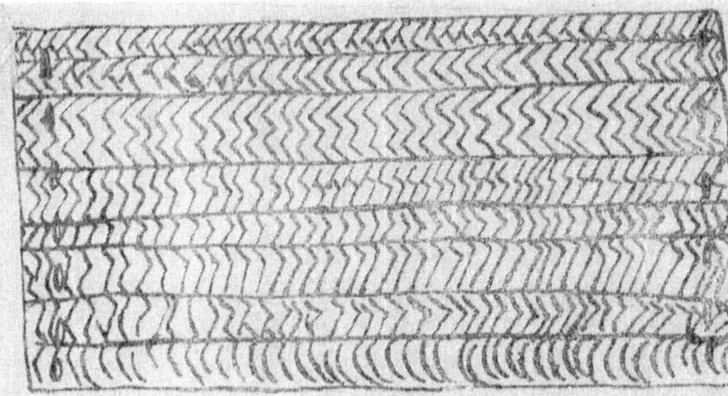

14. Charo (mat)

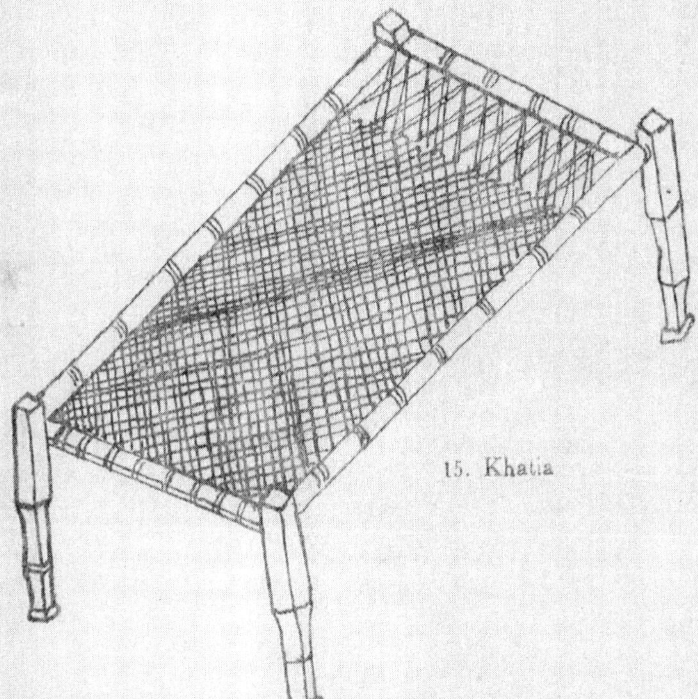

15. Khatia

Plate V.—Mat & string-bed.

(To face p. 97)

the leaves of the wild dwarf-palm (*Phoenix Acaulis*) trees. Mats are also sometimes made of split bamboo. No other leaves or grass or sedge of any kind is used for the purpose. A mat of bamboo is called *Chārō* and of date-leaf *Jhintu*. These mats are generally rectangular in shape and the dimensions vary from 3 to 6 ft. by 7 to 15 ft. The pattern of weaving mats is double-twilled work and the two free leaf-ends are stitched with rope (Pl. V, fig. 14). No mat-loom is used. Mat-making is the work of women at their leisure.

(3) *Rope and string-making.*

The Khāṛiās make ropes of *sabai* fibres (*Ichaemum augustifolium*) and of *chōp* bark (*Bauhimia Scandens*) and also of the leaves of the common aloe plant. Their method of making ropes is as follows:—

The bark of the *chōp* (*Bauhinia Scandens*) or the leaves of the common aloe are steeped in water for a few days. Then they are taken out and the fibres are twined together to form strings and ropes of the required thickness.

(4) *Oil-press.*

The oil-press generally used by the Dūdh and some Ḍhelki Khāṛiās in their houses is of the following type:—

It consists of two wooden planks. The lower plank has a circular groove in the middle with an outlet on each side. In the groove are placed two (rarely one) bundles or *pūṭlis* containing oil seeds ground and steamed beforehand. The *pūṭlis* are made either of plaited fibres of the *Udro* tree or of plaited bamboo. The *pūṭlis* are crushed between the two planks which are fastened together either at both ends with ropes or only at one end. In the latter case another pair of planks or rods of wood are fitted cross-wise into the open end and two or more men press down the open end by sitting upon the cross planks. Oil comes out of the two outlets of the central groove.

(ix) *Travel and Transport.*

The Khāṛiās ordinarily carry things in baskets. The women carry them on their head while the men carry them in carrying-nets slung on the carrying-pole or "*Sikā-bāhingā*" placed over the shoulder.

1. *Sikā-bāhingā*:—It consists of two parts. A pair of "Sikā" nets (Pl. XI, fig. 39) are made of twisted strings, generally of *chōp*-fibre. The baskets to be carried are placed one on the circular bottom-end of each *sikā*, and the free-ends of the two *sikās* are fastened each to one end of the wooden "bāngā" or "*bāhingā*"-pole.

The "bāngā" or "bāhingā" (Khāṛiā, *ārgo*) is a smooth wooden stick about 1 yard long and tapering towards both ends, being about 1½ inch broad at the middle of its length and about ½ inch at each end. The two ends are grooved so that the "sikā" may not slip out. Equal weights are placed on each side, and the middle of the "Bāngā" is placed on the shoulder of the man carrying it. The two baskets are not allowed to touch the ground when thus carried.

2. *Sagaṛ*:—This is the country block-wheel cart drawn by a bullock. The wheels are of solid wood and every portion of the cart is made of wood. The wheel is not generally made of one single piece of wood, but

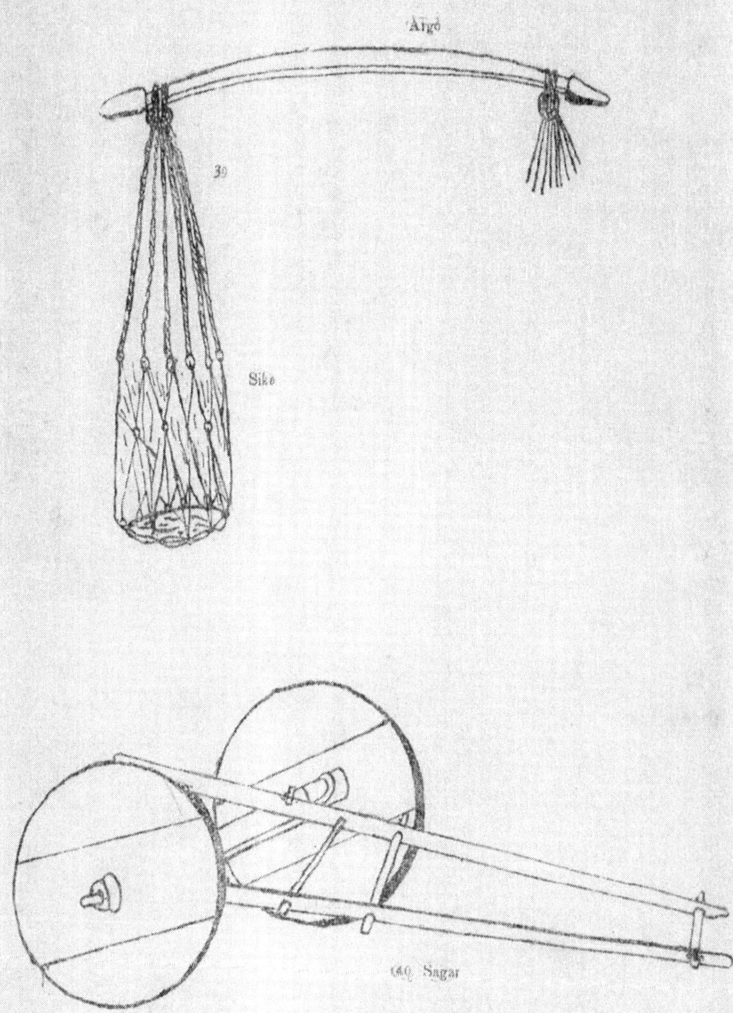

Transport

Plate VI.—Carrying net & pole, and Block-wheel cart.

(To face p. 98)

different pieces, not more than three, are joined together (Pl. XI, fig. 40).

(x) *Clothing and Ornaments.*

1. *Dress*:—Khāṛiā children remain naked till about five or six years of age, after which boys wear only a '*khadiā*'. This is a piece of loin-cloth seven to ten inches in width and about one yard and a half in length. It is passed round the thigh and wound round the waist. This is worn till the age of about twelve.

Adult persons at home wear besides the '*khadiā*' and, over it, a '*kārdhāni*' (which is a piece of cloth twelve to fourteen inches in width and two to three yards in length). This *Kārdhāni* hangs down about twelve inches from the waist towards the thigh. A very old man only wears a *khadiā* like a boy. While going out to market or other places, and in winter, they wrap up their body with a long sheet of thick loin cloth, now-a-days sometimes a blanket. This loin-cloth is known in Khāṛiā as a *Borokā*.

From about 5 or 6 years of age girls wear a '*lāhāng-lūṭni*' which is a piece of loin-cloth, 1½ yards long by 1½ feet in breadth, generally with red or black borders. Adult women wear on the waist a '*lāhāngā*', which is a loin-cloth about two yards long and 2½ feet wide with or without borders and reaching down to the knees. Some women now cover their breasts either by using a *lāhāngā* a little longer than two yards, or by wearing, in addition to the ordinary shorter *lāhāngā*, another piece of cloth called '*Rāgo lūṭni*' round the chest.

Women (particularly young women) decorate their hair and ears with flowers and leaves, particularly on festive occasions.

2. *Ornaments*:—The ornaments of the Dūdh and Ḍhelki Khāṛiā women are generally made of brass, but ornaments made of other metals such as nickel, or even silver are not unknown. Their jewellery consists of glass beads and beads of *Kāsi*-grass-seeds, brass necklace (*Hānsuli*), generally six brass armlets (*Karang*) on each arm, brass earrings—one at the top of each ear-lobe (*Kanbouri*) and another at the bottom (*Lurka*), brass finger rings (*Mū'dhi*) and toe-rings (*Jhunṭiā* and *Kāṭri*), iron hair-pins (*Khōngsō*), and wooden or bamboo hair-combs (*Kānausi*). As their names indicate the use of most of these metal ornaments have been borrowed from their Hindu neighbours and are known by their Hindi names.

Boys use brass *Berā* (Khāṛiā, *Kaṛam*) on both hands. Young people of both sexes wear necklaces made of beads bought from local markets. A Hill Khāṛiā woman wears six or seven brass armlets (*Khāṛu*) on each arm, a brass pin on each side of the nose, and brass-rings (*mūdi*) on the fingers and toes. They tie up their hair at the back with *tasar* silk ribbons.

(xi) *Hunting* (*Lāmṭām*) *and its weapons*.

As has already been said, the Khāṛiās and especially the Hill Khāṛiās are expert hunters. With bows and arrows and sticks, and rarely with spears, they kill almost all kinds of birds and animals. The common game of the Khāṛiā country are the deer and the hare, pea-fowls and jungle-fowls, pigeons and partridges, snipes and occasionally quails.

The different kinds of weapons used in hunting are described below:—

1. *Ghunta*:—This is a sling for throwing stones, and consists of a string with its middle doubled up. In the middle of the string there is a broad position "P" as shown in Pl. VI, fig. 16 A. The pellet is placed there, and the free ends ("A") of the string are held in the hand and the pellet is whirled round and one end let loose in the direction at which the pellet is aimed; and off goes the pellet in a violent motion. It is used for shooting birds.

Kom and *Kā'* :—This is the common arrow made of two parts. The arrow-head called '*chiāri*' or '*kāin-kōm*', made of iron, of different shapes as shown in Pl. VI, figures 18 and 18 B, forms the first part. This is inserted into the second part which is the shaft made of bamboo of a diameter of two inches and a length of about 1½ feet. The junction of the joint is lashed with *landam* or *chōp* (*Bauhinia scandens*) fibre. The *Kā'* is the common bow.

For killing small birds the arrow-head used is blunt and conical-shaped with its point towards the shaft and is called "*Ṭhoṭi*" (Pl. VI, fig. 18 A). The fore-end of the shaft is often decorated with two or three bird's feathers.

2. *Kọm-Thongi*:—This is an arrow-case made of pumpkin-gourd, and sometimes of bamboo (Pl. VI, fig. 19).

3. *Ghuinta* or *Gunta*:—It is a pellet bow (Pl. VI, fig. 20) made of the same materials as the long bow, the difference being that there are two strings separated by a small stick ("S") about two inches long inserted about six inches from one end. There is a small net-work

("N") near the stick for holding the pellet. It is thrown in the same manner as the arrow.

4. *Mahā-Kinkom*:—This is a spear. There are two varieties of it. In the first variety (Pl. VII, fig. 21) the handle, made of solid bamboo about five feet in height, is inserted into the socket of the iron spear-head. In the second variety (Pl. VII, fig. 21 A) the spear-head is inserted with force, generally by heating, into the wooden bamboo shaft. The Khāṛiās, however, do not generally use the spear, but mostly use the bow and arrow.

5. *Buṛhā-kāṇḍē* :—This is a batte-axe. (Pl. VII, figs. 22 B & 22 C.) The iron blade varies in shape and size. The blade is either concave or convex or a mixture of the two. The handle is made of a strong wooden stick, about three feet long and half an inch in diameter. The handle is socketed into the hole or holes of the axe-blade. These axes are particularly made for hunting and killing animals. The edge is very sharp. The *Ḍēnēy* is a smaller axe.

The Khāṛiās generally do not themselves make these metal weapons but buy them either from local markets or from their own village-smiths. They, however make the handles.

(xii) *Honey-collecting and its Methods*.

The Hill Khāṛiās are expert tree-climbers. They collect honey and bees-wax, which they sell to people of other castes and tribes. They are experts in honey-collecting, and practise it almost as an occupation.

The Hill Khāṛiās of Dhalbhūm while starting to collect honey offer oblations of water to the mountain-spirit

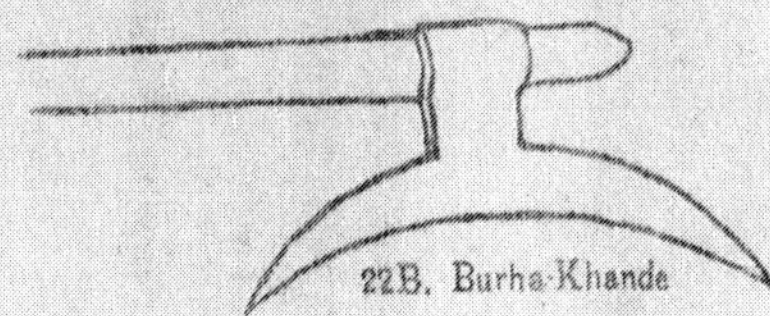

22B. Burha-Khande

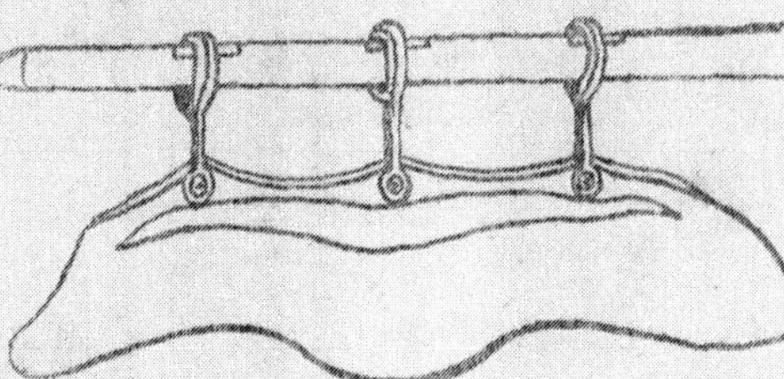

22C.

21. Maha Kirkom

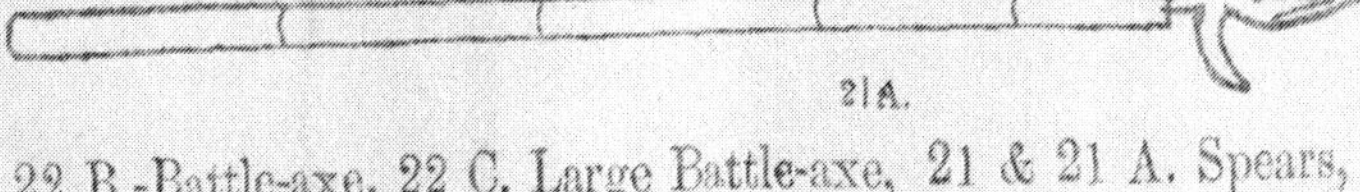

21A.

22 B.-Battle-axe, 22 C. Large Battle-axe, 21 & 21 A. Spears,

Plate VII A.—**Weapons.**

(To face p. 102)

called *Pāṭ*. The Mayurbhañj Khāṛiās offer only a little honey from the first comb as soon as it is collected, to the spirit of the hill (*Pāṭ*) on which the honey is gathered.

It is on a dark night that the Hill Khāṛiās apply smoke to the hives, whereupon the bees fly away. Then on the following morning they take out the white hives in a vessel and extract the honey. If they want to apply smoke in day-light, they cover themselves up with green leaves of trees.

It is very interesting to note that the Hill Khāṛiās of the Simlipal Hills (Mayurbhañj) have divided their native forests and Hills in several portions which they call "*Bhāṇḍārs*" (store-houses). The right to collect honey in particular *bhāṇḍārs* (stores) is recognised by them (though not by the State) to belong to particular families and no one else thinks of encroaching upon another's exclusive right of collecting honey. Every family does not 'own' such a "Bhāṇḍār". Nobody can collect in another's "Bhāṇḍār" without the owner's permission. If any one collects honey from a 'bhāṇḍār' without the permission of its "owner", the trespasser has to pay the owner a fine. Otherwise, the "owner" of the "bhāṇḍār" must be given at least two-thirds of the honey collected.

The hives are generally on the precipitous sides of the hills which cannot be reached on foot. So a ladder, constructed with two ropes made by twisting the fibres of *siāṛi* creepers, with cross-bars made of bamboo-rods, is fastened at the top-end to some tree or heavy stone and let down so as to reach a little lower than the level of the hive. Two more ropes of *siāṛi* creeper are let down, one with a lighted bamboo-torch fastened to it and emitting smoke, and another with a leaf basket placed in a *sikā* attached to it. The ropes are held fast at top-ends by other men at the top.

Honey is collected at night for fear of being otherwise bitten by bees. One man with two sticks gets down by the ladder, and reaches down to the level of the honey comb. He then pokes the hive with a stick to which the torch is attached, so as to graze the hive and scare away the bees. Then the rope with the basket is pushed on with a stick to the bottom of the hive and held fast there, while with the other stick he pokes at the comb and breaks it so that the honey and hives fall into the basket. Then the men at the top pull the basket up.

The man gets up, presses out the honey and stores it, and again gets down and similarly breaks other hives. One hive usually yields about 4 seers of honey and 1 to 1½ seers (2 to 3 lbs) of wax. Honey is generally gathered by honey-bees from mango, *śāl*, and *mohuā* flowers every year, and once every 10 or 12 years from a kind of flower called "*Paiyā*".

Except the "owner" of the "*bhāṇḍār*", the others who assist him in collecting honey get each a small share of the honey or daily wages besides fooding for the days they remain in the hill. As I have said, the spirit of the mountain on which the honey is collected gets an oblation of honey from the first hive. This oblation is dropped by the gatherer over a stone on the hill.

(xiii) *Fishing, & Fishing-Implements*.

Fishing is only a subsidiary and occasional occupation with the Khaṛiā. Fish does not form a regular

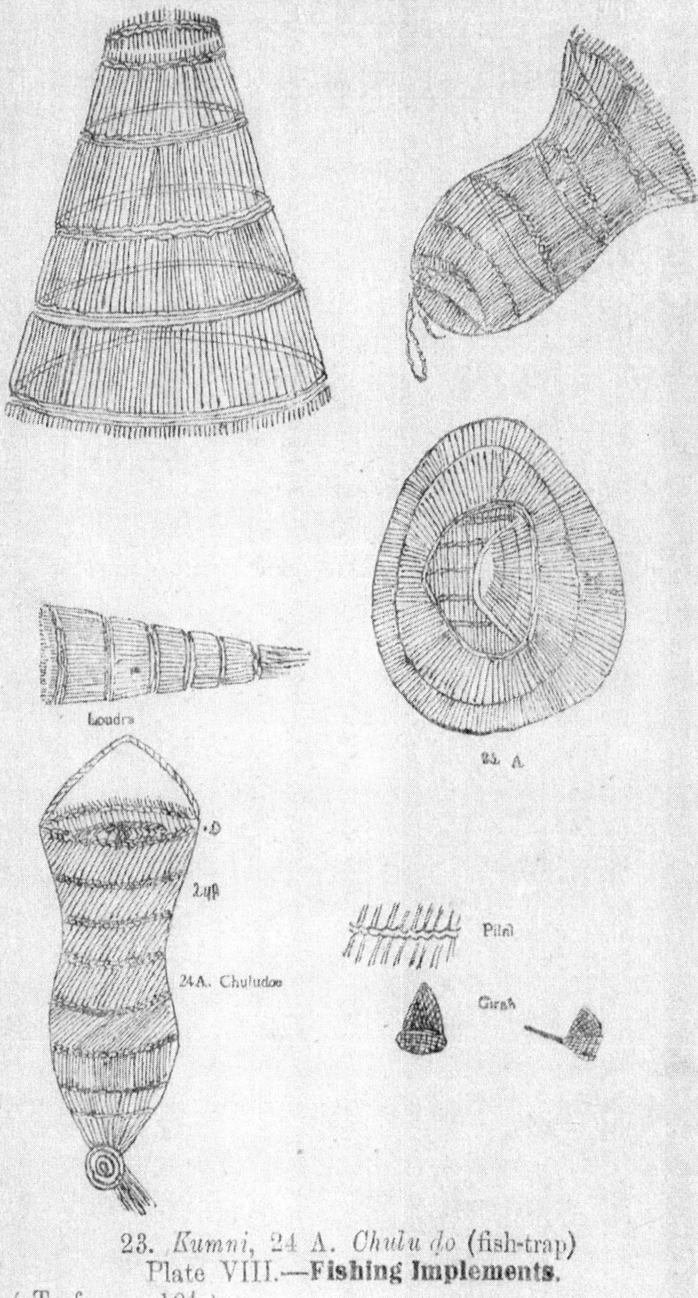

23. *Kumni*, 24 A. *Chulu do* (fish-trap)
Plate VIII.—**Fishing Implements.**

(To face p. 104)

article of food with him nor is it found in plenty in much of the Khāṛiā country. Yet a few kinds of fish-traps are in use. The principal ones are the following :—

1. *Muchu*—This is a fishing trap made of bamboo strips stitched together with rope in such a way as to form a conical cage with a diameter of about 6 inches at the apex and 1½ feet at the bottom. Bark rope is lashed round strong bamboo strips at the bottom, top and at three or four intermediate positions to hold the trap in position. It is held with both hands at the apex, and placed over fish in shallow water. Then the man inserts his hand through the apex and catches the fish.

2. *Londrā*:— This is a self-acting trap made of similar bamboo strips, and is of similar conical shape as the former. It is very long but narrow, being 4 inches at the mouth : and the other end is not stitched but the free ends meet together. It is placed at the mouth of an opening in the ridge of a paddy field through which the water flows out. The small fishes that enter into it cannot move backwards or forwards, as it is very narrow and the free end is tied with a rope. Fish caught in the trap is taken out by unfastening the rope or overturning the trap.

3. *Kūmni*:—This is a little complicated self-acting trap made of bamboo strips. Its shape has been shown in Pl. VIII, fig. 25. It consists of two parts,—the trap as seen from outside (fig. 25) which is nothing but a cage with a door having a hook at the bottom, and the "catching trap" (Pl. VIII, Fig. 25 A), as it might be called, which is placed very near the mouth of the trap and allows the fish to force its way in but does not allow

the fish to come out, as it opens inwards only. It is placed against flowing water in a field or near a pool and when fish is caught in it they are taken out by opening the door (D in Fig. 24 A, Pl D).

4. *Chulu doē*:—This is used both as a fish-trap and as a fish-carrier but more often the latter. It is made of thatching grass, the free-ends of the grass being tied at the bottom. (Plate VIII, fig. 24 A). Dūdh and Ḍhelki Khāṛiās practice terrace cultivation. The water of the higher fields falls down over a lower field; and it is where water from the higher terraces comes down to the terraces lower down that this trap is set so that the water falls through it and passes out leaving within the trap the fishes that the water carries along with it.

The *Pilni* or cast-net, the *Girā* or a round bamboo frame with a net woven at one end, and the *Ḍoirbaiñsi* or line and hook are also occasionally used by the Dūdh Khāṛiās.

5. *Bhāoñr jāl*.—This is the cast-net. Its use is practically unknown to the Khāṛiās in general. Only a few well-to-do Dūdh and Ḍhelki Khāṛiās occasionally take the help of the cast-net to catch fish. The Dūdh Khāṛiās weave cast-nets for themselves (see Illustration). The introduction of the cast-net is, however, of recent date amongst them.

6 *Poisoning fish*:—The most common method of fishing is by letting out water from pools on a hot summer day, and poisoning the water by mixing certain poisonous leaves in it. The leaves of either the *Pāṭwār* or the *Āstā* tree are crushed with stones and mixed with the water. The fish when dead or dying are collected and taken home.

(xiv) *Agriculture and its Implements.*

The Hill Khāṛiās have not yet taken to regular plough cultivation though some of them practise *Jhūming*. It is surprising that Mr. Das[55] did not find *jhūming* among the Khāṛiās he visited. Perhaps his informant took him to be a local Zemindar's agent and concealed from him the existence of *jhūm* cultivation for fear of being assessed to tax. We saw Khāṛiās in Dhalbhūm engaged in *jhūming* upon the hill slopes.

Jhūming :—In the summer months the trees of a large plot of hill-slope is cleared of bushes and shrubs, and all trees standing on it are cut down and the bushes and shrubs are heaped around them, and left to dry for sometime and then set fire to. When everything is reduced to ashes, the ashes are spread out all over the plot of land, which is now ready for *jhūm* or *dāhi* cultivation. In the beginning of the rainy season the seeds of *Māṛuā* (*Eleusine Coracana*) or pulses or maize are inserted with the help of the digging-stick on the ground thus prepared. Weeds are cleared, and the crop is protected from wild animals as best as can be managed and, for the rest, left to the mercies of nature. The crops, when ripe, are gathered and stored in their huts, or bartered in part for other necessary articles in the market.

Some Khāṛiā families have each a small plot of land attached to their dwelling-house, where green vegetables such as beans, pumpkins and the like are grown. Regular plough-cultivation is practised by the Dūdh Khāṛiās in particular and by most of the Ḍhelkis, but by very few Hill Khāṛiās.

55. *The Wild Khāriās of Dhalbhum*, p.11

The different agricultural implements used by the Khāṛiās are the following :—

1. *Ḍeney* :—This is an axe for cutting trees, *etc*. The iron piece (about 4 to 6 inches long) is triangular in shape with a socket fitted at the top of one of the angles, the opposite side being the blade. An wooden handle about a yard long and ½ to ¾ inch in diameter is fitted into the socket (Plate VI, fig. 22).

2. *Koṇḍē* :—This is also a cutting axe but the blade is of a different pattern (Pl. IX, fig. 28). The sharp edge is convex and the handle is socketted as in the preceding type. The axe-head is very heavy, being nearly 2 to 3 *seers* (4 to 6 pounds) in weight.

3. *Khantā*:—This is a digging implement used mostly by the Hill Khāṛiās for digging out roots and tubers, and in sowing seeds in their *jhūm* cultivation and for certain other purposes. The iron blade has a double edge, the two edges being pointed. The blade is about one inch in diameter at the middle. One edge is inserted into a long wooden handle about one yard long and lashed with *chōp* fibres. So the blade outside the handle is conical in shape and has 4 sides, each about 4 inches in length. The handle is held in both hands and the blade is inserted into the soil (Pl. IX, fig. 29).

4. *Gaṇḍirā* :—This is also another kind of digging implement used by the Hill Khāṛiās, particularly in Mayurbhañj. The wooden handle is about 1 ft in length. Its shape is shown in Pl. IX,fig.29 A. At its broad end the pointed long iron blade, with a maximum length of 10 inches or more and a maximum breadth of ½ inch only, is inserted to form an obtuse angle with the handle. The blade juts out about 8 inches outside the

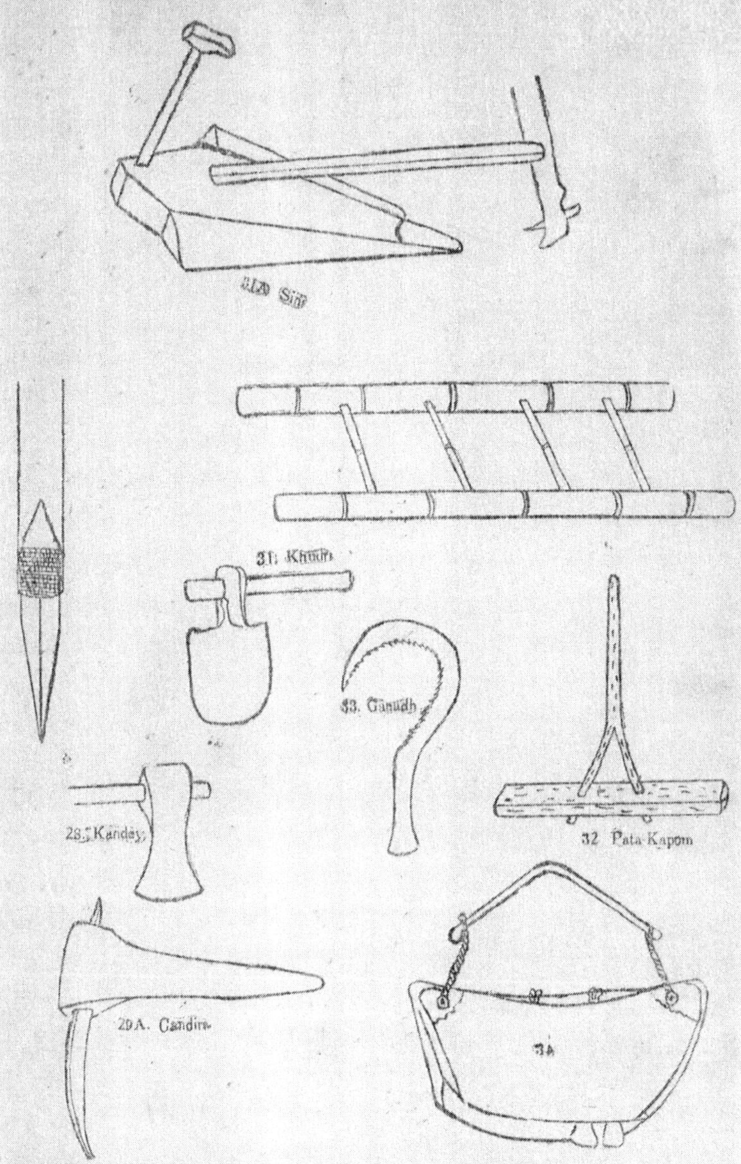

30. Cow-bell. 32. Pāṭā-Kāṭsorn (Harrow)
Plate IX.—Agricultural Implements, *etc.*

(To face p. 108)

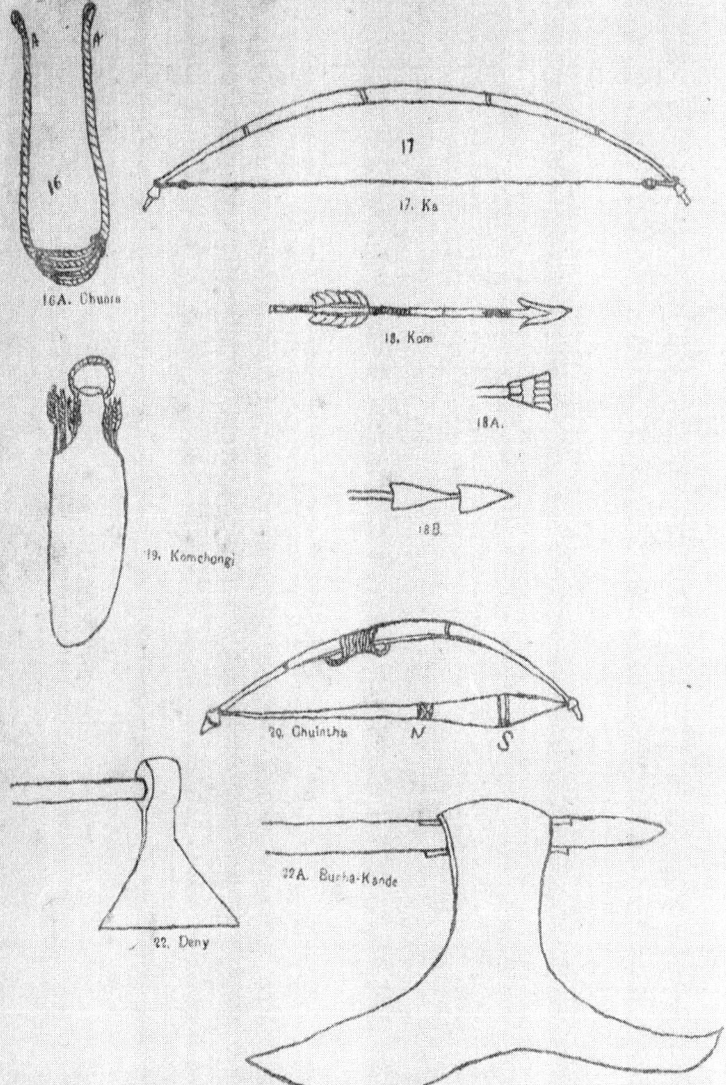

16. *Guinṭā* (sling), 17. Bow, 18. Arrow, 19. Arrow-case, 20. Goṛhā (pellet-bow), 22. Axe, 22 B Battle-axe,

Plate VII.—**Weapons.**

(To face p. 109)

handle and has four surfaces a little concave towards the handle. It can be used either with one hand or with both the hands.

5. *Khudṛi*, or *Kudṛi*:—This is the ordinary modern hoe and has been adopted by the Khāṛiās from their Hindu neighbours. The name "Khūdri", has been borrowed from Hindi (*Kudāri or Kudāli*) and corrupted.

6. *Sini*:—It is the Khāṛiā name for the ordinary country plough in use in the Khāṛiā country. The different parts of the plough are made of wood except the plough-share which is made of iron and called "*luāng*" by the Khāṛiā. The *luāng* is a pointed flat iron piece of about 8 inches in length. The plough-handle (B) is called *Kaṛbā* or *Kaṛbā-Khunṭō* and the yoke (D) is called *Rodkong*. (Plate 31 A).

7. *Pāṭā-Kāṭsom*:—There are two varieties of the harrow. The most prevalent form is represented in Pl. IX, fig. 32, which is made of only a log of wood with a wooden beam fitted into it.

The other variety is most probably imported from Bengal by the Khāṛiās who go there as labourers. It is represented in Pl. IX, fig. 32 A. This is in the form of a wooden ladder laid flat on the ground and drawn by a bullock with a man standing on the harrow.

8. *Kūṛū*.—This is the common earth-remover called *Kārhā* or *Krūr* by the Orāons and some other tribes and castes of Chōṭā Nāgpur. It is used for levelling the uneveness of a newly made rice-field, by carrying the soil from the higher to the lower parts of the field.

9. *Gānādh*:—This is a toothed sickle made of one piece of bent iron, as shown in Pl. IX, figure 33.

The iron implements and weapons used by the Khāṛiās are mostly made by village blacksmiths, although imported implements are now coming into favour. The wooden portions of the implements are mostly made by the Khāṛiā himself.

In the cold weather of 1866-67, V. Ball found some Hill Khāṛiās of the Dalma Range in the Mānbhūm District making and manupulating a kind of primitive forge to sharpen their *Khantās*. We have given a description of this forge (p. 82 *ante*) which is, however, getting rare these days. Now-a-days to get his *Khantās* sharpened the Khāṛiā generally resorts to the neighbouring Kāmārs or blacksmiths who make and mend them as well as whet them for him.

Processes of Agriculture.—The Khāṛiā's methods of manuring, ploughing, harrowing, sowing, transplanting and weeding his rice-fields and threshing and harvesting his crops are the same as those employed by his neighbours—the Mūṇḍās and the Orāoñs. For details of these agricultural operations we would refer the reader to S.C. Roy's *The Orāoñs of Chotā-Nāgpur* (pp. 123-129). Broadly speaking, after three or four ploughings at intervals between February and April, the land is levelled by the harrow and again ploughed, and paddy-seeds are either sown broad-cast on the pulverised soil in May or early in June, or are sown in mud after a heavy shower of rain in June or July; or paddy seedlings reared in a nursery are transplanted about August in fields prepared for their reception. The fields are weeded from time to time, first by picking up grass and weeds by the hand before sowing, then again in July or August with the help of the harrow and the plough, and finally once more by the hand in or about September. The paddy-crops on wet lands are harvested in October and November, and then threshed and stored. The ploughing and sowing must be done by the men and never by women; the weeding is generally done by the women but men may also take a hand in it; and transplantation and harvesting may be done both by men and women.

(xv) *Musical Instruments*.

Khāṛiās use the following musical instruments:—

Rutu:—This is a bamboo-flute of the pattern commonly used in the country. They generally make it themselves. It is only seven to eight inches in length and about three-fourths of an inch in breadth. Six holes are perforated along its length for playing the wind.

Māndri:—This is a two-skin drum. The diameter of one side is greater than that of the other. The maximum diameter is about 1 ft. The shell is mostly of wood hollowed out of a solid block. Its size varies from 1½ feet to 2 feet in length. Leather (cow- or buffalo-hide) is stretched on either end, fastened to the shell, and straightened by interlacing strips of leather,—a number of leather strips passing round the shell over the braces and serving to tighten the instrument at the desired pitch. It is played upon by both hands.

Nagerā (Pl. XII, fig. 43):—This is a drum of the variety know as "kettle-drum". The vellum is stretched over the base of a hollow conical metal pot which serves as the resonater. The vellum is made of leather and kept in proper tension by means of leather interlaced over the body of the pot. It is played upon with two short sticks. A big drum called *Ḍhōl* is also sometimes played upon at weddings.

Chāngu (fig. 44):—This is a kind of drum or rather half-drum in use among the Hill Khāṛiās particularly in the Mayurbhañj State. It consists of a round wooden frame of 4 to 6 inches in breadth and of a diameter of 1 to 2 ft. The vellum is made of leather and stretched on one side only, the other side remaining open. There are small rings fitted on to the instrument which give a jingling sound as the player of the instrument dances. It is played upon by the hand.

(xvi) *Trade and Barter*.

The Hill Khāṛiās procure principally rice by bartering honey, lac, frankincense, silk (*tasar*) cocoons, *śāl* leaves and leaf-plates and leaf-cups, bamboo splinters or *Khāṛikā* used in stitching leaves into plates and cups, horns and skins of hunted animals, and sometimes wild animals and birds caught by them. The Dūdh and Ḍhelki Khāṛiās carry to the weekly markets in their neighbourhood, for sale, the surplus produce of their fields, the medium of exchange being ordinarily the current minted coin of the realm. With part of the money thus procured they buy salt, tobacco, and other necessaries which they themselves do not grow or manufacture.

General Observations.

An examination of the objects of material culture described above shows that almost all the household furniture, utensils, implements, tools, weapons, and other

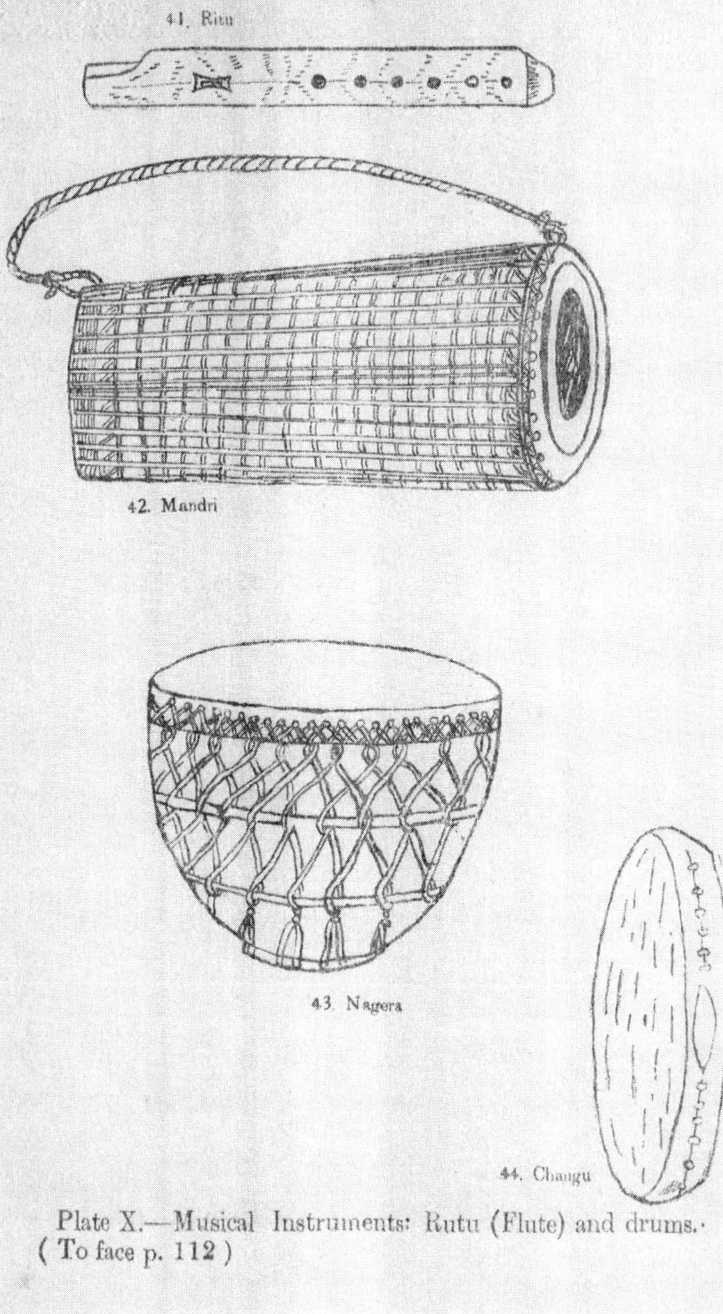

Plate X.—Musical Instruments: Rutu (Flute) and drums.
(To face p. 112)

instruments used by the Khāṛiās are common to them with the other tribes of their respective districts, and form part of the general culture of the area they inhabit. Which, if any, of the various artefacts and technological processes described above have been the original contribution of any particular tribe can perhaps never be determined. The Hill Khāṛiās claim the Khantā or digging implement and the rope-ladder they employ in collecting honey, to be their own inventions. But any such claim would be difficult to substantiate. In fact, some of the primitive elements of the culture of the tribes of the "Central Belt", whether in the economic or in other spheres, must have been evolved in the far past when the Mūṇḍā tribes lived together as one common stock. And these would appear to have been gradually supplemented by other elements derived by one or other of the different component tribes of the Mūṇḍā stock from analogous as well as higher cultures of other racial stocks with whom they came in more or less intimate contact. Whether acquired by chance culture-contact or in some cases perhaps by more or less racial intermixture, culture-elements borrowed by one or more tribes must have been diffused over adjacent areas and passed on to other allied tribes. And in the process of assimilation, alien culture-traits would appear to have been modified and transformed by each recipient group so as to suit their own level of culture. In the following pages we shall come across instances of such culture-loans and their necessary modifications and, in some cases, transformations that are almost beyond recognition. Anyone who has studied the aboriginal tribes of the "Central Belt" of India, cannot fail to be impressed with the idea that the aboriginal tracts of

Chōṭā Nāgpur and the Santāl Parganās, the Feudatory States of the Eastern States Agency and, to some extent, of the Central Provinces and the Central India Agency, would appear to constitute, in essential respects, one homogeneous culture-area .

General Economic Condition .—As may be naturally expected, the agricultural and land-owning Dūdh and Ḍhelki sections of the tribe are in a better economic condition than the Hill or Pārbatiā or Pāhāṛia section who have practically no cultivation . Better economic organization and co-operation have further helped the Ḍelki or Ḍhelki, and more so the Dūdh section in improving their economic condition . The incidence of rent on agricultural land is comparatively light . But in the practical absence of artificial irrigation, their crops are always at the mercy of the monsoon rains, which can never be depended upon . So in years of drought or of excess of rain damaging or destroying their crops, many Khāṛiā families are obliged to borrow grains or cash on high interest from the usurious local *mahājans* or money-lenders ; and some Khāriās are obliged to emigrate for a time to work in the tea-gardens of Assām or the Duars, or elsewhere . Many Christian converts, tide over seasons of stress by borrowing money on easy terms from the Co-operative Credit Societies started by the Missions . Hill Khāṛiās, in consideration of loans advanced by money-lenders are obliged to give them honey, lac, frankincense, jungle birds *etc.* at a valuation considerably below the market-price in payment of these loans and interest . In years of plenty, some sell the surplus produce of their fields in the market, and even in ordinary years they have to sell a portion of the produce to pay their rent with . A

27. A group of Dūdh Khāṛiā hunters.

28. Dūdh Khāṛiās weaving cast-nets.

(To face p. 114)

very few Dūdh Khaṛias engage in petty trade, or work as mechanics, police constables and the like; and still fewer who have received English education work as clerks or as school-masters or as catechists. Two or three better educated Khāṛiās after a course of theological training, have been ordained as Catholic missionaries, and a few more are under training for the ministry. It is not so much either capacity or intelligence that the Khāṛiās or other aborigines on the same level of culture lack, as suitable facilities for education and opportunity in life.

The presents of articles of food which Khāṛiās bring to their relatives on occasions of marriage and other domestic celebrations in the latters' families, besides their value as an expression of the social sentiments of family affection and tribal fellow-feeling have a practical economic value in that they lighten the burden on the celebrants' families. Parade of wealth and unusual liberality in feasts do not, in Khāṛiā society, affect the rank or even tangibly the prestige of the individual or his family, and are indeed almost unknown.

Religious practices are vitally bound up with the Khāṛiā's economic pursuits. In fact, most of the periodical religious rites and festivals of the tribe are intended to bring good luck and avert bad luck in their economic pursuits. Before the Khāṛiā goes out on a hunting expedition and again on return after a successful hunt, and when he has collected honey, and before he begins sowing or harvesting his crop, and while eating the first fruits of his fields, the blessings of the deities and spirits who are believed to control Nature must be invoked as an essential preliminary.

CHAPTER VI.

Social Organisation.

(i) *The Khāṛiā Family.*

Type of Family.

The ultimate basis of Khāṛiā society as of other societies is the family as the elementary unit consisting of parents and their children. A Khāṛiā family centres round the father through whom lineage or descent is traced and who exercises supreme authority or *potestas* in the family. In a few cases, the Khāṛiā family includes an adopted son or a 'domesticated' son-in-law living in the house of his sonless father-in-law, and in a still fewer cases, only among the Dūdh and Ḍhelki sections, it includes more remote relatives such as paternal grand-parents, paternal uncles and first cousins living in the same house. In most cases, however, after his marriage the Khāṛiā son builds a separate hut for himself; and this is invariably the case with the Hill Khāṛiās.

Ownership of family property ordinarily vests in men. A Khāṛiā woman, after her marriage, generally lives in her husband's house throughout her married life except, of course, for occasional visits to her father's place. Thus the type of the Khaṛiā family is patrilineal and patripotestal. The form of mating on which the Khāṛiā family depends is monogamous, although polygamy, while rare, is not altogether unknown.

Possible Relic of Matriliny. It may be noted, however, that the special importance and authority which attaches to the mother's brother and certain suggestive ceremonial functions appertaining to this relation among the Khāṛiās, as among their congeners, would appear to point either to a former state of matriliny or mother-right and *avunculate* (in which the supreme authority is exercised by the mother's brother over her sister's children), or possibly to close contact in the past with some tribes or communities organised on a matrilineal basis. At the present day, however, the Khāṛiās have no matrilineal societies as their neighbours.

Functions of the family. Like the family in other communities, the Khāṛiā family subserves the primary biological function of the perpetuation of the life of the species and the transmission of the biological heritage, the economic function of securing food and shelter and material comforts for its members, and the cultural function of transmission of the social heritage (including the mother-tongue) and the conservation of traditions and folkways and folk-customs. These latter functions it shares along with the clan, the village or other local group, and the community. The family also shares with the clan the sociological function of the regulation of marriage and the determination of the place which each child is to occupy in the community.

As in all patrilineal and patrilocal communities, the duties of the father among the Khāṛiās are to protect his wife and children and to provide them with a habitation and food. The Khāṛiā husband and his wife contribute, each in his or her own way, towards the maintenance of the family. But there is a well-recognised division of labour between man and woman.

Division of Labour among the Sexes.

In the matter of procuring food, we have seen that among the Hill Khāṛiās the duty of procuring food by hunting and occasionally fishing devolves on the men, whereas the task of gathering fruit and tubers and edible leaves or herbs devolves mainly on women, although men also search and dig for tubers when no food is available by hunting or fishing. Among the Dūdh Khāṛiās and Ḍhelki Khāṛiās who have taken to agriculture the men harrow and level the fields, construct and repair ridges and embankments, drive the plough and sow and thresh the paddy, whereas such operations as transplanting, weeding, breaking clods, and reaping the crops devolve on the women. It is the proper function of women to husk the paddy either with the mortar and pestle or with the *ḍhenki* or rice-pounder.

The Dūdh Khāṛiās of the Rānchi District, like their neighbours—the Oraons and the Mūṇḍās,—are so jealous of any usurpation, however temporary or accidental, by women of men's functions in agriculture that should a woman be found driving the plough even for the nonce, she is fined and a ceremonial expedition to drive out the calamities that, it is believed, would otherwise overtake the village, is undertaken. This ceremony is known as "Rōg-Khednā" or 'disease-driving' or 'calamity-driving' expedition. Until recently the offending woman would also be required to expiate her 'sin' by being yoked to the plough she handled, and by ploughing a few feet of ground. She was also made to eat some grass and to go round the village begging for rice with which a feast and drink had to be provided for the village elders to 'expiate her sin' and re-incorporate her into the tribe. Even now this barbarous punishment does not appear to have altogether disappeared, though instances are getting rare. Ceremonial 'purification' of some sort either by drinking a drop of blood of a fowl offered to Pōnōmōsōr, or drinking a little rice-beer after libation to Him and a drink to the Pañch, is still deemed necessary, at least by the orthodox.

Among Khāṛiās, the women also draw water and cook food, and weave mats with leaves of the wild date-palm. Dūdh Khāṛiā and Ḍhelki Khāṛiā women spin cotton; and the spun thread is then given to men of the weaver caste to weave into clothes. When there is any surplus grain or other article to sell, it is generally the women who carry it to the market and sell it. The care of domestic animals is principally the function of men. As in all communities, the women look after the children.

The construction and repairing of houses and sheds is also part of the duties of men. As among the Mūṇḍās, Orāoñs, and some other tribes of Chōṭā-Nāgpur so also among the Dūdh Khāṛiās, should a woman happen even to get up on the thatch of a house or hut, some serious calamity to the village is apprehended and a '*rōg-khednā*' or 'calamity-driving' ceremony has to be undertaken, as in the case of a woman usurping men's function in agriculture; and the offending woman is required to procure rice by begging from door to door, and to prepare rice-beer therewith for libation to Pōnōmōsōr and a drink to the village elders, and thereby to 'expiate' her 'sin'.

Position of Women. The Khāṛiā woman is generally well-treated and is not the family drudge that a primitive woman is popularly supposed to be. Although a Khāṛiā husband exercises more or less general authority over the wife, the latter exercises considerable influence over her children and household and has a potent voice in matters of domestic economy. Her influence over her husband is by no means negligible.

Religious Disabilities. The exclusion of Khāṛiā women from certain religious festivals and ritualistic observances, like their periodical segregation during their monthly course, appears to be due not to any assumed inferiority in their status in society but probably to the primitive man's horror of the menstrual blood, which is supposed to attract evil spirits. This superstitious fear may be also responsible for some of the other disabilities of the Khāṛiā woman, such as restrictions against her accompanying funeral processions to the burial place or cremation ground, and against her going to *sarnās* or sacred groves or attending the Fāgu and Kadleṭā sacrifices. Women may not offer sacrifices themselves, and unmarried girls may not eat sacrificial meat. A Khāṛiā's grown-up daughter or sister will not be permitted to enter his cow-shed which is supposed to be the abode of the *Goṛeā* or the tutelary deity of cattle who is also called "Ahīr Dūbō" or "Dimtāng sāng".

Property Rights. A Khāṛiā woman is not altogether debarred from possessing property. Her dress, ornaments, and articles made by her for her own use or acquired by her, are her own personal property with which she may deal as she pleases. But as for property, either moveable or immoveable, belonging to her husband she may use or enjoy them so long as she lives with him, and, on his death, may inherit a life-interest in them, if he has left no male issue. If the husband dies leaving sons or grand-sons to inherit him she will be entitled to maintenance out of her husband's assests. If the husband leaves no male issue but only male agnates, the widow will be entitled to a life-interest in the property left by her husband; and it is only on her death that the nearest agnates will inherit the property. A Khāṛiā daughter cannot inherit her father's property, but an unmarried daughter is entitled to her marriage expenses and maintenance, until marriage, out of her father's assests at the hands of his heirs.

Relation of Parents to Children.

The Khāṛiās, like other primitive people, have a keen appreciation of the social and economic importance of children. Female children appear to be as welcome as sons. Khāṛiā parents treat their children of both sexes with kindness, often, indeed, with an excess of kindness and indulgence. The practice of infanticide is practically unknown, although a very few instances of abortion of children born out of wedlock have been reported. During infancy children naturally remain under the care of their mothers. But, during respite from their work, most Khāṛiā fathers fondle their children and, when necessary, help their wives in looking after the children. When old enough to tend goats or cattle and help the father in his field-work, boys pass from the mother's tutelage to the father's. Girls remain under the tutelage of their mother until they are married. An unmarried

Khāṛiā daughter helps her mother in her domestic and other duties as much as she can.

(ii) *Clan Organisation.*

The next higher social grouping is the Clan. The Hill Khāṛiās of Mayurbhañj, however, have practically no effective Clan organisation at the present day, although it exists in full vigour amongst the Dūdh and the Ḍhelki Khāṛiās, and also more or less among the Hill Khāṛiās of the Mānbhūm and Singbhūm districts.

Absence of the Totemic Clan system among the Hill Khāṛiās of Mayurbhañj.

In the Mayurbhañj State which appears to be the centre of dispersion of the Hill Khāṛiās and where they are still found in the largest number, there is strong evidence to indicate that this section of the tribe has probably lost their clan organisation as they have lost their original language, unless it may be that they never evolved any such organisation. In some of their settlements we found that they know of no totemic clan names, and recognise no division into *Gōtras* or clans: in some settlements there is a vague idea that all Hill Khāṛiās belong to the Nāg *gotra* or Cobra clan, which is found in most Mūṇḍā-speaking tribes; in some settlements, again, we were told that all Hill Khāṛiās belonged to the *Sāluk* (a kind of bird) *gōtra*; and in a few settlements we were informed that the Hill Khāṛiās are divided into two clans—the *Nāg* clan and the *Sāluk* clan; in still others(as in village Sarsōpal)we were told that the Khāṛias belonged to the *Nāg-Sāluk gotra* (which they named as a single indivisible clan); in some villages (as in Gurguria) we were told by some families that they had only one *gōtra*, namely, *Sāluk*, while some others said they had each two separate *gōtras*, namely, the *Sāluk* and the

Nāg ; in a few villages (as in Khejuria) the Hill Khāṛias gave us as many as six clan-names, namely, *Sūl* (a kind of fish), *Aśoka* (a kind of flower), *Sāru* (a kind of yam), *Bāliā* (a kind of fish), *Sāluk* (a kind of bird) and *Nāg* (cobra). None of these clan names, it may be noted, appear to be known to either the Dūdh or the Ḍhelki sections of the Khāṛiās in the Rānchi district and the adjoining States of Gāngpur and Jāshpur.

It is significant that although such of the Hill Khāṛiās of Mayurbhañj as still retain any totemic clan name abstain from eating or using or harming the object from which their respective *gotra* names are derived, there is generally no interdiction against marriage in the same clan or *gotra*. All this might appear to indicate that, having long ago lost their original totemic organization, they have now no clear notion of totemic clans and clan-divisions but have come to adopt certain totemic clan-names anew, perhaps in imitation of their neighbours the Mūṇḍās, the Hōs and the Sāntāls who have settled in large numbers in the State.[56]

It may, however, be noted that the name *Kili* (pronounced *Khili* by the Hill Khāṛiās) which is still applied by their neighbours—the Mūndās, the Hōs, and the Santāls—to the exogamous totemic clan, is also applied by the Hill Khāṛiās of Mayurbhañj to certain class names or *Sangyās* (*lit.*, name or description) of totemic complexion which they have adopted in imitation of their neighbours

56. The allied tribe of Hill Bhūiñyās in Mayurbhanj and neighbouring States and the Juāngs of Keoñjhar have similarly lost their older exogamic totemism and totemic restrictions; and agnatic relation is practically now the only bar to intermarriage between two families. See *The Hill Bhūiñyās of Orissā*, by S. C. Roy p. p. 146-149,

of Ōṛiyā Hindu castes. Thus the Khāṛiās of the *Sāl* fish clan (*Gōtra*) have adopted *Reṇisia* (another kind of fish), the *Aśoka* flower clan have adopted *Kaṭuri-pāṇiā* bird, those of the *Sāru* or yam clan have adopted the *Pāṇi-oḍiā* (a kind of water-fowl), those of the *Bāliā* fish clan have adopted *Duārbandhiā* (the door-shield), those of the *Sāluk* clan have adopted *Talapāṇiā* (a flowering plant), and those of the *Nāg* clan have adopted *Siāl* (Jackal) as their respective *Sangyās*. The *Saluk* or *Nāg* or *Sāluk-Nāg* clan of village Gurguria name *Patra-bichhā* (a caterpillar) and also *Pani-Oḍiā* (a kind of water-fowl) and also *Sañkh* (the conch-shell) as their *Sangyā* or *Khili* names. Again, many Hill Khāṛiā families of the Mayurbhañj State have adopted *Padits* or family surnames in imitation of their Ōṛiyā neighbours. The *Dehuri* or priest as a surname of priestly families and *Nāek* as a surname of families of secular headmen is common to the Khāṛiās and other tribes of Ōṛissā and Chōtā Nāgpur. But distinctly Ōṛiya *Padits* adopted by some Hill Khāṛiā families are *Jau-rāndhā*, *Khomāe*, *Digar*, *Sihōr*. and *Doṇsoṇā*.

It is again significant that, at first some Mayurbhañj Khāṛiās told us that the *gōtras* or clans were exogamous; some asserted that the families distinguished by different *Sangyā* or *Khili* names were exogamons, and some said that the families designated by particular *padits* or surnames were exogamous. But on closer enquiry it turned out that neither the possession of a common *gōtra* name, nor that of a common *sangyā*, nor of a common *padit* was a bar to inter-marriage. The Mayurbhañj Khāṛiā may marry in his own village, in his own *gōtra* or clan, in his own *padit* and in his own *sangyā*.

The only regulation that now restricts marriage among the Hill Khāṛiās of Mayurbhañj is based on consanguinity or kinship traced through either side of the family except that a man may marry his mother's brother's (including mother's cousin's) daughter, and father's sister's daughter, and mother's sister's daughter (provided the latter is not his agnate). In no case may therebe union between children of two brothers or those of two agnatic cousin-brothers.

Dāśarathī Dehuri of Sarsopāl said, and scores of Khāṛiās who were present with him admitted, that a Hill Khāṛiā may marry in the same *gōtra*, same *padit* (surname), same *sangyā* (class) and same village as his own. The only restriction to marriage is that a Khāṛiā must not marry in a family with whom no previous relationship by marriage either of his own family or of some related family (*Bandhu-bāsiā*) can be traced nor in a family very closely related, save and except such cross-cousins and parallel-cousins as have been just named above.

Totemism among other Hill Khāṛiās.

Among the Hill Khāṛiās of the Singbhūm and Mānbhūm Districts, however, the division into exogamous clans is recognised for purposes of marriage. But most of their clan names are different from those known to the Dūdh Khāṛiās and Ḍhelki Khāṛiās or any other tribe of the Mūṇḍā stock. Mānbhūm Hill Khāṛiās name the *Gūlgū* or *Sāl-gūlgū* (the *sāl* fish), the *Bhūiyā* (said to be the name of a fish), *Jāru* (a kind of rat), *Badya* (a kind of tuber), *Tesa* or *Ubusari* (a kind of bird), and *Hembrom* or *Guā-Hembrom* (the bettle-nut) as their clan totems. None of these clan names are those of the original clans of the tribe as given by the Dūdh and the Ḍhelki sections of the tribe, although *Hembrom* is the name of a totemestic clan among some allied tribes such as the Mūṇḍās and the Sāntāls; and the Birhōṛ tribe has *Bhūiñyā* as one of its clan names. Mr. Das[57] mentions six clan-names of the Hill Khāṛiās of Singbhūm (two of which were supplied to him by one informant and four by another). These are—*Kusli*, *Khelnā*, *Hujur*, *Āngaria*, *Kuicha* or *Bhuiya*, and *Golgu*; but he could not ascertain the meaning of any of these names except that of *Kuicha* or *Bhuiya* which is a kind of fish. The term for 'clan' among the Hill Bhūiyās of Ḍhalbhūm and Mānbhūm is 'Goṣṭi', which is really the Hindu's name (*Goṣṭhi*) for 'lineage'. One or two of these *goṣṭi* names given by Mr. Das may not improbably be merely titles or *Sangyās* rather than clan-names. Risley [58] wrote in 1891, " I have been unable to ascertain whether the wild Khāṛiās commonly known as Banmanush, 'men of the woods', have any similar [clan] divisions."

The Clan System—the basis of Dūdh Khāṛiā and Dhelki Khāṛiā Societies.

In the case of the Dūdh Khāṛiās and the Ḍhelki Khāṛiās, however, although the ultimate basis of their society, as of all human societies, is the family, and although the local grouping of the aboriginal village community is to some extent the unit of their socio-economic and socio-political life, the real and effective unit on the social side is now the exogamous totemic clan. It is the exogamous patrilineal clan which for them regulates kinship and marriage.

---

57. *The Wild Kharias of Singhbhum*, p, 23.

58. *Tribes and Castes of Bengal*, Vol. II, Appendix; p. 78.

Supposed Descent through common male Ancestor.

These Khāṛiās have a vague belief that the members of a clan are all descended from a common male ancestor, although the names of their supposed clan ancestors are not known or remembered, and descent from such ancestors can no longer be geneologically traced. From this traditional belief in descent from a common ancestor the sexual taboo necessarily follows. Each member of a Khāṛiā clan regards the other members as his brothers; all the members feel a kind of social solidarity akin to that of an enlarged or extended family; and accordingly marriage or sexual union within the clan is rigorously tabooed. Sexual union between persons bearing the same clan name is regarded with abhorrence as incest by the Dūdh and Ḍhelki Khāṛiās. This they characterise by the significant term "*gotra badh*" or "clan-murder".

There can be no question that the primary feature of the Khāṛiā clan is its exogamy. And the primary function of the clan in the social economy of the Dūdh and Ḍhelki Khāṛiās is, as we have said, to regulate marriage and to some extent assign to each child its proper place and status in the community.

Clan Totemism.

The feeling of social solidarity of the Khāṛiā clan is strengthened by the possession of a common totem.

The Ḍhelki Khāṛiās name eight exogamous clans as their original clans. These clan names are :—1. *Mūrū* (Tortoise), 2. *Sōren* or *Soreng*, or *Sereng*, also called *Tōreng*, (rock or stone), 3. *Samad* (a kind of deer ?) *alias Bāgē* (the quail), 4. *Bārlihā* (a fruit), 5. *Chārhād* or *Chārhā* (a bird), 6. *Hāṅsdā* or *Ḍūngḍūng* or *Āind* (the eel), 7. *Mail* (dirt) also called *Kiro* (a tiger), and 8. *Tōpnō* (a bird).

Respective Social position of Different Dhelki Khāriā Clans.

Of these eight clans, the *Mail* and the *Tōpnō* are regarded as lower in social rank than the others. They are sometimes called by the other Ḍhelki Khāṛiās as *Chhōṭ Khāṛiās* (The Dūdh section, as we have seen, is called by this name by the Ḍhelkis who assume for themselves the name "Baṛ Khāriās.") The other Ḍhelki clans do not take food cooked by persons of the *Mail* and *Tōpnō* clans, although they eat cooked food even at the hands of the Bhũiñyās, Kherwār, and Kāwār tribes and the Rāutiā and Mahākūṛ (Gouṛ Āhīr) castes of their country. The other Ḍhelki Khāṛiā clans may, however, intermarry with the *Mail* and *Tōpnō* clans. The *Muru* clan, on the other hand, is regarded as the highest in social rank and next to it comes the *Samad* clan. Men of these two clans alone—the *Muru* and the *Samad*—act as heads of tribal councils or Pañchāyats. In tribal gatherings and feasts, such as at birth, death and marriage celebrations,—men of the *Muru* clan are accorded the rank of *Pāndihā* or "giver of water" and men of the *Samad* clan that of the *Bhāṇḍāri* or steward. A man of the *Muru* clan must eat the first morsel at a social feast of the Ḍhelki Khāṛiās, after which alone others may begin eating. Thus a sort of class division came in time to be super-imposed upon the older clan-divisions.

The traditional origin of such differences in status of these Ḍhelki Khāṛiās was thus related to us by

Khāmāri Khāṛiā and others of village Bāndhātoli in the Gāngpur State :— After a funeral feast the elders (*Siāñs*) of the tribe bathed in a stream. The ancestor of the present *Mail* clan took his bath lower down the river than where the men of other clans were bathing. He had thus to bathe in water soiled by the dirt (*mailā*) of the bodies of his companions who bathed higher up the stream, and he was accordingly dubbed by his companions as *Mail* ; and this name stuck to him and his descendants as their clan-name. The ancestor of the present *Muru* clan bathed higher up the stream than those of the other clans and so he became the leader and head of the tribe. According to another account it was because the *Muru* clan preceded the other clans in their migrations from the ChōṭāNāgpur plateau to Gāngpur and then to Jāshpur, that this clan was accorded the highest rank among the Ḍhelkis and as the *Tōpnō* clan was the last to enter Gāngpur and Jāshpur, and "cooked their meals at hearths and in vessels already used and dirtied by other clans," the *Tōpnō* was accorded as low a status as that of the *Mail* clan. Dūdh Khāṛiās, as we shall see later on, identify the *Mail* clan with the *Kirō* or tiger clan, and have a different myth to account for the origin of the clan name. Such legends would appear to be *ex post facto* stories invented to satisfy natural curiosity.

Although the eight clans named above are believed to have been the original clans of the Ḍhelkis, most of these clans have now more than one sub-division. We came across the following sub-divisons of the different clans: The *Bāgē* clan has at least five sub-divisions known respectively as (1) *Ānkulia Bāgē*, (2) *Dādhūg-*

kūliāBāgē, and (3) *Karpāṭoliā Bagē.* Of the *Chārhād* clan we found only one sub-division known as *Bāndhākelhiā Chārhād*. The *Hāṅsdā* or *Ḍūngḍūng* has at least three sub-divisions, namely,—(1) *Masoda Hāṅsdā*, (2) *Dhāṛṛo Hāṅsdā*, (3) *Kaserdā Hāṅsdā.* We have come across three sub-divisions of the *Mail* clan, namely,-(1) *Tāmkūi Mail*, (2) *Kōil Mail*, and (3) *Bilūng Mail*. We have not come across any sub-division of the *Tōpnō* clan or the *Bārlihā* clan. Clan-subdivisions such as *Tapkāriā*, *Sirigbiriā*, *Karpāṭoliā*, etc., are derived from the names of places where they presumably settled down after they had branched off from their parent clans. Such names as *Bilūng Mail* and *Tāmkui Mail* might have been otherwise derived. Besides the original clan-names and their subdivisions noted above, we have come across a few other clan-names among the Ḍhelki Khāṛiās of the Jāshpur State in the Central Provinces. These are *Ṭeṭeṭehōiṅ* (which, some say, is a variant of *Bāgē*), *Bilūng* (Salt), and *Tiru* (a kind of bird), *Ḍumar* (a fig), and *Barwa* (a small cocoon). Of these Ḍhelki Khāṛiā clans in the Jāshpur State, the largest population is that of the *Muru* clan with as many as 99 families, and *Soreng* or *Suren* clan with 91 families out of 455 Ḍelki families in the whole State. Next to that comes the *Hāṅsdā* or *Ḍūngḍūng* which comprises 75 families. Next in numerical strength is the *Samad* or *Kerkeṭā* clan comprising 68 families, and then comes *Kirō* with 52 families. The other clans comprise each a few families only (see Appendix III).

Dūdh Khāriā Clans.

The Dūdh Khāṛiās recognise nine clans as the original clans of the tribe who first came to Chōṭā-Nāgpur along the banks of the Koel from the north-west. These are :—1. *Ḍūngḍūng* (the eel), 2. *Kūlū* (Tortoise) 3. *Samad* or *Kerkeṭā* (the quail), 4. *Bilūng* (salt), 5. *Soreng* (stone), 6. *Bā'* (paddy), 7. *Ṭēṭetohoiñ* (a kind of bird), 8. *Ṭōpō* (a kind of bird), and 9. *Kirō* (tiger). The other clans are said to have originated as offshoots from these original clans. Of these the first three clans are regarded as superior in rank to the rest. The social heads or *Karṭāhās* of the tribe are elected from the first three clans. At social feasts they must begin eating before the other clans. The *Ḍūngḍūng* clan is called the Rājā (king), the *Kūlū* clan the Rāṇī (queen), and the *Samad* or *Kerkeṭā* clan is called the *Bhāṇḍāri* (barber), in most places.

Risley in his *Tribes and Castes of Bengal* gives a list of 34 supposed different clan-names of the Khāṛiā tribe as a whole. The names and their meanings as given by Risley are as follows :—

1. *Bāgē*, a bird ; 2. *Bar*, *Ficus Indica* ; 3. *Bārlā*; 4. *Baroā*, an animal ; 5. *Bilūng*, *Nun*, or *Nonā Maila*, salt ; 6. *Ḍemṭā*, red ant ; 7. *Dhān*, paddy ; 8. *Dhanuār*, (can't eat rice soup); 9. *Ḍhelki*, a bird ; 10. *Ḍungḍung*, *Aind* or *Ind*, eel ; 11. *Durang*, a fish ; 12. *Hāthi*, elephant ; 13. *Kasi* ; 14. *Kerkeṭā*, a bird of that name ; 15. *Kiro* or *Bāgh*, a tiger ; 16. *Kulu* or *Kachchuā*, tortoise ; 17. *Mailwar* ; 18. *Murgear* ; 19. *Nāg*, cobra ; 20. *Naik* ; 21. *Naniār* ; 22. *Pardhan* ; 23. *Pathal* ; 24. *Purti* ; 25. *Sāhul* ; 26. *Samdiā* ; 27. *Saur*, fish ; 26. *Suraniā*, a rock ; 29. *Telga* ; 30. *Tetetēyin* or *Bagiār*, a bird of that name ; 31. *Tirkoār* ; 32. *Ṭiṭiṭihu*, a bird ; 33. *Ṭopo*, a bird ; 34. *Ṭuṭi*, vegetable.

To this list Risley appends the following note :— " The above groups are found among the settled Khāṛiās.

I have been unable to ascertain whether the wild Khāṛiās, commonly known as *Ban-Mānush*, ' men of the woods ', have any similar divisions ".[59]

Risley appears to have been misled in his enumeration of clan-names by three or four erroneous assumptions. His first error is that he has included what he calls " Mūṇḍā-Khāṛias" and " Orāoṅ-Khāṛiās " among the true Khaṛias and has thus included a few Mūṇḍā clan names and Ōrāoṅ clan-names in his list. As a matter of fact, the people whom he calls Mūṇḍā-Khāṛiās and Ōrāoṅ-Khāṛiās respectively are, as we have said, mostly cross-breeds between Khāṛiās (men or women) on the one side and Mūṇḍās or Ōrāoṅs (women or men) on the other. In such cases in conformity with the usage of patrilineal societies when the male parent of the original cross-breed was a Mūṇḍā, the Mūṇḍā clan-names and totems have been retained in the family; and so, too, where the male parent was an Ōrāoṅ, the Ōrāoṅ clan-name has been retained. This would appear to be the reason why in Risley's list we find such Mūṇḍā clan names as *Ḍemṭā* (the red ant), *Ṭuṭi* (a vegetable), *Pūrti* (crocodile), and *Nāg* (the cobra) which is a clan common to most primitive tribes of Chōṭā-Nāgpur and Ōṛissā and is named, as we have seen, by some Hill Khāṛiās of Mayurbhañj as their clan-name. Of course, as Mūṇḍāri and Khāṛiā are cognate languages the same words may and do occur for the same things in both the languages in many cases. The Mūṇḍāri name '*Bārlā*' in Risley's list appears to be the same as the *Bā*' clan of the Dūdh Khāṛiās. The names spelt by Risley as *Saur* and *Sahul* as those of two different clans probably refer to one and the same clan

59. *Tribes and Castes of Bengal*, Vol. II, Appendix, pp. 77-78.

totem, namely the *Sāl* fish, which is common to both the Ōrāoñs and the Mūṇḍās, but has not so far been found by us among any section of the Khāṛiās.

Risley's second error is his enumeration of the same clan-name more than once under different forms as belonging to different clans. Thus, he gives the Khāṛiā name of the *Soreng*, or *Soren* or *Surin* (rock, stone) clan, which he spells as *Surania*, and again gives its Hindi name *Pāthal* (stone) as the name of a different clan; the name of one and the same *Ṭeṭeṭehōiñ* or *Ṭēṭēṭēiñ* clan (the *ṭhiṭhāi* bird) of the Dūdh Khāṛiās, which is the same as the *Bāgē* clan of the Ḍhelkis, has been repeated three or four times by Risley as the names of three or four different clans under three or four different names, namely, *Ṭeṭeṭeyin* or *Bāgiār*, and again as *Ṭiṭiṭihū*, and also as *Bāgē* and also as *Tirkoār*. Competent Khāṛiās (e.g. Nuas Kerkeṭā, now a teacher in a High school) informed us that *Tirki* or *Tirkoār* is "a new form of *Ṭeṭeṭehoiñ* adopted by the Khāṛiās" from their neighbours, for both the Ōrāoñs and the Mūṇḍās name *Tirki* as one of their clans. The *Bā'* or paddy clan of the Dūdh Khāṛiās is put down in Risley's list under its Hindi name of *Dhān* and then again as *Dhanuār*. The *Samad* clan of the Khāṛiās is also known under the Hindi name of *Kerkeṭā* and sometimes under the name of *Hāthi*, but Risley gives the three names as belonging to three different clans. *Mailwār* of Risley's list obviously refers to the *Mail* clan of the Dūdh Khāṛiās which is the same as the *Kiro* or Tiger clan; but Risley names these as two different clans. *Bilūng*, *Nūn* or *Nōnā Mailā* (salt), which Risley names as an independent clan, is merely a sub-division of the *Mail* clan (see *ante*, p.130).

The name *Naniār* which Risley enumerates as a separate clan-name is obviously the same as the *Nūn* or *Nona Mailā* (Khaṛia, *Bilūng*) sub-clan.

The last case is also an instance of Risley's third error which is to confound sub-clans with clans. Similarly he gives *Murgear* as a separate clan name, although it is probably the *Murgi* sub-clan of the *Muru* or Tortoise clan of the Ḍhelki Khāṛiās (same as the *Kūlū* clan of the Dūdh section), unless it be another name for the *Bilūng* clan of the Dūdh Khāṛiās whose ancestors are said to have brought salt from village Ghāgrā to *Murgu* or *Mukṛu* where the clan had first settled in the Rānchi district.

Risley's fourth error is that he confounds titles with clan-names. The names *Nāik* and *Pardhān* in his list of clans are not really clan names at all but titles of certain village headmen which have in some cases been adopted by their families. 'Ḍhelki' is not a clan name at all but the name of the Ḍhelki or Ḍelki section of the tribe which some of his informants (or rather the informants of his non-Khāṛiā correspondents through whom he appears to have collected the clan-names and other data), must have carelessly given him as a clan-name. In the course of our investigations we have often come across similar careless and vague general answers given in the first instance by Khāṛiās who remain either suspicious of or indifferent to such enquiries, unless the enquirer can inspire confidence in his informants or, what is more helpful to an ethnologist, can make them appreciate the object of the inquirer, so that they may enter into the spirit of the questions and the questioner, and (as our experience shows) heartily co-operate with him.

We have not yet been able to trace the remaining clan-names, namely, *Durāng*, *Kāsi* and *Telgā*, that occur in Risley's list. As for the *Hāthi* clan, our inquiries, as noted above, show that the *Kerkeṭā* or *Samad* clan is sometimes called the "*Hāthi*" clan by the Khāṛiās.

As we have seen, the social organisation of the Hill Khāṛiās of Mayurbhañj has now the family and not any totemistic clans for its basis, and marriage is regulated by kinship or geneological relationship alone. Although in Mayurbhañj some Hill Khāṛiās recognise one or more totemic clan names, marriages and sexual relations between families owning the same clan name or even belonging to the same local group are not generally forbidden. Thus they furnish an instance of a people who recognise totemic groups which are no longer generally exogamous. As for the Hill Khāṛiās (or *Kheṛeys*, as they are locally called) of the Mānbhūm and Singbhūm districts, though they recognise a few clan names, these names are not among the totem-names known to the Dūdh and Ḍhelki sections of the tribe and, at the present day, although these Hill Khāṛiās, too, are strict in their observance of clan exogamy, the usual taboo on eating, using, or harming the totem-species is often disregarded. V. Ball noticed some Hill Khāṛiās on the Dalmā hills in Mānbhūm abstaining from the use of mutton and of woollen rugs, and some subsequent writers have quoted him and suggested that sheep must have been a totem of a section of the Khāṛiās. With all our best efforts we have not been able to discover any trace or tradition of taboo against mutton or wool or the existence of a sheep clan.

Very few traditions regarding the origin of the clan-totem names are remembered. Such traditions as exist are obviously fanciful. Of the origin of the *Kiro* (Tiger) *alias* '*Mail*' clan the following myth is recounted:— Once God (named in the myth as Bhagwān or Mahādeo) went to the jungles to cut wood for making a plough with. As he was late in returning from the jungle, his spouse Pārvatī wiped off some sweat from her body and with the dirt of the sweat fashioned a *Kiro* or tiger and named it *Chāōn̄rā Bhāōn̄rā*. She directed the Kirō to go to Bhagwān and frighten Him so that He might return home without further delay. The Kirō did as it was bidden and roared as loud as it could to frighten Bhagwān. Bhagwān cast a glance of contempt at the Tiger, took up a *chailā* or piece of split-wood and threw it at *Chāōn̄rā Bhāōn̄rā*, addressing the *chailā* thus: "Go, thou, *Khoiāmuā* (*lit*., dog-faced), rend Chāōn̄rā Bhāōnrā to pieces". Then out of the split wood there at once issued a number of wild dogs (*Barwa*) who rent the tiger to pieces. When Bhagwān returned to Pārvatī, she told Him that she had sent Chāōn̄rā Bhāōn̄rā to threaten Him. Bhagwān informed Her, "I had your Chāōn̄rā Bhāōn̄rā killed by my *Chaila*". As Pārvatī created the *Kirō* or Tiger out of the dirt (*Mailā*) of Her body, the *Kirō* clan is also named the *Mail* clan. The narrator of this myth (Sōmā Ḍūngḍūng of village Birkerā in the Simḍegā sub-division of the Rānchi District) did not actually ascribe the origin of the ancestors of the *Kiro* clan to Chāōn̄rā Bhāōn̄rā or to the torn pieces of its body. But the Khāṛiās believe every clan to be somehow ultimately related to its totem on which the clan depends

Origin of Clan Names.

for its identity and which constitutes a mystic bond between the members of a clan. Though the Khāṛiā, whether Dūdh or Ḍhelki, has a vague idea of a sympathetic relation between him and his totem, he does not claim nor is he credited by his neighbours with any of the qualities of his totem or any influence over his totem species.

The following legend, which seeks to trace the descent of the original clans from a common ancestor, is told by some old Dūdh Khāṛiās:—[60] In the remote past, a terrible flood swept over the land where the Khāṛiās then lived, and carried away men and beasts. One old Khāṛiā and his nine sons saved themselves by taking shelter in a cave. When the flood subsided, they came out of the cave, and began to maintain themselves by hunting in the forests. Once the brothers spent one whole day in search of game and strayed far from their encampment but to no purpose. The next day, however, they were more fortunate and succeeded in bagging a deer in the dense forest. They cut the deer into nine pieces and each brother took one piece for himself. But there was no water in sight and they all felt thirsty. So the brothers left their respective shares of the meat carefully stowed away and went out, each in a different direction, in search of water. They agreed among themselves that within a specified time they would return to the spot. By the appointed time they all reassembled, and one of them reported he had found a pool of water in a

---

60. This legend and the account that follows as to the establishment of the Bhūiñhāri villages of the Khāṛiās was supplied by Mr. Nuhās Kerketā a Khāṛiā school-teacher, who heard them from old Khāṛiās.

particular direction. The brothers went there by turns to drink water; and curiously enough, each met with a different creature or other object there. One saw a *Kerkeṭā* bird drinking water, one saw a *Ḍūng-ḍūng* fish (eel), another saw a *Kulu* or tortoise, another saw a *Ṭopo* bird, another saw a quantity of *Bilūng* or salt near the pool, another saw some *Bā'* or unhusked rice; another saw a *Teṭeṭehōiñ* bird, another met with a *Kiro* or tiger, and the remaining one saw a *Sereng* or a block of crystalline rock. When, one after another, they had all allayed their thirst at the pool and went back, they tied up their respective shares of meat each in his napkin (*gāmchhā*) and returned home together. Father and sons rejoiced at meeting after about two days. And the sons hastened to unfasten their napkins and place the meat before their father. To the great astonishment of all, on opening their napkins, they found a different kind of flesh in the napkin of each brother. The brother who had met with a *Kiro* or tiger by the side of the pool had in his napkin tiger's flesh instead of deer's flesh, the brothers who had seen a *Kerkeṭā*, a *Ṭopo*, a *Ḍūngḍūng*, a *Ṭeṭeṭehoin*, and a *Kulu* respectively had in their napkins the flesh of Keıkeṭā, Ṭopo, Ḍūngḍūng, Ṭeṭeṭehoiñ and Kulu respectively. The brothers who had seen *Bilūng* or salt and *Ba'* or paddy respectively found a quantity of salt and paddy instead of venison in their respective napkins, and the brother who had seen *Sereng* had a piece of crystalline rock in his napkin. The sons then told their father all that had happened in the jungle. And the old father in his wisdom decided that the line of each of his nine sons should adopt as their respective clan name the respective bird, beast, fish or other object that each had seen in the pool and found in his napkin. This is how these became the original *gotras* or *gotars* of the Dūdh Khāṛiās.

As for the first settlements of the nine original clans of the Dūdh Khāṛiās in Chōṭā Nāgpur, the following traditional account is recounted by old Khāṛiās:—

Original Settlements of the different Clans.

The *Soreng* or *Surin* clan was named after a rock (*Sereng*) upon which their ancestors offered sacrifices at a place called Khāṛiā Ghāṭ (hill pass). The original habitat (*mūdā*) or *Bhūiñhāri* village of the *Soreng* clan in the Rānchi District of Chōṭā Nāgpur was Semrā. The *Bilūng* or *Mailwār* clan was so called because their ancestor who came to Chōṭā Nāgpur brought salt (*Nūn* or *Bilūng*) from village Ghāgra to Mūṛgu. Their Bhūiñhāri village was Muikarunḍā Mukṛu. The *Ḍūngḍūng* or *Āind* or *Indwār* clan originally settled in Chōṭā Nāgpur at Bongloe which was their original Bhūiñhāri (*mūdā*) village. So, too, the Ṭeṭeṭehōiñ or Ṭirki clan had Āmkuli for their original Bhiūñhāri village; the *Kulu* or *Kachuā* clan had Panderiā Sodapudul for their Bhūiñhāri village; the *Samad* or *Kerkeṭa* clan had Porhā or Porā for their original Bhūiñhāri village; the *Bā'* or *Bārlā* clan had their Bhūiñhāri at Sisāi; the *Kiro* or Bāghwār clan had Bāghimā for their original Bhūiñhāri village; and the *Ṭopo* clan had Barway or Barwē Ḍāirgāoñ for their original Bhūiñhāri village. This is why the clans are also sometimes named after their original (*mūdā*) villages in Chōṭā Nāgpur. Thus men of the *Ḍūngḍūng* clan are also called *Bongloe-wārs*, those of the *Soreng* clan are called *Semriārs*, and so forth.

We have said that on their arrival in what is now the Rānchi District, each Dūdh Khāṛiā clan cleared jungles, reclaimed lands and established each its original (*mūdā*) village which came to be called their Bhūiñhāri villages. In course of time they also founded other villages. Thus men of the *Ṭopo* clan also established village Pādur-soadā or Padaria; the *Ḍūngdūng* clan also established village Sedem; the *Bilūng* clan also established village Ghāghir or Ghogher; the *Kiro* clan also established village Turnḍukārla; the *Kulu* clan also established village Sosom; the *Bā'* clan also established village Papatya Rendo, and so forth. Accordingly, these, too, became the Bhūiñhāri villages of the respective clans. In course of time, as the population of each clan increased, other lands were reclaimed and other Bhūiñhari villages of the Khāṛiās were established. Thus, among these later Bhuinhāri villages claimed to have been founded by the Khāṛiās of the Kerkeṭā clan are Sodē, Gālāiṭoli, Ṭā'krom or Ṭākarmā, Gyongdā' (Gongdiā), Jhikirmā, Pāṛhāṭoli, and Ā'ghrom or Aghirmā with its hamlets Ṭangartoli, Koronjṭoli, Jongorṭoli, Chiroṭoli, Karma-ṭoli, Dolongser, *etc*.

Among similar later Bhūiñhāri villages of the Kulu clan are named Kailga or Kulgā, Koṭengserā, Mājhikel Pāt'ol, Pānthā, and Sidijbir. Among the later Bhūiñhāri villages claimed to have been founded hy the Khāṛiās of the *Soreng* clan are, Ichāguṭu, Sālēguṭu, Bāngru, Jhāro, Chorbindhā, Bhunḍonkel, Konoskeli, Rāmpur, Kita, Banaiḍegā, etc.

Among the later Bhūiñhāri villages claimed to have been founded by the *Ṭeṭeṭehoiñ* clan are Kurloe, Tanrāe *etc* ; and by the *Kiṛo* clan— villages Lukir, Lowkerā, Nākṭi, etc.[61] From the names given above and also at pp. 36-37, it will be seen that different villages are claimed to be the original villages of one and the same clan. The probable explanation is that different branches of the same clan founded different villages as their *Bhuiñhāri* villages.

As we noticed before, a Khāṛia is not believed to possess any influence over his totem species as is the belief among the allied tribe of Birhōṛs. Nor does a Khāṛiā clan perform any rites or ceremonies for the preservation or multiplication of its totem species, as some Australian clans, for example, do; nor does the Khāṛiā clansman observe any totemic ceremonies in which the flesh of his totem animal or bird may be eaten. Beyond the taboos on the eating or using or killing or injuring the animal or bird or other object that constitutes his totem, there does not appear to be any evidence of a religious or quasi-religious attitude in the Khāṛiā towards the totemic species. It is said that until recently, the Khāṛiās of such clans as the *Kirō* (tiger), *Nāg* (cobra), and *Kulu* (tortoise), would make obeisance to their clan-totems when they came across one of the totem species ; but this exhibition of veneration to the totem-animal appears to be out of fashion at the present day. The use of totem-badges is not in vogue, nor have different clans any differences in dress or in the mode of

61. This account of the establishment of Bhuiñhāri villages and the preceding account of the origin of the *gotras* or clan-names was supplied by Mr. Nuas Kerkeṭa, a Khāṛiā school teacher, who obtained them from old Khāṛiās. The account of the origin of the clans was given to him in detail by Rev. Samuel Bāgō, an old Khāṛiā Pastor of the Lutheran Mission.

wearing hair to indicate their respective totems. Individual totems and sex totems are unknown.

Sex-taboo. Exogamy and totemism and the emphasis laid on the patrilineal system of reckoning kinship are the main features of the Dūdh and Ḍhelki Khāṛiā clans. Marriage or sexual union is tabooed within the clan, and even the member of one sub-clan may not marry a member of a different sub-clan of the same parent clan.

The penalty for disregarding the sex-taboo is social ostracism of the offender and his family. The offending man and woman may be taken back into the tribe only on the man giving up the woman and atoning for his "sin" by drinking the blood of a white fowl offered to Giṛing or the Sun-God, and providing a feast to his tribe-fellows. The procedure adopted in restoring an excommunicated family to 'caste' will be described in the next section.

Food-taboos. A Khāṛiā may not eat or otherwise use or injure or kill the beast, bird, plant or other object which constitutes his totem. But as such things as paddy and salt are indispensable articles of diet, this taboo has had to be modified by a workable compromise. Thus Dūdh Khāṛiās of the Bā' or Paddy clan eat rice but abstain from eating only its gruel or rice-soup or, more generally, the scum which gathers over the rice when it is being boiled; and Dūdh Khāṛiās of the *Bilūng* or Salt clan take food cooked with salt but abstain only from eating raw salt and, even if raw salt must be eaten, two or more fingers must be used in conveying salt to the mouth. Khāṛiās of the *Soreng* or Rock clan do not use stone for their ovens which they make with clods of earth only. Any infringement of such taboos is believed to bode misfortune but does not render the offender liable to any social penalty.

A Khāṛiā woman belongs to her father's clan so long as she remains unmarried and has to observe the food-taboos attaching to that clan, but after marriage she is regarded as a member of her husband's clan and has to observe the taboos appertaining to her husband's clan. Khāṛiās may take cooked food at the hands of their married daughters, and a married daughter may eat food cooked by her parents or parents' kin but a married woman may not enter the kitchen or cattle-shed of her parents' place. The probable reason for this taboo appears to be that the kitchen is the seat of the ancestor spirits and the cattle-shed that of the *Goreā*-spirit.

The principal clan-names that we actually found or heard of among the Dūdh Khāṛiās are the following :— 1. *Ba'* (paddy), 2. *Bilūng* (salt), 3. *Ḍūngḍūng* or *Āind* or *Hañsda* (the eel), 4. *Samad* or *Kerkeṭṭā* (bird), 5. *Kirō* or *Mail* (tiger), 6. *Kulu* or *Muru* (tortoise), 7. *Soreng* or *Suren* (rock, stone), also sometimes identified with the *Ṭoreng* bird, 8. *Ṭeṭeṭehōiñ* or *Bāgē* (the quail), 9. *Ṭōpō* (a bird), 10 *Bārlihā* or *Bārlā* (a fruit), 11. *Ṭirki* (mice), 12. *Bar* (a tree), 13. *Nāk* (Nag ?), 14. *Tōpnō* (a tree), 15. *Char*, *Charad*, 16. *Lugun* (a tree), 17. *Hembrom* (betel or *pān*), 18. *Kanḍūlnā* (bird), 19. *Keñdu* (fruit), 20 *Koro*, 21. *Pōṛh* (fruit), 22. *Pātiar*, 23. *Demṭā* (red ant), 24. *Kūjri* (fruit), 25. *Bānḍā* (jackal), 26. *Bāyāng* (?), 27. *Bakāiñ* (tree), 28. *Bari*, *Bariā*, 29. *Tiru* (bird), 30. *Muchu*, 31. *Ṭuṭua*.

The clan-names (leaving out sub-clans) that we found among the Ḍhelki Khāṛiās are the following:—

1. *Ḍūngḍūng* or *Hāṅsdā*, 2. *Samad* (said to be same as *Kerketā*) 3. *Mail* (said to be same as *Kiro*), 4. *Muru* (same as *Kulu*), 5. *Soren*, 6. *Bāgē* (said to be same as *Ṭeṭeṭehōiṅ*), 7. *Ṭōpnō* (a tree), 8. *Bārliha*, 9. *Bā'*, 10. *Bilūng* (salt), 11. *Tirki* (mice), 12. *Panidh* (a water-fowl) 13. *Chung*, 14. *Pail*, 15. *Tetar*, 16. *Mahnandiā*, 17. *Barwā* 18. *Nākh* (*Nāg?*), 19. *Ṭōpō* (a bird), 20. *Charhād*, 21. *Ḍūmar* (fruit) 22. *Besha*, 23. *Bachwar*, 24 *Jharo* .

Among the Hill Khāṛiās we heard of the following clan-names:—1. *Hembrom* (betel-nut), 2. *Tesā* (a bird), 3. *Sāluk* (a bird), 4. *Golgu* or *Sāl* (a fish), 5. *Bāliā* (a fish), 6. *Bhūiyā* (a fish), 7. *Sāru* (a yam), 8. *Badiyā* (a tuber), 9. *Nāg* (a cobra). Besides these Mr. T.C. Das speaks of *Kusli*, *Khelna*, *Hujur*, and *Andaria*, of which he could not get the meaning .

Now, if we compare these clan-names met with among the different sections of the tribe, we find that of the first eight clan-names of the Ḍhelki Khāṛiās, which are said to be the original clan-names of the tribe, the Dūdh Khāṛiās have all the eight, but of these they do not count *Bārlihā* and *Ṭōpno* as original clans but regard them as subsequently-acquired clan-names, and add three more, namely, *Ba'*, *Bilūng*, and *Kerketā* as their original clans . Thus, between these two sections, eleven clans are regarded as the original clans of the tribe, and both sections still have those clans amongst them . But the Hill Khāṛiās do not possess any of these eleven clans, at the present day at any rate . These eleven supposed original clans would be:—1. *Ba'*, 2. *Bilūng*, 3. *Ḍūngḍūng* or *Āind* or *Hāṅsdā*, 4. *Kerketā* or *Samad*, 5. *Kirō* or *Mail*, 6. *Kulu* or *Muru* or *Kachua*,

7. *Sōreng* or *Suren*, 8. *Teṭeṭehōiñ* or *Bāgē*, 9. *Ṭōpō*, 10. *Ṭōpnō*, 11. *Bārlihā*.

The Hill Khāṛiās do not name any of these clans. Of the clans named by some sections of them, only the *Nāg* occurs as a minor clan amongst the Ḍhelkis, and *Hembrōm* amongst the Dūdh Khāṛiās. As noted above, these two clan-names are also found among the Santāls, Mūṇḍās, Bhūiyās and some other Mūṇḍā tribes. The probabilities are that either the Hill Khāṛiās separated from the main body of the tribe before the clan-system developed amongst them and they subsequently adopted these clan names from their neighbouring Mūṇḍā tribes, or that only a few minor clans of the tribe constituted the section that first separated from the main body of the tribe and migrated to the Hills of Mayurbañj, whence some families went further north to Mānbhūm and Singbhūm. These, owing to their small and scattered population, were obliged to marry within the clan and thus practically lost their totemic clan organisation and the totems and the sentiments connected with them. The latter supposition might perhaps appear in the circumstances to be more probable than the former. The fact that although the Mayurbhañj Khāṛias have long forgotton their own language but still use the Khāṛiā and Mūṇḍā terms "Khili" (*Kili*) meaning a totemic clan, might appear to lend support to this conjecture. Their older clan organisation would appear to have been more or less replaced among the Hill Khāṛiās of Mayurbhañj by the class organisation of *Padits* (titles) to which the name *Khili* has since been transferred. It may be noted that the Hill Bhūiyas of Ōṛissā and the Juāngs of Keoñjhar, both belonging to the Mūṇḍā stock as the

Khāṛiās do, are also remarkable for the absence at the present day of a totemic organisation. On the other hand, two other among the most primitive Mūṇḍā tribes,–namely, the Koṛwās and the Birhōṛs,–still retain the totemic clan organisation more or less intact as also their Austric speech.

In Appendix III is given the local distribution of Dūdh Khāṛiā clans in the Rānchi District in Chōṭā Nāgpur and the Ḍhelki Khāṛia clans of the Jāshpur State in the Central Provinces, and also both Dūdh and Ḍhelki Khāṛiā clans of the Gāngpur State in Ōṛissā.

(iii) Kinship System.

For a fuller comprehension of the social organisation of the tribe, it is necessary to study the system of Relationship nomenclature and the natural rights and duties, functions and disabilities appertaining to different relations. We accordingly proceed in this section to give a brief account of the Relationship System of the Khāṛiās.

The Bilateral Kin-groups.

As we have seen, the exogamous kinship group of the patrilineal clan is the basis of the social organization of all sections of the tribe except the Hill Khāṛiās of Mayurbhañj among whom the social unit is the village. Except among the latter sub-section, the Khāṛiā is born to the clan-name of his father and resides with his father and father's kin under a system of father-right. Among the Hill Khāṛiās of Mayurbhañj, marriage is regulated exclusively by degrees of relationship including village relationship. Among the other sections of the Khāṛiās matrimonial regulations are based primarily on exogamous clans but secondarily also on degrees of relationship. The Kinship system of all three sections of the tribe is mainly of the type named by Morgan as the "Classificatory system". The fundamental feature of this system is that the same relationship term is used for most, though not all, relatives of the same generation and sex. Relationship is reckoned between groups rather than individuals, and collateral lines are not always kept distinct from the lineal. Although clan relationship is regarded by the Dūdh and the Ḍhelki sections of the Khāṛiās as more vital to society than other relationships, yet both paternal and maternal kindred are regularly recognised and definite relationship terms are employed with regard to relations on both sides of the family. The Hill Khāṛiās of Mayurbhañj employ Ōṛiyā terms of relationship and those of Mānbhūm and Dhalbhūm use Bengali terms.

The following tabular statement of the terms of relationship and mutual address in vogue among the Dūdh and Ḍhelki Khāṛiās has been arranged by generations and sexes. The terms of relationship and mutual address have been obtained by the geneological method. In collecting genealogies we found that the Khāṛiā usually remembers the personal names and and clan names of relatives up to the third generation or his grand-father's generation only and, only in a few cases, up to that of his great grandfather's generation, but has no special Kinship nomenclature beyond the third generation in the ascending or descending line.

Although no section of the tribe is now composed of only two exogamous moieties, the Khāṛiā's classification of the children of father's sisters and those of mother's brothers in one group as distinct from the children of father's brothers, and the prevalence of cross-cousin marriage which would be a natural result of the dual organisation, may lead to the inference of the probable existence of such an organisation in the past.

List of Kinship Terms.

1. *Speaker's own generation.*

English term of relationship.	Khāṛiā Term for the relationship.	Term for addressing the relative.
Brother ...	Bhāi	Eh Bhāi !
Elder brother ...	Dādā	Eh Dādā ! Dādā jōe !
Eldest brother ...	Dādā	" "
Younger brother ...	Bhāi, Kōnōn bhāi	Eh Bhāiyā ! Eh Bābu! Eh (name)!
Youngest brother ...	" "	" "
Father's elder brother's son ...	Baḍāk' beṭdōm ; Bhāi or Dādā	Eh Bhāi ! or, Eh Dādā ! (according to age).
Father's younger brother's son ...	Kākāk' beṭḍōm	" "
Father's elder sister's son ...	Mamiāk' beṭḍōm	" "
Father's younger sister's son ...	Māmiāk'beṭā	Eh Bhāi ! or, Eh Dādā! (according as he is junior or senior).
Mother's sister's son ...	"	" "
Mother's elder sister's son ...	"	" "
Mother's younger sister's son ...	"	" "
Mother's elder brother's son ...	"	" "
Mother's younger brother's son ...	"	" "
Husband's elder sister's husband ...	Dādā	Eh Dādā !

English term of relationship.	Khāṛiā Term for the relationship.	Term for addressing the relative.
Husband's elder brother ...	Bāo	(Not addressed)
Husband's younger brother ...	Bōker	Eh Bābu ! Eh (name) !
Wife's elder sister's husband ...	Sāṛhu, or Mahā Sāṛhu	Eh Sāṛhu ! Eh Dādā !
Husband's younger sister's husband ...	Bhāi	Eh Bhāiyā ! Eh Bābu !
(Man's) Elder sister's husband ...	Ba'ṭhi	Eh Ba'ṭhi !
(Woman's) Elder sister's husband...	"	" "
(Man's) Younger sister's husband...	Kulāmḍāe ārām; or Bahin-ārām	Eh Bābu ! Eh (name) !
(Woman's) younger sister's husband ...	"	" "
Wife's younger brother ...	Boker	Eh Bābu ! Eh (name) !
Wife's elder brother ...	Bāotāng	Eh Dādā !
Mother's sister's son ...	Bhāi or Dādā (according to age)	Eh Bhāiyā ! Eh Dādā! (according as the speaker is senior or junior)
Wife's elder sister's husband ...	Mahā Sāṛhu, Dādā	Eh Bhāiyā ! Eh Dādā !
Husband ...	Kenḍōr	(not addressed by any particular term).
Son's wife's father ...	Samdhī	Eh Samdhi !
Daughter's husband's father ...	"	" "
Wife ...	Kānṛāe	Eh ge !
Husband's elder brother's wife ...	Donku, Mahā Ḍonku	Eh Nānā ! Eh Didi!
Eldest sister ...	Dai, Nānā	Eh Nānā ! Eh Dai!

English term of relationship.	Khāṛiā Term for the relationship.	Term for addressing the relative.
Elder sister ...	Kulāmṛā, Boi	Eh Māi !
Youngest sister ...	„	,, Eh (name) !
Younger sister ...	Kulamṛā, Boi	Eh (name) !
Mother's elder brother's daughter...	Māmā' beṭ ḍōm	Eh Nānā (if older) ! Eh Māi (if younger) !
Mother's younger brother's daughter ...	„	„ „
Mother's elder sister's daughter ...	Baḍiāk bichḍōm	Eh Nānā! Eh Dai! Eh Māi !
Mother's younger sister's daughter	Mij bichḍōm	„ „ „
Husband's elder sister	Nānā	„ „ ,,
Husband's younger sister ...	Bōksel	Eh Boi! Eh(name)!
Husband's younger brother's wife...	Bokerdā, or Kōnōn ḍonkin	Eh Boi!(Eh name)! „ „
Husband's elder sister ...	Nānā	Eh Nānā! Eh Dai!
Wife's elder brother's wife ...	„	„ „
Wife's younger brother's wife ...	Kulamḍāe	Eh Mai ! Eh Boi !
Father's elder sister's daughter ...	Māmīā' bichḍōm	Eh Nana ! Eh Dai !
Father's younger sister's daughter	Māmiā' bichḍōm	Eh Nānā! Eh Māi!
Father's elder brother's daughter...	Baḍa' bichḍōm	,, „
Father's younger brother's daughter ...	Kākā' bichḍōm	„ „
Wife's elder sister ...	Aijker	Eh Didi ! Eh Dai !
Wife's younger sister ...	Bokesl	Eh Māi! Eh(name)
Younger brother's wife ...	Kimin	Eh Mai! Kimin ki!
Elder brother's wife ...	Āji	Eh Āji ! Āji joe !!

English term for relationship.	Khāṛiā Terms for the relationship.	Term for addressing the relative.
Son's wife's mother ...	Dewān	Eh Dewān !
Daughter's husband's mother ...	Dewan	" "

II. Generation next above the speaker.

Father :	Āppā	Eh Āppā !
Father's elder brother ...	Baḍā	Eh Bāḍā ! Eh Bā
Father's eldest brother ...	"	" "
Mother's elder sister's husband ...	Baḍā	Eh Baḍā !
Father's youngest brother ...	Kākā	Eh Kākā !
Father's younger brother ...	"	"
Step-father ...	Kākā	EhKākā! EhĀppā !
Mother's younger sister's husband	Mosā, Kākā	Eh Kākā!
Father's elder sister's husband ...	Māmā	Eh Māmā !
Father's younger sister's husband...	"	"
Mother's elder brother ...	Māmā	Eh Māmā !
Mother's younger brother ...	"	"
Husband's father ...	Sasūr	Eh Bā !
Wife's father ...	"	"
Mother ...	Mā.	Eh Mā ! Mā jōe ?
Step-mother ...	Mij, Mosi,	Eh Mā !
Father's elder brother's Wife ...	Baḍī	Eh Baḍī !
Father's younger brother's Wife ...	Mij	Eh Mij !
Mother's elder sister ...	Mij	Eh Mij ! Eh Mā !

English term of relationship.	Khāṛiā Terms for the relationship.	Term for adressing such relative.
Mother's elder brother's wife ...	Māmī	Eh Māmī!
Mother's brother's wife ...	„	„
Mother's younger sister ...	„	„
Father's elder sister ...	„	„
Father's sister ...	Māmī	Eh Māmī !
Father's younger sister ...	„	„
Wife's mother ...	Kinker	Eh Mā !
Husband's mother ...	„	„

III. Generation Next below the speaker.

Son ...	Beṭā	Eh Beṭā!Eh Bābu!
Elder brother's son ...	Bhātijā	Eh Beṭā! Eh Bhā-tijā! Eh Bābu !
Wife's elder sister's son ...	Bhātijā	„ „ „
Husband's elder brother's son ...	Bhātijā	Eh Bēṭā! Eh Bhā-tijā! Eh Bābu!
Wife's younger sister's son ...	Baḍa	Eh Baṛa!Eh Bābu!
Husband's younger brother's son ...	„	„ „ „
Husband's younger's sister son ...	Bhāgnā	Eh Bhāgnā ! „
(Woman's) Elder brother's son ...	Bhāgnā	Eh Bhāgnā ! „
„ Younger brother's son ...	„	„ „ „
(Man's) Elder sister's son ...	„	„ „ „
(Man's) Younger sister's son ...	„	„ „ „
Husband's younger sister's son ...	„	„ „ „
Wife's younger brother's son ...	„	„ „ „

English term of relationship.	Khāṛiā Terms for the relationship.	Term for addressing the relative.
(Woman's) elder sister's son ...	Bhātijā	Eh Bhātijā! Eh Bābu!
Daughter's husband ...	Ārām, Arāmkuḍu	Eh Bābu!
(Man's) Elder brother's daughter...	Bhātiji Pūtri	Eh Māi! Eh Bhātiji!
Husband's elder brother's „ ...	„ „	„ „
(Woman's) Elder brother's daughter	Bhāgnī	Eh Māi! Eh Beṭi! Eh Bhāgni!
Husband's younger sister's daughter	Bhāgni	Eh Mai! Eh Beṭi! Eh Bhāgni!
(Man's) Elder sister's daughter ...	Baḍī	„ „ „
(Woman's) „ „ „ ...	„	„ „ „
Husband's „ „ „ ...	„	„ „ „
(Man's) Younger sister's daughter	„	„ „
Wife's elder brother's daughter ...	„	„ „ „
Wife's younger brother's daughter	„	„ „ „
(Woman's) Younger sister's daughter ..	„	Eh Bāḍi! Eh Māi! Eh Beṭi!
(Man's) Younger brother's daughter	„	„ „ „
Wife's Younger sister's daughter	„	„ „ „
Son's wife ...	Kimin, Beṭākimin	Eh Kiminki!

IV. Third generation from speaker.

Son's son ...	Bokḍū	Eh Bōkḍu! Eh Nāti! Eh (name)!
Daughter's son ...	„	„ „ „
Son's daughter's husband ...	„	„ „ „
Daughter's daughter's husband ...	„	„ „ „
Sister's son's daughter's husband...	„	„ „ „
Sister's son's son ...	„	„ „ „

English term of relationship.	Khāṛiā Terms for the relationship.	Term for addressing the relative.
Sister's daughter's son ...	"	" " "
Son's daughter ...	"	" " "
Daughter's daughter ...	"	" " "
Sister's son's daughter	"	" " "
Sister's daughter's daughter...	"	" " "

It may be noted that in addressing persons of either sex who are younger than the speaker, Khāṛiās, both male and female, often use the proper name of the person addressed. When a male speaker calls another man or boy, he often uses the vocative expletive "Le", e. g. "Eh Le!" (in the sense of 'Come here!'). A female in such a case would say 'Eh Ri!'. When addressing a relative of a higher generation (such as the father, uncle, *etc.*) both men and women often use 'joi' after the term of address instead of prefixing 'Eh' before the term of address.

From the above table of kinship terminology the following features of classification appears to emerge :—

Main features of Khāṛiā Kinship system.

1. There are in many cases two distinct groups of terms to express relationship,—one in *speaking of* relatives and another in *addressing* them. The terms of address are used in a much more general sense, and as they are more comprehensive and of more extended application they are necessarily fewer in number.

2. Although a general kinship term is employed in addressing a number of relatives of the same generation and sex, two different terms are in many cases employed for each class of such relatives, according as they are older or younger than the person speaking. Thus, most men of the same generation-level (e. g. one's own brothers, one's father's brother's sons, father's sister's sons, mother's brother's sons, and mother's sister's sons) are classed together and regarded as 'brothers' to whom the term '*Bhāi*' is applied, if younger in age, and '*Dādā*', if older. It may be noted that the term '*Dādā*' is also applied by a Khāṛiā woman in addressing such a relation by marriage as her husband's elder sister's husband, and the term "*Bhāi*" is used by a woman for her husband's younger sister's husband; the term '*Nānā*' is applied to one's own elder sister, husband's elder sister, and wife's elder brother's wife; the term "Bōkḍu" is applied to son's sons, son's daughters, daughter's sons, daughter's daughters; and the term "Bhāgnā" to one's sisters' sons, wife's brothers' sons, and husband's sister's sons.

3. Different terms are often employed for relatives by marriage according as they belong to a man's or a woman's own side of the family, or to one's wife's or one's husband's side of the family. Thus, a man terms his own elder sister's husband as *Ba'ṭhi*, but his wife's elder sister's husband as *Sāṛhu* or *Mahā-Sāṛhu*, his own younger sister's husband as *Ārām* or *Bahin Ārām* or *Kulāmḍāe Ārām*, but his wife's younger sister's husband as *Sāṛhu* or *Kōnōn Sāṛhu*; his own elder brother's wife as *Āji*, but his wife's elder brother's wife as *Nānā*; his own younger brother's wife as *Kimin*

but his wife's younger brother's wife as *Kulāmḍāe*. A woman calls her own elder sister's husband as *Ba'ṭhi* but her husband's elder sister's husband as *Dādā*; her own younger sister's husband as *Ārām*, her husband's younger sister's husband as *Bhāi* or *Bōkselingā Kenḍōr*, her own elder sister's son as *Bhātijā* but her husband's elder sister's son as *Bhāgnā*; her own elder brother's wife as *Āji*, but her husband's elder brother's wife as *Ḍonku*; her own younger brother's wife as *Kimin* or *Bhāi-kimin* but her husband's younger brother's wife as *Bokerḍāe*.

It may, however, be noted that the same terms are applied by a Khāṛiā wife to certain relatives of her husband which the husband applies to her wife's relatives of the same or similar class. Thus, a man refers to his wife's younger brother as 'Boker', and a woman calls her husband's younger brother as 'Boker'; a man calls his wife's younger sister as 'Boksel' and a woman applies the same term also to her husband's younger sister; a man terms his younger brother's son and also his wife's younger sister's son as 'Baḍa' and a woman terms her younger sister's son and her husband's younger brother's son as 'Baḍā'; a man terms his elder brother's wife as 'Āji' and a woman applies the same term to her elder brother's wife.

4 A few reciprocal relationships are designated by a common term. Thus, the term 'Baḍā' is used by a Khāṛiā for his father's elder brother, who in his turn calls his younger brother's son as "Baḍā". Again, a Khāṛia calls his wife's younger sister's son as "Baḍa" and reciprocally a Khāṛiā also calls his mother's elder sister's husband as "Baḍā". The term *Baḍi* is used for the

father's elder brother's wife and for the mother's elder sister as also for the reciprocal relations, namely, a man's younger brother's daughter and wife's younger sister's daughter and a woman's younger sister's daughter.

Among social correlations of terminological features the following may be mentioned :

Social correlations of Kinship terms.

(1) The same kinship term "Māmā" is used for father's sister's husband and mother's brother, and these two relationships are necessarily combined in one and the same person where cross-cousin marriage is practised. Such marriages are customary among the Khāṛiās, although now very close relatives of the class are generally avoided.

(2) The same term 'Bā 'thi' [62] is used by the Ḍhelki Khāṛiā for mother's brother's daughter, father's sister's daughter, mother's sister's daughter, and father's brother's daughter. When two brothers marry two sisters, the relationship of mother's sister's child and father's brother's child are combined in one and the same person. Exchange marriage by which a brother and a sister are married respectively to the daughter and son of the same father is in vogue among the tribe. The fact that a man's younger sister and his wife's younger brother's wife, are both classed together under the same kinship term "*Kulāmḍāe*" also points to a similar social correlation.

(3) The same term 'Kākā' is used by the Khāṛiā for a step-father, a father's younger brother, and a mother's younger sister's husband. When a man marries his deceased elder brother's wife he is both uncle

62 Dūdh Khāṛiās apply the term 'Ba'ṭhi' only to an elder sister's husband.

(father's brother) and step-father to his elder brother's children. The custom of junior levirate is in vogue in the tribe and explains the identity of the relationship term for both father's younger brother and step-father. Again, when a man marries a younger sister of his elder brother's wife, he combines in himself the relationship of father's younger brother and mother's younger sister's husband to his brother's children.

Such are some of the salient features of kinship nomenclature of the Khāṛiās. We have discussed certain social correlations of kinship terminology to show how Khāṛiā kinship nomenclature gives us some insight into the social system and social condition of the tribe. The entire kinship terminology of the Khāṛiās cannot, however, be referred to social causes but some must be referred to borrowing mostly from their Hindu neighbours, as for example, the terms 'bhātijā,' 'baḍā,' 'Kākā,' 'Samdhī,' 'Sāṛhū,' and 'Dewān'. To the Khāṛiā a son and a brother's son are both 'sons,' and a father and father's brothers all come under the category of 'father' and are distinguished as 'elder father,' 'younger father,' and 'father,' when it is required to distinguish and specify each of them separately.

We shall conclude this chapter by noticing some of the rights and duties which Khāṛiā society attaches to certain relationships.

Father:—It is the duty of the Khāṛiā father to shave the first lock of hair of his new-born babe at its first ceremonial purification (known as *Kānsōng Kāraenā*) ceremony. Whether this custom was in origin intended to signify a recognition of fatherhood, it is difficult to say.

Mother's brother :—Among the Ḍhelki Khāṛiās the mother's brother has to officiate at the name-giving ceremony of his sister's child. In his absence some other elderly relative takes his place. Among the Hill Khāṛiās, however, preference is given to the father's mother.

The mother's brother has also his part in the marriage ceremonies of his sister's son, as will be seen in the chapter on Marriage.

Mother's father :—At the first hair-tying ceremony of a Khāṛiā baby, the mother's father and, in his absence, the mother's brother has to take the principal part.

Relationship Taboos.

Certain relatives are called by the Khāṛiās as "Bārenā" or Tabooed relatives, as between whom not only are marriage or sexual relations regarded as social 'sins,' but even close contact must be avoided. Thus the husband's elder brothers or elder cousins, particularly the husband's mother's brother's sons, if older in age than the husband, are 'taboo' to a Khāṛiā woman. Neither she nor such a relative must even "tread upon each other's shadow", much less touch each other or sit on the same mat, or even talk to or take the name of each other. Such a relative is regarded as the woman's "*Somārbo Bāo*" or the tabooed *Bāo* or *Bhaisur* (husband's elder brother or cousin). A similar reciprocal taboo is imposed by society upon a Khāṛiā and his *wife's mother's brother's daughter* if older than him in age; she is regarded as a tabooed sister-in-law (*somārbō āijker*); and the local Hindi term " Jeṭh-sās" (*lit*; aunt-in-law) is applied to her.

A similar taboo has also to be observed between a woman and her husband's elder brother (*Bāo*), but she may serve food and drink to her *Bāo.* A Khāṛiā must not talk to, touch, or take the name of his younger brother's or cousin's wife. He has to observe the same taboo in relation to his sister's son's wife. A Khāṛiā woman is not permitted to jest or joke with her *Ārām* or younger sister's husband, and a Khāṛiā man is not permitted to joke with his wife's elder sister or wife's elder brother.

Joking Relations or "Landā-Nātā".

There are, however, certain near relations as between whom Khāṛiā society not only permits, but regards as appropriate, jests and jokes and a bantering mode of conversation suggesting, though not actually indicating, undue familarity. This relationship is termed in the Khāṛiā language *Lāndā-Nātā* (literarlly, 'Laughing' or joking relationship). Such relations exist and such liberties are permitted between—

(1) A man and his wife's younger brothers and sisters.

(2) A man and his brother's wife's brothers and sisters.

(3) A woman and her husband's younger brothers and sisters, and her sister's husband's younger brothers and sisters.

(4) Grand-parents and grand-children.

As regards the above-mentioned joking relationships, it may be noted that a Khāṛiā may marry—(i) his wife's younger sister; and (2) his brother's wife's sister; and a Khāṛiā widow may marry either her deceased husband's younger brother or her sister's husband's brother. As for joking relationship (*lāḍā nātā* between grand-parents and grand-children, this is supposed by some to be the survival of an archaic social regulation which permitted marriage or sexual relations between persons two degrees apart or related to one another as grand-uncle and grand-nephew, in a classificatory sense. But Khāṛiā society now abhors sexual union within the clan as incest, and would resent any such suggestion.

In the table of kinship terms, we have seen (p. 153 *ante*) that the term "Bōkḍu" is applied in common to all relatives of the third generation below the speaker. Male relatives of the third generation above the speaker (*viz.*, father's father or uncle, and mother's father or uncle) are termed 'Ājā' and addressed as 'Eh Ājā', and female relatives of the third generation above the speaker (*viz.*, father's mother or aunt, and mother's mother or aunt) are "Yā'yā" and addressed as 'Eh Yā'yā'!.

Artificial Relationship:—Besides blood-relationship and relationship by marriage, Khāṛiā society has devised artificial forms of relationship by which two persons may enter into a ceremonial bond of friendship, regarded as equally sacred. The main features of these ceremonial alliances between individuals are generally the sprinkling of water with mango-leaves from a brass-jug (*lōṭa*) on each other by the contracting parties, feasting each other and exchanging new clothes, and subsquently inviting each to the other's house on the occasions of all feasts and festivals, and exchanging presents. Another interesting point about it is that such relationship may be contracted by a Khāṛiā with a non-Khāṛiā neighbour as much as with a Khāṛiā. The two friends do not take the name of each other but call each other by the relationship name. There are various forms of ceremonial alliances between individuals, of which the "Sahiā" form is sociologically the most important, as it really involves a close bond of relationship between two families. A fairly detailed account of this and other forms of alliance such as the "Gōi", "Karamḍāiṛ", "Iār", and "Sangi" forms which the Khāṛiās have in common with the Ōrāōns, has been given in the monograph on *The Orāōns of Chōṭā Nāgpur* (pp. 396-405) to which the reader is referred.

Among other forms of artificial relationships are the different forms of "flower-friendship" and "tree-friendship" such as "Keorā", "Gulāichi", "Karam ḍāiṛ", *etc.*, among women, young or old, in which the two friends insert into each other's hair flowers of the particular species from which the relationship takes its name. The *Iār* form of friendship between men and the *Gōi* form of friendship between girls have also a social significance. A man's brother and his wife's sister, and a man's sister and his wife's brother, are also said to be related to each other as "Gōi". As exchange marriage is not unknown to the Khāṛiā, these two classes of "*Gōis*" may marry each other. The *Mitān* form of ceremonial 'friendship' may be contracted even with neighbours of other castes and tribes, sometimes for some mutual economic advantage, and may be terminated or renewed after a fixed period.

Thus, we find Khāṛiā Society, in its efforts to secure the utmost *social integration*, has devised artificial bonds of relationship not only within the tribe but with their alien neighbours as well.

CHAPTER VII

Tribal Government.

In the last chapter, we examined the social and kinship grouping of the tribe. Khāṛiā social organisation with its body of traditions, that constitute the social environment of the individual, produces appropriate social sentiments. These mould the character and behaviour of the individual in society, and mark off members of Khāṛiā society from other societies. Traditional usage crystallised into customary law. It is the business of Tribal Government to enforce obedience to such law and custom. The machinery of tribal government varies in size and complexity with the size and culture of a particular tribe or group.

Hill Khāṛiās. The Hill Khāṛiās living in inhospitable mountain fastnesses and often wandering over jungles and barren wastes in search of small game and wild fruits and edible leaves and roots, seeds, nuts and berries, are compelled to live in small groups of from four or five to eight or ten families. The limited extent of their food-supply prevents these groups, mainly of food-gatherers and hunters, from increasing in size. Each such group of families, as we have seen, compose one settlement occupying the slope, or the foot, of a hill and are generally known in the locality as the "Kheṛeys" of that particular hill. This group is mostly genetic, each group being ordinarily composed of agnatic families, although in some instances a near relation by marriage is included,—a son-in-law, for example, coming to live in the settlement of his father-in-law. Thus a Hill Khāṛiā settlement is essentially an enlarged household group. But even the closest ties of relationship are not always sufficient to prevent an individual member of such a group from detaching himself from one settlement and joining another. Thus, to cite one instance out of several that came to our knowledge, Ḍōm Dehuri of village Kānchhiṇḍā in the Mayurbhañj State had two sons, Bānkā and Jaiyā. The latter migrated to village Kusumbandi after his marriage with a girl of that village; and although Ḍōm's younger son Bānka Dehuri lived on at Kanchhiṇḍā, yet the latter's four sons—Srīpati, Srīdhar, Sankarā, and Dāśarathī,—tempted by the prospect of securing lands for cultivation at village-Sarsopāl, subsequently migrated to the latter village. Such shifting of individuals or families from one settle ment to another appears to have been going on among the Hill Khāṛiās from very remote times.

Favoured by more bountiful environments on the comparatively fertile valleys of the Sankh, the Koel and the Ib, the Ḍhelki and the Dūdh sections have congregated in much larger groups ; and these groups have more or less held together for countless generations. Larger aggregation and greater co-operation and more stable association have naturally resulted among them in relatively more extended social activities and relationships and a relatively greater economic progress than among the more primitive Hill Khāṛiās. Although in most Ḍhelki and Dūdh Khāṛiā villages, a few families of artisan and menial castes, such as blacksmiths and weavers, have settled down, and have been serving the economic needs of the Khāṛiās, these castes have no recognised place in the social polity of the tribe.

Social Authority: The Village Council.

As there can be no group-life without a leader, even in the rudest societies some sort of authority comes to be generally accorded to the oldest or wisest or most clever among the elders of a group. So we find among the Hill Khāṛiās, as among the Ḍhelki and the Dūdh Khāṛias, each settlement acknowledging the leadership, in social as well as religious matters, of the sacrificer or priest of the settlement who is generally its seniormost member. He is styled the 'Dehuri' or 'Dihuri' among the Hill Khāṛiās and the 'Kālo' among the Ḍhelkis and variously as 'Kālo' or 'Baiga' or 'Pāhān' in the Dūdh section.

But this head-man is not the sole authority in the group. In all matters of any importance he may not act without consulting the more influential heads of families. In fact, the Dihuri or Kālo and the village elders, or practically all the adult males together, form the village-council now known in the Khāṛia country, as elsewhere in India, by the name of the Village-*Pāñch* or *Pāñchāyat*, literally,—the "Council of Five".

It is interesting to note that the Hill Khāṛias of Mayurbhañj prefer to adopt, as their tribal name, the term "Dehuri" in place of "Khāṛiā", just as a Sañtāl prefers to be called "Mājhi" rather than Santāl. Though 'Mājhi' or "Māñjhi" is, properly speaking, the name of the secular head-man of a Sañtāl village, it has, in fact, come to be now locally applied to the Sañtāls as their tribal name. Similarly, though "Mūṇḍā" is, really in origin, the name of the secular head-man of a Mūṇḍā (Hōṛo) village, it is now the recognised name of the tribe as a whole.

The Village Council:— Its powers and functions.

The village council or Panchāyat settles all social (including socio-religious and socio-political) matters of local interest, particularly violations of minor social or religious taboos, and disputes about partition. The headman in consultation with the elders of the settlement also arranges for raising contributions from the villagers for periodical public worship and religious feasts, and for the propitiatry sacrifices to the spirits in times of epidemic to men or cattle. Among the Ḍhelki and Dūdh Khāṛiās when a widow or a minor owner of fields cannot arrange for the proper cultivation of their lands, the village headman and the village-elders direct the other villagers to cultivate, each in his turn, the lands for the benefit of the helpless widow or minors, as the case may be. In a marriage or a funeral in a Khāṛiā family, the village Pañch consisting really of all adult members of the village, as also the Pañch of two or three or more neighbouring related villages are informed, and they attend the ceremonies unless the family in question is under a sentence of social excommunication. When a Khāṛiā desires to take a *ghar-jīā*, that is to say, a young man to be married to his daughter and adopted in his family as a residential member, the Pañch of his village accompany him to the house of the parents of the selected young man, and there in the presence also of the Pañch of the latter's village ask and receive the consent of the parents of the young man and of the Pañch of his village; and again on the arrival of the *ghar-jĩã* to reside permanently in the house of his prospective father-in-law the latter treats the Pañch of his village to a feast or at least drink, and declares before them that he has taken the young man as his *ghar-jĩã*.

At the *Chaṭṭi* ceremony by which the ceremonial pollution of a family in which a birth has taken place is ceremonially removed and at a marriage ceremony and also at a funeral feast, the village elders constituting the Pañch, and (in the case of families who can afford to invite them) the village elders of one or more neighbouring villages also, attend not only as guests but as witnesses to the ceremony. In the public worship of village deities and spirits, too, the village Pañchāyat assemble at the place of *Pūjā* or sacrifice and the village-priest (Dihuri or Kālō or Baigā or Pāhān, as he may be variously called at various places) performs the pūjā in their presence.

Taboos.

Among the social and socio-religious taboos of which the breach is dealt with by the tribunal of the village-Pañch the following may be mentioned as the more important ones:—

(1) The taboo imposed upon a Khāṛiā woman against attending the *Phāgu* Pūjā or the *Kadleṭā* Pūjā or the *Kharrā* Pūjā, or to enter the *Jhāñkōr* or Sarnā or sacred grove during these Pūjās, or to eat the sacrificial meat of these Pūjās.

(2) The taboo upon a woman against eating the meat of the head of any animal or fowl sacrificed to the village-deities.

(3) The taboo upon a woman against going to and touching or drawing water from a well or spring

in the village during her monthly course or during birth-pollution.

(4) The taboo upon a woman against getting up on the roofing thatch of a house.

(5) The taboo upon a woman against touching or handling a plough or sowing a field. [The customary orthodox punishment for such an offence is to yoke the offending woman to the plough and make her plough a few feet of ground and eat a little grass, and finally go round the village begging for rice with which she must prepare and provide rice-beer for the Pañch; but, as already noted, the "ploughing" and "grass-eating" part of the punishment is now falling into disuse.]

(6) The taboo upon a married Khāṛiā woman against entering the cattle-shed of her parents' house or of the house of any other Khāṛiā except her husband's. [The breach of this taboo is believed to perturb the spirit presiding over cattle and the cattle-shed and thereby bring calamity to the family.]

(7) The taboo upon a Khāṛiā returned from jail or from a sojourn to some distant country against entering his own house or that of a tribe-fellow and even against touching a tribe-fellow, including his own wife and children, until he has undergone ceremonial purification by drinking (or rather licking from a leaf) a drop of blood of a white cock or a white he-goat sacrificed to Pōnōmōsōr or Bhagwān or Beṛo, as the Supreme Being is variously named, or at any rate by drinking rice-beer after libation of it has been offered to Him.

(8) The taboo upon a Khāṛiā against getting his hair shaved or nails pared or his clothes washed by a non-Khāṛiā. [This taboo is in most cases no longer observed.]

(9) The taboo upon a Khāṛiā against carrying the palanquin or *ḍōli* (litter) of a Mahomedan, or a weaver, or a barber, and a similar taboo against carrying a Mahomedan 'Tāziā'. [This is reported only of the Khāṛiās of parts of the Central Provinces.] [63]

Penalty and Expiation.

Breaches of even the very gravest social taboos such as those upon the sexual union of a Khāṛiā with a non-Khāṛiā, or upon marriage or sexual intrigue within the clan, or upon the killing, whether intentional or accidental, of a cow, calf, or bullock, are also punished by excommunication by the village Pañchāyat in the first instance; and, if the accused denies the charge and contests the soundness of their decision and sentence, he may convene a tribal assembly or *Kuṭumb Sabhā*, (sometimes called by the name of *Pāṛhā Pañchāyat* as among the Mūṇḍās and the Orāõns) for fresh investigation; and, in any case, this tribal Council has to be called if the excommunicated family desire to be readmitted into the tribe. The penalty of excommunication can only be called off, in cases in which this is permissible, by the tribal assembly after ceremonial purification and a communal feast to be described later. Punishment for breaches of other taboos are proportioned according to their respective gravity in tribal estimation. Breaches of taboos next in order of gravity to those like sexual union either with non-Kharias or within the clan or the exogamous group, or the killing of cows or bullocks, are generally expiated by the offender by the drinking of the blood of a white cock or he-goat sacrificed in the name of the Sun-God and treating the Pañch to rice-beer. Compara-

63 *Vide* Russel, *Tribes and Castes of the Central Provinces*, Vol. III, p.451

tively lighter taboos are removed by offering a libation of rice-beer to the ancestor-spirits, or by sprinkling water mixed with pounded or powdered turmeric on the person of the breaker of the taboo. The offence is considered as comparatively light if the breach of taboo was unintentional or done in ignorance. The breach of such minor taboos as that against giving away fire from his house to an outsider on the day in which a Khāṛiā takes out paddy-seeds from his house for sowing in his fields, affects only the luck of the individual or family concerned (e.g., their crops may fail) and is therefore not dealt with by the Pañch.

Customary Law of Inheritance.

The *Pañchāyat* is also the custodian of the customary law of seccession and inheritance, and of tribal custom in general. The customary law of inheritance among the tribe is, in its broad features, as follows :—

Customary Law among the Hill Khāṛiās.

Partition and Inheritance:—Among the Hill Khāṛiās all sons get equal shares of their deceased father's property. Daughters receive no share but are maintained by their brothers until their marriage. The widow of the dead man is also supported till death by her sons. If the widow and the sons fail to agree the former is given by the Pañch a small share out of the property, if any, left by her deceased husband; and such share reverts to the sons on her death. If so required, the village Pañch may themselves effect the actual partition. A sonless widow is entitled to a life-interest in the immoveable property left by her husband.

Adoption.—A sonless Khāṛiā may adopt a Khāṛiā boy as his son (*Pōth-Pō*). The adopted boy is generally a brother's son or a sister's son, for only such a near relative, if adopted, is entitled to inherit the entire property of the adoptive father on his death. But if an unrelated boy has been adopted, the Pañch allots only a small fraction of the deceased's assets to him by way of maintenance and the rest to the nearest agnates of the deceased. An adoption, in order to be recognised, must be made in the presence and with the approval of the Pañch and relatives and tribe-fellows. In a few cases in the Mayurbhañj State, the fact of the adoption is reported to have been recorded in writing by a literate person called for the purpose to the assembly.

Ghar-Jāmāi.—A sonless Khāṛiā may also take into his family a *Ghar-Jāmāi* or a prospective bridegroom for his daughter to live in the house as a son. Such *Ghar-Jāmāi*, if duly taken in accordance with tribal custom, inherits, on the death of his father-in-law, any property left by the father-in-law; and in case he predeceases his father-in-law, his wife (daughter of the deceased owner) inherits her father's property; and in case she, too, perdeceases her father, her sons, if any, may inherit the property. The procedure prescribed by tribal custom for taking a *Ghar-jāmāi* is as follows: In the presence of assembled relatives and tribe-fellows, the Khāṛiā who desires to take a Khāṛiā boy as *Gnar-jāmāi* has to declare that he has decided to take this boy (who must be present) as his *Gahr-jāmāi* and to make him the heir of all his property. No written record of this adoption of a *Ghar-jāmāi* or *Gharjīā* is known to have been hitherto kept.

On a subsequent day the marriage is duly celebrated according to tribal custom, and relatives and tribe-fellows are treated to a marriage-feast.

It may be noted that though inheitance is in the main patrilineal as among other Muṇḍā tribes, the customary law of the Hill Khāṛiā differs from the custom among the other sections of the Khāṛiās and generally among other Muṇḍā tribes in one important respect, namely, that the Hill Khāṛiā recognises the right of a sister's son, if adopted as a son by his mother's brother, to inherit the entire property of his adoptive father.

Customary Law among the Dūdh and the Ḍhelki Khāṛiās.

Partition and Inheritance.—The sons of a Khāṛiā owner are entitled to equal shares in his father's properties with this exception that, as among the Muṇḍās and the Orāoñs, the eldest son receives a somewhat larger share of the family lands. Cattle, money, and other moveable properties are equally divided among the sons. But in case partition takes place before the father's death, a share is reserved for the father; and the son or sons who may live with him and work for him and take care of him till his death, and meet his funeral expenses, will get his father's share of land and moveables, in equal shares if such sons have been more than one in number. Daughters are not entitled to any shares in their father's property, but unmarried daughters are entitled to maintenance out of her father's assets until their marriage; and the expenses of their marriage have also to be met out of their father's assets, if any.

Ghar-dāmād.—A Dūdh Khāṛiā as well as a Ḍhelki Khāṛiā may take a *Ghar-dāmād* in the same way and under the same formalities as prevails among the Hill Khāṛiās as described above. But a *Ghar-dāmād* among the Dūdh and Ḍhelki sections usually gets half the lands of his deceased father-in-law, the other half going to the nearest *bhāyāds* or agnates of the deceased owner.

Adopted son.—A sonless Khāṛiā may adopt a son with the consent of his agnates and the Pañches of his own village and that of the village of the adopted son's father if it be different from his own. If a brother's son is adopted, the adopted son will inherit the entire property of his adoptive father, provided he lays no claim to a share in the property of his own natural father, nor receives any such share. With regard to an adopted son other than a brother's son, he is ordinarily entitled to half the *rāiyati* lands left by his adoptive father unless there has been a written document purporting to be a gift or bequest of a larger share or of the whole. The rest of the *rāiyati* lands will go to the nearest *bhāyāds* or agnates in the absence of any such document. But, in any case, no portion of Bhūiñhāri lands, if any, of the deceased owner can be taken by an adopted son other than the brother's son of the deceased owner. Such Bhūiñhāri lands will be inherited by his nearest surviving agnates or *bhāyāds*. If a Khāṛiā leaves sons by a wife married (while a maiden) in the regular *Bihāi* form, and also one or more sons by a wife (a widow or divorced woman) married in the *Sāgāi* form, the sons by the *bihāi* wife will, among themselves, receive a much larger share (two or three times more according to the custom of the locality) than the sons by the *Sāgāi* wife.

Formerly disputes among the Khāṛiās of a village regarding possession of lands, payment of debts, and the like, and other minor differences used to be settled by the village Pañch; but now-a-days these disputes are generally taken to the law courts.

Sexual offences and breaches of sexual taboos, breaches of taboos against taking forbidden food and eating and drinking at the hands of an excommunicated Khāṛiā or of forbiden castes and tribes come up to the village Pañch in the first instance. If proved, the guilty parties are excommunicated and fined by the village Pañchāyat; but if the condemned party is dissatisfied with the order, and in every case in which the accused or guilty person belongs to another village or another tribe or caste, the Pāṛhā or tribal or inter-village council is invited to adjudicate and pass sentence according to tribal custom. And, further, the restoration to 'caste' of a Khāṛiā outcasted either by the village Pañch or by the inter-village Assembly is the function of the latter alone.

Inter-village Federations : *The Federal Assembly or Pāṛhā Pañchāyat or Kuṭumb Sabhā; and its Constitution and Functions* :—As has been indicated above, in the matter of tribal government, the Khāṛiās have worked out an organisation higher than the mere village-community with its Village Council or Pañch. All the three sections of the tribe, including even the Hill Khāṛiās, have long since developed a social organisation higher than that of separate settlements or village-units, each under the leadership of a village headman and village-council. Among the Hill Khāṛiās, representatives of different related groups, settled on the slopes or at the foot of different neighbouring hills occasionally meet in council to discuss matters of vital interest believed to affect the 'luck' of the clan or tribe, and the eldest or wisest or most clever among the Dihūris of these different settlements is recognised as the social head of the federation and presides over this tribal or inter-village Pañchāyat known among the Hill-Khāṛiās as a *Bhīṛā* (*lit.*, Assembly) and the presiding headman is called the Ḍāṇḍiā of the Bhīṛā. Besides the Dāṇḍiā headman, there is no other office-bearer of a *Bhīṛā* of the Hill Khāṛiās.

Among the Hill Khāṛiās there is no distinction of rank as between different families except that the elders of the village and the Dihuri or village-priest, as the seniormost or the wisest among the elders, are accorded some amount of respect, and at village Pañchāyats and at *Bhīṛās* or tribal assemblies they act as the guides and mouthpieces of the assembly.

Among the Ḍhelki Khāṛiās, too, there is no standing Pañchāyat of a group of federated villages called Pāṛhā or Gādi, nor a permanent *Mūkhiā* or superior headman of a Gādi Assembly. But a man of the *Muru* clan among the Ḍhelkis must act as the "Pāin-dihā" (a corrupt form of "Pāni-dihā" or "water-giver") or master of the ceremonies and a man of the *Samad* clan must act as the *Bhanḍāri* (barber) in a tribal feast and their services are indispensable at Pañchāyats for restoring an outcasted member of the tribe to 'caste', that is, to his or her former tribal status and rights. On the tribal assembly or Pañch deciding to restore a person to 'caste', it is a man of the *Muru* clan who, as "Pāin-dihā ", has to administer the purifying potion to the hitherto excommunicated person; and a man of the *Samad* clan has to perform the same services that a barber has to do amongst the Hindus at their purification ceremonies meant to remove birth-pollution, death-pollution, *etc*.

A tribal council of the Ḍhelkis is composed of villages of more than one clan. Thus a four-village *Gāḍi* (*chār-khanḍa-pāli*) of the Ḍhelki Khāṛiās of the Gāngpur State (in Ōṛissā) is composed of the Khāṛiās of villages—Bairāgi Bāhāl (*Muru* clan), Ḍumā Bāhāl (*Kiṛō* clan), Barḍihi (*Hāñsdā* clan), and Mahulpāli (*Kiṛō* clan). Another four-village *Gādi* similarly consists of the Ḍhelkis of Raj-bāhāl (*Muru* clan), those of Sipu-kachchhā (*Muru* clan), and those of Mohulpāli (*Kiro* clan, and also *Hāñsdā* clan newly arrived)—all of the Gāngpur State, and the Khāṛiās of Haldijharia (*Chārhād* clan) belonging to the neighbouring State of Rāigaṛh in the Central Provinces. It is interesting to note that in some cases one and the same village may attach itself to more than one *Gādi* and take part in the tribal (or inter-village) councils of both the groups. It may also be noted that some *Gādis* contain a larger number of villages than others. Thus villages Ujalpur, Ṭāngar-pāli, Kanak-jūṛā, Kāṭrā, Dhūñri-pāṛā, Indar-pūr, an d Telengḍihi form one *Gādi* in the Gāngpur State.

In every *Kuṭumb Sabhā* or *Pāṛhā Pañchāyat* or *Gādi* or *Bhīrā*, of any section of the tribe there must be present both *bhāyads* and relatives by marriage (related either in the present generation or in a former generation) so that villages belonging to different and related clans may take part in the deliberations. It may be noted that the Hill Khāṛiās of any other village with whom the Hill Khāṛiās of a particular village may enter or did enter in a past generation into marital relations are termed by the Hill Khāṛiās their *Bandhu-bāsiās*.

Pāṛhā officials:—A Dūdh Khāṛiā *Pāṛhā* or group of federated villages is also composed of villages of more than one clan, and the post of *Karṭāhā* of a Pāṛhā is now generally hereditary and cannot be held by a man of any clan other than either the *Ḍūngḍūng*, or the *Kūlū*, or the *Samad*. Among some Khāṛiās of the Central Provinces, the *Karṭāhā* or Pārhā headman is styled the *Pradhān* who 'gives water' to caste offenders on readmission, and must belong to the ***Samar*** (*Samad* ?) clan, and a man of the *Soreng* or *Soren* clan officiates as the *Negi* and a man of the *Baṛṭha* (?) clan as the *Gāndā* or messenger, whose duty it is to summon tribe-fellows to a "caste-feast".[64]

In the *Census Report for Bengal, Bihar and Orissa* for 1911, speaking of the 'Pañchāyat' system among the Khāṛiās (of the Rāñchi District) Mr. O'Malley wrote:- "The Kharias also have a Kārṭāhā who restores men to caste. He is not a permanent officer". This no longer appears to be quite correct in respect of the main body of the Dūdh Khāṛiās of the Rāñchi District. Thus, in a Pāṛhā composed of villages Tāmṛā, Tābāḍih, Kūmbāṭoli, Sirsurā, Bheṛi-kudar, and Pharsā-beṛā, in thānā Simḍegā in the Rāñchi District, Chāṛā Māhto was the Karṭāhā, and, on his death, was succeeded in the post by his son Ḍeṛem; and since Ḍeṛem's death his son Chārā II, the present Karṭāhā, has been holding the post.

64. *Idem.*, Vol. III. p. 451

Jurisdiction of the Federation Council. :— The Kuṭumb Sabhā or Pāṛhā Pañchāyat, besides exercising jurisdiction over disputes and controversial points which the Village Council cannot satisfactorily decide or cannot finally deal with, is vested by tribal custom with exclusive jurisdiction in matters of tribal interest. The restoration of an individual or a family who have been excommunicated by the village council or (as often happens) are, owing to some breach of social or socio-religious taboo, automatically treated as "outcastes" by the village community, is the function of the *Pāṛhā Pañchāyat* or *Kuṭumb Sabhā* or *Gādī* or *Bhiṛā.*

The paramount interest and vital concern of the tribe is the maintenance of **tribal solidarity** and strength. Anything that causes or threatens to cause depletion in its ranks or is calculated to attract supernatural dangers to it, is necessarily a matter of the utmost tribal solicitude. The two principal classes of offences that, in the

Social Offences.

Khāṛiā's estimation, threaten the social order and tribal integrity are sexual connection of a Khāṛiā woman with a man of another caste or tribe and the eating of forbidden food and eating cooked food at the hands of tribes or castes at whose hands such food is tabooed, or at the hands of even Khāṛiās who or whose families eat or may have eaten such food or who may be under a tribal sentence of excommunication. It is not primarily from a sense of pride of superior blood, and much less is it from any high code of abstract ethics or morality as the civilised man understands it, that Khāṛiā society bans such sexual union; nor is it from any hygienic principles that such food is tabooed. It is the intensity and force of their tribal feeling, their primitive zeal for maintaining the solidarity, security and strength of the group that makes Khāṛiā society instinctively, as it were, abhor these breaches of social taboo as the gravest of social offences. Such an offence not only constitutes an attack on the social solidarity of the tribe but further serves as a channel through which supernatural dangers are apprehended to visit the community.

The intrigue or union of a Khāṛiā woman with a man of another tribe or caste means to the community not only the social "death" of the woman who by the very act becomes "lost" to the tribe and thus depletes its number, but she also becomes, in the tribe's estimation, the medium of **social pollution** and of evil spiritual infection or "**sin**" to her family through the evil contagion of a stranger. Some Khāṛiās attribute this taboo against sexual congress of a Khāṛiā with an alien man to the fear of the malignant influence of the tribal or tutelary spirit of the stranger; but the Khāṛiā's behaviour, both individual and collective and his words in this connection, would further appear to indicate that his almost instinctive fear of such defilement has behind it also the sub-conscious and, to all appearance, instinctive fear of a mysterious dangerous power of the nature of **mana** infecting the erring woman and her family and calculated to prove contaminating and destructive as Death. As soon as the misbehaviour or 'sin' is detected and admitted or proved before the village Pañchāyat, the woman and her family are forthwith excommunicated. But an excommunication from 'caste' has to be confirmed by the tribal council if the woman or her family appeal to the heads of the villages of the *pāṛhā* or group of "*Kuṭumb*" villages. And, in any case, for the restoration of the remaining members of the delinquent woman to their tribal status and for the punishment of the seducer, if possible, the tribal council has to be assembled by the family. And if the seducer or the seduced woman or both deny the charge, the tribal council makes a thorough inquiry into the matter before taking further action.

Procedure.—The tribal council convened to deal with such a case follows the procedure prescribed by ancient custom. It proceeds in an orderly method to examine the parties and hear evidence, consider the pleas, if any, of the offenders, and finally after due deliberation forms its judgment. If the charge is admitted, or, failing that, if it is considered as duly substantiated, the President of the *Pañchāyat* or *Sabhā* or *Bhiṛā* or *Gādi*, after consultation with the other members, pronounces judgment and passes sentence on the seducer in conformity with tribal custom. Among the Dūdh Khāṛiās, if there is any literate member present among the *Pāñch*, the proceedings are now-a-days sometimes recorded in writing. The sentence consists principally of a fine sufficient to compensate the family of the seduced woman for the cost of the necessary sacramental feast to the tribe-fellows which the family has to provide for its own restoration to the tribal fold; and the offender is further required to take the erring woman in his keeping and to maintain her. But unless the man voluntarily submits to the penalty, the Khāṛiā Pañchāyat has now-a-days no means of enforcing it, however much they may curse and abuse him and utter empty threats in order to satisfy the emotional need of venting their tribal indignation and dismay. Indeed great must be the shock to the intense group-sentiment that pervades these simple societies by the attack made on their tribal integrity and the disruption caused to their society and social order, and greater must be the dismay at the supernatural dangers to the family and to the tribe apprehended from the sexual congress of one of its women with an alien man.

Sometimes the offender, though he may be willing to take charge of the woman, may lack the means or, at any rate, may plead inability, to pay the fine. In such a case unless the husband of the seduced woman choses to seek redress in the law-courts (which he rarely does) the man, in some cases is and formerly used always to be, punished with a severe thrashing, if with nothing worse. But if the alien seducer be a resident of the village he naturally apprehends that unless he could make peace with the Khāṛiā village-community they might make the village too hot for him. And he may therefore consider it prudent to throw himself at the mercy of the village community and accept such other penalty as the Pāñchāyat may think fit to substitute for the fine. In such a case, some humiliating (even indelicate) punishment indicative of ridicule and contempt may be imposed. In any case, the man has to take charge of the erring woman.

Their tribal self-respect being thus vindicated and the intense emotional tension of the assembly being thus relieved, and the erring woman and her alien seducer being thus disposed of, the assembly next turn their attention to what is indeed more important to the tribe, namely, making arrangements for the restoration of the remaining members (survivors, so to say) of the unfortunate family to communion of the society. This requires expiation or atonement ('at-one-ment') or reconciliation with man and God. This is effected by the offering of a libation of rice-beer and sacrifice of a white fowl or white goat to Beṛo or Giṛing or Bhagwān or Pōnōmōsōr (as the Sun-God or Supreme Deity is variously named by the Khāṛiā), and by each member of the hitherto excommunicated family drinking one or two drops of the sacrificial blood, and, finally, by a common meal with the tribe-fellows in the manner described below.

Method of Purification.—The purificatory rite employed to restore an excommunicated Khāṛiā to 'caste' is as follows: The excommunicated person and his family have to remain fasting the whole day. In the afternoon either a white fowl or a white goat is sacrificed to the Sun-God or Supreme Deity. The Pāin-dihā (among the Ḍhelkis) or the Karṭāhā (among the Dūdhs) or the Ḍānḍiā (among the Hill Khāṛiās), drops one or two drops of blood of the sacrificed fowl or goat into a leaf-cup containing a little turmeric juice and water or pounded turmeric and water. In some places a bit of copper is also put into this cup. The cup is then handed over to the excommunicated person who drinks the sanctifying potion while the Karṭahā or Pāin-dihā declares before man and God as follows:–

Tubhlūnglē Pōnōmōsōr, tutātē Pañch utē-elē dokosile'. Elē utē tāmā ḍōkōsilē'. Ukiārtē rē ḍibhārteglē. Ukiār tāng elā'-surigā ỹō-gē uḍekiār. Tāngkō ukiārtē āning-jo tērēning beṭi āning-jō dōṛening. Tāngkō bitar karāioning".

[*Translation*]

"O God on high, and O Pañch (tribal council) below! Here we are now assembled (lit., are sitting).

We are now taking them [back] into [our community]. They will henceforth eat with us, drink with us. Henceforth we shall also give our daughters [in marriage to them]. We shall [also] take their daughters [in marriage]. Now then we [have] incorporated them [into our tribe]." The Dāṇḍia of the Hill Khāṛiās, too, makes a similar declaration of reassimilation of the family into the tribe.

Thus purged of their ceremonial pollution and reassimilated into the tribe, the head of the hitherto excommunicated family goes about making his *jōhār* or obeisence to the President and other elders. And all rejoice at the reintegration of the tribe. Thus is the sense of **tribal solidarity** refreshed and reinforced.

After being thus ceremonially purified and reunited with their community, one or more members of the excommunicated family, all of whom have till then remained fasting, serve a little *bhāt* (boiled rice) on the plate of each tribe-fellow present. In some cases, the head of the hitherto excommunicated family touches the heap of the *bhāt* prepared for the feast. When rice has been served on all the leaf-plates, the members of the family now 'purified' or, at any rate, the head of the family sit down to dinner with the assembled tribe-fellows. The social head of the *Pāṛhā* or *Kuṭumb Sabhā* or *Gādi* or *Bhīṛā*,—the *Karṭāhā* among the Dūdh or the *Pāin-dihā* among the Ḍhelki sections, or the *Ḍāṇḍiā* as he is called among the Hill Khāṛiās,—takes up the first morsel of rice and puts it into his mouth and then accords permission to the others to fall to. This common meal shared with the members of the family that had so long remained excommunicated completes their readmission into "caste" and restoration to their former tribal status.

At each such "caste-" feast, the President receives a present or perquisite in cash from the host. The Karṭāhā among the Dūdhs generally gets a sum of about five rupees out of which the Karṭāhā pays four rupees or so to the members of the Pañchāyat for a drink and keeps the balance for himself. Anthropologists may be inclined to infer that as the Karṭāhā eats the first morsel at a feast for restoration to "caste", he stands in the position of a scapegoat, who takes upon himself the 'sin' of the 'out-caste', and that by providing, with the perquisite paid to him, a drink to his tribe-fellows he atones for the 'sin' of having eaten at the hands of an outcaste. But the Khāṛiās themselves have no such notion, at any rate at the present day. They simply explain it by saying that this drink-money is paid to the *Karṭāhā* as his '*mān*' or '*mānya*', that is to say, as a recognition of his dignity and social position.

It is significant that these rites are virtually the same as those performed for the ceremonial purification of a Khāṛiā family at the termination of the customary period of "death-pollution".

If the family of the outcast lack the means to meet the expenses of the required sacramental feast, the Pāñchāyat raises the required amount by contributions or subsciptions either in cash or kind from the assembled tribe-fellows.

The only case in which the union of a Khāṛiā man with a woman of another tribe is sometimes conditionally permitted is marriage with a Mūṇḍā woman, the condition being that if the Khāṛiā husband eats cooked food at the hands of his Mūṇḍā wife, he will be forthwith excommunicated. Children born of such a union are, in any case, regarded as "outcastes" unless and until they undergo ceremonial purification by drinking sacrificial blood and sharing in a common tribal meal as described above. This exception made in favour of the Mūṇḍā tribe is explained by the tradition still extant that the Mūṇḍās and the Khāṛiās once formed one and a single tribe.

But a Khāṛiā woman, whether a maid or a widow or a divorced woman, marrying a man of the Mūṇḍā tribe, becomes *ipso facto* an outcast, and her parents are also excommunicated and have to be restored to 'caste' by the same method of ceremonial purification and communal meal as described above.

It is not only sexual union of a Khāṛiā woman with a man of another tribe or caste that is a matter of grave concern to the Khāṛiā tribe. The Khāṛiā regards with suspicion, verging on fear, strangers even belonging to their own branch (Dūdh or Ḍhelki or Hill section, as the case may be) of the Khāṛiā tribe but with whom his family or his relatives, or any of his relatives' relatives have had no previous social and marital relations, or who are known to have taken tabooed food or to follow tabooed customs. Therefore, as we have already noted, marital connection of a Khāṛiā with such Khāṛiā families, even of his own section, are tabooed. Should such an union take place, the breach of the taboo is punished with excommunication. When the family thus excommunicated desires to be restored to their former tribal status in the community, a tribal assembly (*Bhīṛā* or *Gādi* or *Pāṛhā Pañchāyat*) has to be convened, and this assembly, after due deliberation, names the customary terms on which the ostracised family may be readmitted into the tribe. Thus, Nandu Dehūri, a Hill Khāṛiā of village Sarsōpāl (now of village Purnāpāni), gave his son, Mākṛu by name, in marriage to the daughter of a Khāṛiā of village Bhuāsuni. The Khāṛiās of Bhuiāsuni were reputed to eat cooked food at the hands of Santāls and 'Kols', and so the Khāṛiās of Sarsopal had up till then entered into no marital relations with them. Accordingly, the relatives and fellow-villagers of Nandu did not attend his son's marriage, and his family was excommunicated. Afterwards, at Nandu's instance, a *Bhīṛā* or tribal assembly composed of the headmen and adult Khāṛiās of villages Sarsōpāl, Rengelbeṛā, Kānchhinḍā, Asṭo-beṛā and Rangāmāṭiā assembled at Sarsopāl (in Mayurbhañj). At Nandu's solicitation the *Bhīṛā* discussed the terms on which Nandu and his son and their family might be taken back into the community. The council decided that Nandu might be allowed to retain the girl as his son's bride but that he and his family must give up all social intercourse with the Khāṛiās of Bhuiāsuni including the parents of his son's wife, and must provide a fine of one rupee and four annas to the Pañchāyat (for drink) besides the usual ceremonial feast to his tribe-fellows before he could be restored to "caste". Nandu paid the fine and provided a feast at which the new bride served a little rice on the plate of every guest and was thus re-admitted into the Hill Khāṛiā community.

Among other offences of a similar kind which come within the jurisdiction of the *Pāṛhā Pañchāyat* or *Bhīṛā* or *Gādi* are marriage within prohibited degrees of relationship, and marriage within the same totem clan (except in the case of the Mayurbhañj

Khāṛiās, among whom the totemic clan system hardly exists).

Another heinous social offence, according to Khāṛiā ideas, is sexual union within the clan. This is characterised as *Gotra-badh* or "clan-murder". In the case of a marriage within the clan or of premarital love-intrigue of a Khāṛiā with a married daughter of a fellow-clansman or with a Khāṛiā girl or woman within prohibited degrees of relationship, the offenders and their families are excommunicated, and can only be readmitted into the tribe after the prescribed ceremonial purification of the erring man and woman by their drinking sacrificial blood and arranging for a communal feast as described above, provided the erring man and woman take a solemn vow to abstain from all undue relations with each other in future.

In the case of a love-intrigue between a Khāṛiā and the wife of another Khāṛiā, not standing within prohibited degrees of relationship, the man may marry the woman in the *Sāngā* form, provided the woman belongs to a different clan and her husband agrees to give her up, which he may do on receipt of adequate damages.

As for a pre-marital love-intrigue between a bachelor and a maiden belonging to the same clan or standing within prohibited degrees of relationship, generally it is the village Pañch who take disciplinary action and see to it that such breach of sexual taboo do not recur and the family purify themselves by drinking the blood of sacrificial fowl as described above. Should the girl in such a case be found to be in the family way, abortion is procured, if possible, and steps are taken to marry the girl into some distant village. Sometimes the couple may run away to some tea-garden in Assam.

As for a pre-marital love-intrigue between a young man and a maiden, of different clans and not within prohibited degrees of relationship, not much is thought of it except how to arrange for the marriage of the couple: For such intrigue neither involves any spiritual or supernatural danger as is apprehended from union within the clan nor involves depletion of membership of the tribe as union with a non-Khāṛiā would involve.

Other important matters which may come up for decision before the tribal council are the restoration to the tribe of a Khāṛiā who has purposely or inadvertently caused the death of a cow or ox or calf, or one who has been afflicted with leprosy or with malignant sores infested by worms or flies. Leprosy and maligant sores are believed to be the result of some 'sin' and are called "Māchhi Pātak" (lit, "fly- sin"). The deliberate or accidental killing of a cow or ox or calf or the affliction of leprosy, *ipso facto*, places the delinquent and his family out of the pale of the tribe. For his 'purification' and restoration to communion with the tribe, the delinquent and the other adult members of his or her family have to remain fasting a whole night, and on the following day at about noon, in the presence of the assembled tribe-fellows, they have to stand with their faces to the east, and the social head of the Pañchāyat standing before them (with his face to the west) pours water mixed with pounded turmeric on the joined palms, fiirst, of the delinquent's hands and then of the hands of the rest of the family, and each of them drinks a little of the sanctifying water administered by the Kārṭāhā or Pain-dihā, and throws the rest over his or her own head. Then follows a communal feast such as has been described above in respect of readmitting into the tribe outcastes for sexual offences.

Commensality.

The saying, "*Jetek Khāṛiā tetek hāñṛiā*", has been taken by Dalton and Risley to mean that every Khāṛiā must have a separate cooking-pot and that a Khāṛiā "may not allow even his wife to cook for him" [65]! This notion appears to be due altogether to a misapprehension. The real meaning appears to be, " [There must be] as many cooking-pots as there are clans among the Khāṛiās." Among the Dūdh Khāṛiās and the Ḍhelki Khāṛiās, members of one and the same clan living in a village and its adjoining villages observe ceremonial pollution on the death of a member of the clan and, on the termination of the period of pollution, have to throw away their old cooking-pots (*hāñṛiās*). This would appear to explain why members of a clan are said to constitute " one *hāñṛiā*". An important ceremony connected with a marriage among the Dūdh and the Ḍhelki Khāṛiās is that a new bride has to cook rice, in a new *hañṛiā*, and the bridegroom has to offer that rice to his own ancetor-spirits, and then he his people, and all clan-fellows present eat the food cooked by the new bride. In fact, a Khāṛiā's wife, if she is not an alien or an outcast, is the principal cook in his household. It is only a married daughter who cannot cook for his parents in the latters' kitchen, for by her marriage she has passed over to a different family and clan and the kitchen is the seat of the family spirits and no stranger may enter it.

65 Dalton, *Ethnology of Bengal*, p.100, *foot-note*; Risley, *Tribes and Castes of Bengal*, vol I, p 400.

Again, at the annual ceremony of the eating of the first-fruits of up-land rice in the month of Bhādo (August-September) in the house of a well-to-do Khāṛiā, members of his own clan living in the same village and in adjacent villages are invited, and a fowl is sacrificed and offerings of the first-fruits are made to the ancestor-spirits of the clan, and all join in the sacrificial feast and partake of food cooked by the members of the same clan. It is not only members of the same clan (*bhāyāds*) at whose hands a Khāṛiā may eat cooked rice and other food, but also with members of other clans related (as *Kūṭūmbs*) to them or to their ancestors through marriage. But a woman of another clan (and even a Khāṛiā's daughter or sister married necessarily to some other clan) is not permitted to enter the kitchen of a Khāṛiā family. In a communal feast of the *Gādi* or *Pāṛhā* or *Bhīṛā*, given on the occasion of the restoration of an excommunicated Khāṛiā to his tribal rights, all his *Bhāyād* villages and *Kuṭumb* villages, as we have seen, have to be invited, and all partake of the communal meal. At this feast the first handful of rice on the plate of each guest is served by the person who (or the head of the family which) is being readmitted to the community. Even the married daughters and married sisters of the head of a *Khāṛiā* family eat cooked rice and other food at the hands of the members of her parents' or brother's family. It is only in the case of a Khāṛiā girl married into a family with which or with whose ancestors her parents' family either in the present has had, or in any past generation had, no marital relations, that she will no longer eat cooked rice at the hands of the members of her parents' family and when she happens to go on a visit to her parents' or brother's house, she will cook her own food. In fact, even among the Hill Khāṛiās, such a marriage into a family which is not among their "Bandhu-bāsiās", that is to say, families with which marital relations have at any time in the past been contracted, entails excommunication.

Witch-craft. Another matter of great importance in the tribal estimation is the punishment of witches or sorcerers declared by Dēoñṛās or witch-finders and spirit-doctors to be responsible for death or repeated or prolonged illness in a family or epidemic and death to men and cattle. In all such cases the Khāṛiā always suspects that the calamity has been brought on either by some outside evil spirit egged on to it by a witch or sorcerer, or has been caused by some village-deity or family-spirit who has been displeased by some neglect or omission on the part of the family or the village-community concerned in offering the periodical sacrifices. Accordingly, in cases of such illness and epidemics, recourse is had to a Dēoñṛā or ghost-finder and witch-finder to discover the author of the trouble and the means of deliverance. By one or other of the different current methods of divination, which will be described in a subsequent chapter (on *Magic and Witchcraft*), the Dēoñṛā works himself up to a state of spirit-obsession, and sees, as in a vision, the form of the miscreant (usually an old woman of the affected village and rarely a male sorcerer) and describes his or her appearance and the location of his or her house, and finally reveals the name of the spirit who has brought on the calamity and the sacrifices demanded by that spirit. In cases of epidemics, the ghost-doctor generally declares that it is some omission on the part of the village-community in offering the proper sacrifices to some village-spirit or spirits which is responsible for the epidemic. In a few cases of prolonged or repeated illness in a family, he may also declare that it is the remissness of the family concerned in offering the regular sacrifices to the family-spirits or in fulfilling a vow of sacrifice to some spirit or other that is responsible for the trouble in that family. In the former class of cases the village-priest on behalf of the village-community atones for their omission or neglect, by arranging for and offering the sacrifices demanded by the offended spirit through the mouth of the Dẽoñṛā. In the latter class of cases the head of the family hastens to appease the offended spirit by the required sacrifices. But in cases in which the Dẽoñṛā declares that the repeated cases of illness or death in a family have been due to some 'outside' spirit (who has no fixed 'seat' or *āsthān*), as distinguished from a village-deity or a family-spirit who has an appointed place of sacrifice, the Dẽoñṛā's services are requisitioned to appease the offended spirit or spirits and to rid the afflicted family of their attentions by appropriate rites, incantations, and ceremonies, which will be described in a later chapter.

Whether it is a public calamity such as an epidemic to men or cattle or a private calamity such as disease and death in a particular family, the witch or sorcerer who is believed to have brought it on is the object of severe public reprobation and punishment. The anti-social activities of the witch and sorcerer are believed to cause the depletion of the community and its wealth in cattle or crops and thus to constitute a crime against society. Their activities also constitute a challenge and an affront to the beneficent village-spirits on whom the village-community depend for protection of their 'luck'. Thus the witch and sorcerer is regarded with abhorence as an enemy to society and to the gods. Consequently excommunication is the inevitable punishment, and the least part of it, that falls to the lot of the suspected witch or sorcerer. Insult and persecution dogs the steps of this enemy of society so long as he or she continues to live in the village. Formerly a person adjudged to be a witch or sorcerer used to be ignominiously expelled from the village as a mass-murderer, so to say; and sometimes, in some cases, a declared witch or sorcerer would be lynched to death. Now-a-days, however, for fear of the law-courts, such extreme steps are avoided; but the locality is generally made too hot for the witch or sorcerer to live in. In some cases, the persecuted witch, generally with the rest of her family, accepts Christianity to avoid persecution. As the acceptance of the Christian faith is believed to free the convert from the power of the evil spirit with whose aid the witch or sorcerer was so long enabled to work harm to others and whom the witch or sorcerer had to keep in good humour by periodical sacrifices, for otherwise the spirit might bring calamity or even death to its votary, such a convert escapes further molestation.

General view of Khāṛiā Social Organisation.

Such is a rough sketch of the social mechanism, kinship system, tribal government and the customary law of the Khāṛiās. This tribe, in its three branches, furnishes an apt illustration of the correlation of physical conditions with the stage of evolution, particularly in the lower culture. We have seen how the limited food-supply and other unfavourable physical conditions in their native hills and jungles limit the size of Hill Khāṛiā local groups, and keep them much lower in the scale of social and cultural development than the other sub-tribes. Yet they are not really what are called savages.

All social groups acknowledge the authority or accept the guidance of some leader or body of leaders. Even on the most primitive social level in which each family is a law unto itself the authority of the head of the family is acknowledged. The Hill Khāṛiā local group which is composed of but a few families acknowledge, in local matters, as we have seen, the authority of its headman or priest who is usually the oldest man of the group and who, in village affairs, consults the other village-elders; and all of them together constitute the village council or *Pañch*. Again, the Hill Khāṛiās, like the more progressive Ḍhelki and Dūdh sections of the tribe have, as we have seen, even advanced beyond this stage, and evolved a more extended grouping of the nature of an inter-village 'federation'. This is the *Bhīṛā* which, like the *Gādi* of the Ḍhelkis and the *Kuṭumb Sabhā* or *Pāṛhā Pañchāyat* of the Dūdh Khāṛiās, is something like a tribal council to which matters of general tribal interest, besides inter-village disputes, are referred for discussion, decision and disposal. Among the Hill Khāṛiās as among the more advanced Ḍhelki and Dūdh sections of the tribe, the tribal council is composed of headmen and other representative elders from the different neighbouring and related villages forming a federation, so to say. The only difference is that whereas in the more advanced sections the President of the tribal council is either fixed or must come from one or other of particular clans, this is not so among the Hill Khāṛiās who are even more democratic than the more advanced sections of the tribe.

Social Precedence.

Although no occupational classes have yet developed among any section of the Khāṛiās and there is no differentiation of social function except, to a little extent, in the case of the village-priest, yet among the Ḍhelki and the Dūdh sections, some difference of rank is recognised in respect of some of the clans. Thus, as we have seen, in the Ḍelki or Ḍhelki section, the *Muru* clan is regarded as the highest and the *Samad* clan as the next highest in social rank, and it is from amongst them that the President of the tribal council is selected; and in tribal gatherings and sacramental or purificatory feasts a man of the *Muru* clan must give the purifying draught of water to an excommunicated tribe-fellow who has to be readmitted into the tribe, and a man of the *Samad* clan has to act as *Bhaṇḍāri* or barber, and a man of the *Muru* clan has to eat the first morsel at the 'caste-feast' before any one else may eat. The *Mail* and *Ṭōpnō* clans, on the other hand, are regarded as the lowest in social rank, so that the other clans do not eat at their hands though they may, however, intermarry with them. Similarly in Dūdh Khāṛiā society, as we have seen, the social heads of the tribe and tribal councils must be selected from either of the three clans of *Ḍūng-ḍūng*, *Kulu*, and *Samad* or *Kerkeṭṭa* who take rank one after the other, and have social precedence over all the remaining clans.

Again, among the Dūdh Khāṛiās of the Rāñchi district, some families who still occupy their Bhūiñhāri villages which their ancestors established, and are thus in occupation of the privileged tenures known as Bhūiñhāri tenures, enjoy some sort of prestige. Besides this slight distinction based on property, and the social distinction attached to the few clans named above, the Khāṛiās know no other social distinction based either on personal wealth or on purity of descent.

Among Khāṛiās of all sections, there is, as a rule, no notion of the rank or social prestige of a family being enhanced by lavish liberality or extravagance in feasts or by other parade of wealth. The Khāṛiās, like their other aboriginal neighbours, are essentially democratic in their social outlook. Co-operation on equal terms is the keynote of their social relations. The gifts or presents of rice and other articles of food which, according to immemorial custom, Khāṛiās of all sections bring to a relative's family on the occasion of certain domestic celebrations have, besides their immedite economic value, considerable social significance as an expression of the social affections. There is a reciprocity in these presents, for it is the recognised duty of each receiver of such gifts to make similar presents to the givers on similar occasions in the latters' families. This lightens the burden on the receiving family.

Ideas of Private or Individual Property.

Among the Hill Khāṛiās the spoils of hunting are often shared out; and communal life in the settlement is, to a certain extent, more strongly marked than among the more advanced sections. Yet the idea of private property appears to be fairly developed even amongst the Hill Khāṛiās. The ownership of a man in his house and household articles, in his personal dress, ornaments, hunting implements and other scanty belongings, is definitely recognised. So, too, is the right to separate possession of any plot of land which a comparatively enterprising family may choose to take up for *jhūm* clearance and cultivation. An archaic instance of the idea of private property is the Hill Khāṛiā's "Bhāṇḍār" or individual 'reserve' for honey-gathering. It resembles in type the division of hunting-grounds between neighbouring hunting tribes. As little effort is exerted, much less any work done, by any particular family on any particular hill to rear bees or to make them form honey-combs, this primitive type of 'ownership' does not conform to the conception of property as individual acquisition through work done. Yet, like the Ḍhelkis and the Dūdhs, the Hill Khāṛiās, too, possess a clear idea of work giving right of property to the produce of labour. The ownership of persons to trees planted by them not only on waste lands but even on lands actually belonging to another person is definitely recognised by all sections of the tribe. Instances occur of more than one person being recognised as owners of trees reepectively planted by each on a piece of land admittedly owned by another.

As regards social organisation, the **family**, in all the three sections of the tribe is, as we have seen, patrilineal, although there are some usages suggestive of a former state of matriliny and avunculate. The position of women is not so low in Khāṛiā society as might be supposed. Though a Khāṛiā woman labours under certain social disabilities as to inheritance of property and participation in certain religious and quasi-religious ceremonies, yet she has a position of some influence in the household.

The mechanism of the regulation of **marriage** is the clan, which is totemic among all sections of the tribe except among the Hill Khāṛiās of the Mayurbhañj State. These latter have practically lost their totemic system. It has been superseded by what may be called the territorial system which now partly regulates marriage among them. The clan sentiment is strengthened by the belief in the traditional descent from a common ancestor. Co-operation for economic, socio-political, and religious purposes has futher strengthened clan solidarity. And clan incest is abhorred as one of the deadliest 'sins'. Kinship-grouping, though unilaterally emphasised in the male line, is yet bilateral to some extent. As their genealogical memory hardly extends beyond the third generation, relatives through the mother are generally taken into account up to the third generation. The possession of a common totem and, to some extent, the habitation of a common territory, are, however, regarded as evidence of relationship. Parallel cousins are classified with brothers and sisters, but cross-cousin marriage is permitted. As the Khāṛiās have, from as far back as tribal memory extends, more than two clans, it cannot be confidently asserted that cross-cousin marriage among them definitely points to the past existence of a dual organisation.

The system of **kinship** is classificatory. Their kinship nomenclature reflects their system of relationships, such, for instance, as the prevalence of the junior levirate, cross-cousin marriage, and exchange-marriage. The reciprocity in the use of certain kinship terms would appear to indicate that these terms denote relationships rather than relatives.

The Pañchāyat or **tribal council**, as we have seen, is the custodian of tribal law and custom. Property devolves in the male line, but a widow, so long as she does not remarry, is allowed a life-interest in the property of her sonless deceased husband. Daughters do not inherit but an unmarried daughter is entitled to maintenance and, if available, to the expenses of her marriage, out of her father's property.

We have further seen how the tribal council's greatest concern is the maintenance of the solidarity and security of the tribe. This it does by enforcing various taboos under threat of excommunication or other sanctions in proportion to their gravity, and by taking proper measures to purge the 'contamination' and expiate the 'sin' incurred by an individual or family through contact with the evil *mana* of strangers or other persons or of maleficent beings or objects. The commensal meal by which an outcaste is readmitted into the tribe would appear to be more "restorative" than piacular. It is meant to communicate afresh to the outcaste the "**tribal mana**" which he is supposed to have more or less lost through contaminating evil contact.

Finally, we have seen how **witchcraft** or maleficent magic is regarded with intense fear and abhorrence as a secret treason to society and an insidious peril from which nobody is safe. And woeful indeed is the lot of the suspected witch in a Khāṛiā village.

CHAPTER VIII.

Birth, Childhood and Puberty Rites.

The turning-points in the life of an individual are the critical occasions of birth, puberty, marriage, and serious illness which may possibly end in death. For these critical junctures of the individual's life, when confidence is shaken by fear and anxiety, the primitive man, like most of his civilized fellow-men, seeks to satisfy the emotional need of restoring hope and confidence to his mind by methods expected to enlist the help of invisible supernatural powers believed to be potent enough to help him in tiding safely over each crisis. The methods devised and organised by each society for this purpose, constitute what have been called '*Rites de passage*' and include the socio-religious ceremonies relating to birth and childhood, puberty and marriage, disease and death. In the lower culture these ceremonies generally increase in complexity with the degree of culture. This is why these *Rites de passage* are very simple among the Hill Khāṛiās and much more elaborate among the comparatively more advanced Ḍhelki and Dūdh sections of the tribe; but the underlying motive and principles are the same in all the sections. But, it has to be noted, that among the comparatively more progressive Dūḍh Khāṛiās, the old rites and customs have lost much of their vitality and meaning, and are no longer quite as full and elaborate as among the Ḍhelkis.

Birth, Childhood and Puberty Customs among the Hill Khāṛiās.

1. **During Pregnancy.**—Neither a pregnant Hill Khāṛiā woman nor her husband is required to observe any particular taboos or restrictions. At parturition no one except a midwife (generally a relative or other woman of the tribe) besides one or two female relatives of the expectant mother is allowed to remain in the compartment or new shed (*kūmbā*) set apart as the lying-in room (*sūtnā kuṛi*). In a case of difficult labour no magical ceremony is resorted to. Only oil is rubbed on the abdomen, and God's help is invoked. On safe delivery, an offering of rice, vermilion and flowers is made to Bhagwān or Dharam or Parameswar as the Deity is variously named.

2. **Disposal of the Navel-string:**—After birth, the umbilical cord is severed by the midwife with a shell or a knife, a copper coin (pice) being placed underneath the cord at the point at which it is severed. The midwife gets the coin as her perquisite. The babe is then bathed in tepid water, and the navel-string is, among the Mānbhūm Khāṛiās, buried at one corner of the hut, and, among the Dhalbhūm Khāṛiās, either buried under the door-way or threshold of the hut or under the eaves or thrown into a flowing stream. The Hill Khāṛiās of the Mayurbhañj State put the navel-string into an earthenware pot and bury it under a tree close by the hut. The stump of the navel-string, when it dries up and drops off, is also buried under the same tree along with the ashes of the fire that was so long kept up in the lying-in room or shed.

The mother and the babe are regarded as ceremonially unclean until the ninth day from the birth. During this period they must not leave the hut; and, except female relatives and the children of the purturient woman, none else is admitted into the lying-in room during these days. Food and water are brought to her there, and, in some families, she cooks her own food. Except meat no other food is taboo to her. In fact, for these nine days no member of the family may take fish or flesh. Generally the only food given to the mother during these nine days consists of rice, salt and raw garlic.

3. **Ceremonial Purification**:—On the ninth day mother and babe have to undergo ceremonial purification by taking a ceremonial bath and by anointing their bodies with turmeric paste, if available. Families living in the neighbourhood of Hindu villages have also adopted from the Hindus such supplementary processes of purification as sprinkling on the limbs of the mother and babe and other members of the family water into which leaves of the sacred basil or *tulasi* plant (*Ocimum sanctum*) have been dipped, and getting the nails of all the members of the family pared and their hair cut short by some tribe-fellow, and not, as among Hindus, by a man of the barber caste. In most Hill Khāṛiā settlements, however, purification by shaving or cutting the hair and paring the nails is practised only to remove death-pollution. It may also be noted that the ceremonial purification on the *ninth day* after birth is known by the Hill Khāṛiās under the Hindu name of *Nartā*. This would appear

to indicate that the nine-days' ceremonial impurity is also a borrowed custom. Again, in some places a second period of impurity for the mother and the babe only (and not for the whole family as during the first nine days) is also observed up to the twenty-first day of birth. On the twenty-first day (called *Ekusā* as among the Hindus of the State and elsewhere) the mother and babe have their nails pared again and clothes washed, and they take the final purificatory bath. Until then the mother and her babe may not enter the family kitchen or touch cooked food or drinking-water meant for others. During these twenty-one days of impurity the mother's meals are in some places served not even on leaf-plates but on the bare floor of the confinement-room. In some places, again, the mother may not eat any meat except fowl's within six months of her delivery.

4. **Name-Giving:**—At the termination of the birth-pollution on the ninth day (*Nartā*) after birth, and in some places (as in village Kusumbandhi and its neighbourhood in the Mayurbhañj State and among the Hill Khāṛiās of the Dhalbhūm Parganā in the Singhbhūm District) on the twenty-first day (*Ekusā*) or even later, a name is ceremonially selected for the child. Relations and friends are invited to the house. The babe's father's mother (*gūs-mā*), if alive, or some other senior relative, either male or female, sits with his or her face to the east, taking the babe in his arms on the *āngan* or courtyard where the relatives are assembled. A brassplate or a leaf-cup filled with water (in which in some places pounded turmeric is put), is placed before this relative; and into it the latter drops,

first, a sesamum seed to represent the child and, then, a grain of unhusked rice in the name of some deceased member of the family, of a generation not below the babe's father's, but ordinarily in the name of the father's father or father's mother, according to the sex of the baby. If the two grains meet each other on the surface of the water, the name of the particular deceased relative is selected for the child. If the two grains do not meet, or if one or both sink down, two more grains are similarly dropped, one to represent the child and another that of some other deceased relative not below the child's father's generation. If the grains unite, the child is named after the relative in whose name the rice grain has been dropped; if the grains do not unite, the same process is repeated until the desired result is obtained and a name is accordingly selected. In dropping rice in the name of deceased relatives, the names of grandfathers and grand-uncles and uncles on the mother's side are not taken before all eligible names of similar deceased relations on the father's side are exhausted. In some places both the grains employed are of rice (unhusked) and neither is of sesamum. The orthodox belief is that the deceased relative in whose name one grain meets the other has been reincarnated in the babe. In some places, while dropping the sesamum into the water, the officiant actully asks, "Who art thou"? and, while dropping the rice-grain, some deceased relative's name is pronounced. In some villages, again, (as in Kānchhiṇḍā in Mayurbhañj) no such ceremonial test is gone through, but the father's mother or, in her absence, some other elderly female relative chooses a name and proclaims it in the presence of the assembled relatives. In any case, even where a name is selected by the grain-test described above, a second name for every-day use is selected by the father's mother (*Gūs-mā*) or, in her absence, by some other old female relative. In these cases, the name selected by the grain-test resembles to some extent the "soul-name" of such tribes as the Ibo of West Africa. After the name is selected, rice-beer is served to the guests, and they are treated to a feast. Relatives and fellow-villagers help in partly making up provisions for the feast by bringing presents for the occasion. The mid-wife is on this occasion presented with a cloth, if possible, or a few *annas* in cash. But when, as often happens, she is a near relative, such present is generally not needed.

5. **Ear-Boring**, &c:—A Hill Khāṛiā child's ear-lobes are generally perforated at the age of five or six years with no religious rites whatsoever. Two tribe-fellows, whether related to the family or not, are generally employed to bore the ears, and are treated to a drink of rice-beer.

No special ceremonies are also observed by this section of the Khāṛiās either at cutting the first hair of a child or at tying up its hair for the first time, or in tattooing (*kechā*) a girl.

6. **First Mensuration**.— The Hill Khāṛiās regard the first mensuration after marriage as very dangerous, and if the husband cohabit with the wife within seven days after the first menses, it is apprehended that either the one or the other of the couple

may die. So if the first menstruation occurs in the husband's house, the parents of the bride take her to their own home. There she lives in seclusion for seven days in such a way that she may not see the face of any male persons. For these seven days she is regarded as ceremonially unclean. On the eighth day she is conducted to the village-spring (*ḍāri*) or tank, and there she takes her bath with water mixed with turmeric, and smears her hair with oil. She then puts on a new cloth. On the day after ceremonial ablutions, she is taken back to her husband's place.

II. Birth and Childhood ceremonies among the Ḍhelki and the Dūdh Khāṛiās.

1. **Lying-in of the Mother:**—From about a week before delivery the pregnant woman is confined in the "*Sūtnā Kuṛiā*" or "*Kōchā Dōklō Kūṛiā*" in which no male person is allowed to enter. Among the Khāṛiās of the Rāñchi District and the Gāngpur State the "*Sutnā Kuṛiā*" or "*Kōchā Dōklō Kūṛiā*" is generally a corner of the house or a portion of the *Verandā* screened off by means of a partition of bamboos and leaves. Among the Ḍhelkis of Jāshpur it is often a separate shed near the main hut.

2. **Difficult Labour:**—In a case of difficult labour, God or 'Pōnōmōsōr' is invoked for relief.

3. **Birth:**—At brith, a woman belonging to the tribe officiates as midwife and nurse (*Sutrāin*). She cuts the umblical cord with either an arrow or a knife over a copper coin placed underneath the cord; and the knife and the pice are taken by the midwife as her perquisites. Formerly a bamboo splinter served the purpose

of a knife but now-a-days an iron or steel knife is generally used. The umblical cord is then buried in a pit under the door-way. The Dūdh Khāṛiā generally digs the pit with a hair-pin, for the child's teeth are believed to become large or small in proportion to the size of the instrument used in digging the pit. The Dūdh and the Ḍhelki Khāṛiās do not throw the after-birth into a running stream as the Hill Khāṛiās of Dhalbhūm do.

Among the Ḍhelkis, as soon as a baby is born, the midwife notifies the fact by giving two strokes with a small stick against a copper or brass vessel. Some Khāṛiās say that this is done in order that the baby may not be deaf. As a matter of fact, as soon as the baby is born, people exclaim : "Strike a *dūbni* (metal cup) and strike the thatch". (*"Ginākē būgōṛpē. Tilūngtē gilgōṛpē"*). At the sound, one of the men assembled on the court-yard strikes the thatch of the lying-in-room twice with a wooden stick. This is supposed to be done to see if the child is deaf. The baby is then bathed in tepid water, and then the midwife warms her own hands over fire and applies her hands on the limbs of the baby. The mother is given soup of the '*kurthi*' (*Dolichos biflorus*) pulse mixed with the bark of a plant called *rohin* (*Soymida febrifuge*), if available, to drink. She is not allowed to take any solid food that day. And from the next day until after purification she is given only one meal a day at about mid-day.

The services of the mid-wife are generally dispensed with after two or three days or as soon as the mother is strong enough to move about. Usually the midwife attends upon her until the babe's navel dries up, and in some cases for seven days or until the *Shudhōm* ceremony. She receives as her remuneration some money and rice according to the means of the family. This remuneration generally varies from one to four *annas* in cash besides one to six measures (about a pound each) of rice.

The custom of Couvade is not known among any section of the Khāṛiās or, in fact, among any other Mūṇḍā tribe, such as is reported to be found amongst some Khoṇḍs. But no member of a Khāṛiā family may eat flesh for the nine days during which the mother and the baby are regarded as unclean. The new mother and child as well as the nurse are not permitted to touch any water-vessel or any article used in the household.

Some Khāṛiās told us that flesh is regarded during the nine days of polution as identical with the entrails of the new-born child and is therefore taboo in the household. The mother sits with the child apart when food is served to her. Female neighbours or relatives calling to enquire after the health of the baby and its mother sit apart as as to avoid contact with them and with the nurse. Anyone contracting pollution by coming into contact, however accidental, with the babe or its mother or nurse or their belongings in the lying-in room until the *Sudhōm* ceremony has to undergo 'purification' by a fast until mid-day of the following day and by the sacrifice of a white cock to Pōnōmōsōr and the drinking of a drop or two of this sacrificial blood mixed with turmeric powder and water. Among the Ḍhelkis an unmarried young man of either the *Muru* or the *Samad* or the *Bārlihā* clan acts as the sacrificer in such a case.

Among Dūdh Khāṛiās and the Ḍhelkis of the Gāngpur State, bathing in cold water and washing the clothes with ashes are now generally regarded as sufficient for purification in such a case, and neither fasting nor sacrifice nor drinking of sacrificial blood is required.

The ceremonial impurity of mother and babe and of the whole family continues till the falling off of the stump of the navel-string. If it falls off earlier than the sixth day, it is kept by the mother till then; and the dried-up stump of the navel-string (*rā'rā*), along with some ashes, is then buried under the threshold of the lying-in room. Some Ḍhelki, Dūdh and Hill Khāṛiās, however, bury it at the back of the house, and, as we have seen, the Hill Khāṛiās of Kusumbandhi bury it in an earthenware pot under a tree near the house. When the dried-up part of the navel-cord falls off, the whole family, with the exception of children, observe a fast until noon of the following day.

4. **Shudhōm**:—That day, usually on the seventh day after birth, if the babe and its mother are in good health, they are bathed in water mixed with pounded turmeric; but if they are not in good health, turmeric water is only sprinkled upon them. The babe's mother washes her clothes and all things in the "*Sūtnā Kūṛiā*" or lying-in-room. All metal vessels and utensils in the house are scrubbed and cleaned and washed. Female relatives from each house, particularly among the Dūdh Khāṛiās, bring a little oil and rub it on the head of the baby and its parents. Among Dūdh Khāṛiās, the *Kūsrāin* (midwife) pounds the bark of the *Gāmhār* (*Gomelina Arborea*) tree and dilutes it in cold water

brought by her in a jug from the village stream or spring, and this is given to the baby's mother to drink. Among Dūdh Khāṛiās of the Rāñchi District a few leaves of the *Bael* (*Aegle Marmelos*) are also put into this water. A portion of this is drunk by the mother and the rest is sprinkled inside the house. For this occasion about half-a-dozen jars of rice-beer or *golāng* are requisitioned. As rice-beer brewed in the house before the ceremonial purification of the family is taboo to others, the master of the house gives a quantity of rice (up to one *maund* or eighty pounds in the case of a male baby, and half that quantity in the case of a female baby) to some of his neighbours to prepare for him rice-beer for the occasion. The first jar of rice-beer is known as the "medicine-pot" as the mother of the babe is given the first cup of beer from this pot in order to "revive" her, as it is said. It is said that she was so long "dead" and is restored to life by this 'medicinal' rice-beer (*dāoāi hāṇḍi*). A portion of this rice-beer is sprinkled all over the house. The residue of the beer in this jar is drunk by the women present. The second jar is for the men to drink; and the remaining jars of beer are shared by all.

After this *Shudhōm* ceremony all the taboos imposed on the members of the family other than on the mother and child are withdrawn. The rest of the family may henceforth eat meat and join in dances and songs as before. The *Shudhōm* (Hindu, *Nartā*) ceremony removes the ceremonial pollution of the rest of the family and they can now eat at the hands of the mother of the babe, but people of other Khāṛiā families must abstain from taking food or drinking water touched by her until the final purification about a fortnight or three weeks or even a month later.[66]

3. Name-giving, and Second Purification (*Nimi-Rāenā*, or *Nimi-Tāñjnā* [*Dudh*]; and *Kānsōng Kāraenā* [*Ḍhelki*]):—Among the Dūdh Khāṛiās, the name-giving ceremony of the child takes place on the day of the final purification. But among the Ḍhelki Khāṛiās of the Jāshpur State it generally takes place on the day of the first purification or on the following day. In many Ḍhelki families of Gāngpur, again, there is no second purification ceremony; and the name-giving ceremony is performed along with the first or only 'purification' which is generally held on the seventh day after birth, and may, for want of means, be held on the tenth, twelfth or a later day. For the sake of convenience we shall give an account of the name-giving and final purification ceremonies together.

On the day appointed for the ceremonial purification and the selection of a name, relatives and, if possible, villagers are invited by the father. All the adult members of the family except unmarried young men and women remain fasting from the preceding day. In the morning the house is cleaned and the members of the family take their bath. In the forenoon the invited guests arrive, some bringing with them rice-beer and some bringing rice or other provisions. All assemble in the courtyard. Among the Dūdh Khāṛiās the head of the baby is shaved or rather the hair clipped by the father, or, if he is not a practised hand at shaving, by some other person, prefer-

66. Compare the similar second purification ceremony called "Chhoṭā Ṭhhaṭhi" among the allied tribe of *Bīrhōṛs*. *Vide*, S. C. Roy's *Birhōṛs*, (Ranchi, 1925), pp 232-233.

ably the babe's mother's brother ; but the father of the babe must start the shaving. Among the Ḍhelkis some married man of the *Samad* clan must shave the head or, at any rate, start the shaving, but the father, even if he belongs to the *Samad* or to the *Muru* clan, must not do it.

The babe is anointed with oil and turmeric by women, one from each family of relatives and neighbours, who bring these with them. The man who shaves the head, and among the Ḍhelkis a man of the *Muru* clan, sacrifices a white cock immediately in front of the *Sūtnā-kūṛiā* (lying-in-room) and drops the blood into a cup of cold water mixed with turmeric brought from his own house. In some places, besides turmeric, a copper coin or a few leaves of the *Bael* tree or both are, in imitation of the Hindus, dipped into this water by way of sanctification. Then the man pours a little of this sanctifying mixture into the joined palms of the hands of the babe's mother. She drinks a little of it and sprinkles the rest over her own head and then, with the babe in her arms, enters the house. Similarly, the babe's father, too, drinks a little of the sanctifying mixture and follows his wife and child into the house. The officiant next enters the house and sprinkles the sanctifying mixture all around, and over the roof of the house.

After this, among the Ḍhelkis, the officiant usually holds a mango-leaf in his hand and, taking up one rice-grain and one grain of sesamum in it, drops them, one after the other, into the vessel with a prayer to God (*Dharam* or *Pōnōmōsōr*) to bring the two grains together. And the two generally meet. Then the officiant takes up another grain of sesamum and a grain of rice, and one or more of the persons present ask him,

"In whose name are you throwing the rice?" The man names some ancestor, dead or alive (a male in the case of a boy and a female in the case of a girl), as suggested by the members of the family or other relatives. Ordinarily, the first name suggested is that of the babe's father's father or father's mother, according as the babe is male or female. If this grain floats and meets the other grain, then the babe is named after him or her. If the two grains do not meet, the procees is repeated by naming other deceased relatives, one after another, with each pair of grains until the two grains meet. And the baby is named after the relative in whose name the two grains meet.

Among Dūdh Khāṛiās generally two grains of *āruā* (sun-dried) rice are used and no *til* (sesamum). The officiant (a relative) takes up one grain of rice and drops it into the vessel in the name of God. This first grain is called the "*Sākhi*" or "witness". As this rice-grain keeps floating, another rice-grain is thrown in the name of some deceased relative (father's father or father's mother, to begin with, according to the babe's sex). If this grain does not sink but floats on and meets the "*Sākhi*" grain, that relative's name is selected. Otherwise another rice-grain is dropped and another name is taken and so on till a grain meets the "*Sākhi*" grain.

Almost invariably a second name is given to the child without any preliminary ceremony, when it is old enough to sit down. The first name is kept secret, lest some malicious person may work mischief through that name which is called the *āsli* or 'real' name.

While the name-selecting ceremony is going on, the assembled relatives relieve the monotony by some such jocular exhortations to the relatives named or rather to the grains representing them,—"Speed up (*Inārā-gōmtām*), So-and-so! the beer-vessels are staring [at you for the delay]. Come on (*ḍel bhānā*), So-and-so! We are dying of thirst!"

Among most of the Ḍhelkis, when the name is selected, the baby is taken to the officiant of the ceremony. He joins the babe's hands and feet together and washes them with rice-beer. He then dips his own finger into the beer and puts it into the babe's mouth. He next fastens round the babe's waist an unbleached cotton-thread woven by himself and saturated with a little sanctified mixture of sacrificial blood, turmeric and water. All present now take up, by turns, the babe in their arms or touch or caress the baby and make a present usually of from one to four copper pice each. With this money, the babe's parents usually buy one or more fowls which are set apart as the individual property of the child.

Among the Dūdh and some Ḍhelki Khāṛiās, the person after whom the child has been named, if alive or, if he or she is dead, his or her heir, ties the cotton thread, referred to above, round the babe's waist; and such person is thenceforth called the babe's '*mitā*'. The *mitā* gives some presents to the babe. The babe's feet are also washed by him. The officiant then throws the water of the cup ove the roof of the hut and puts down the cup, bottom upwards. This closes the ceremony. Then all have a hearty drink of rice-beer, several jars of which have been brewed for the occasion; and they enjoy the rest of the day in dancing and singing, with beer-drinking at intervals. The parents of the baby observe fast that day. A feast is provided to relatives and tribe-fellows. This is prepared in a relative's house, as the parents are finally purified only by sitting at a communal feast with the tribe-fellows.

Ordinarily the name of a deceased relative is given to the child, and it is believed that the *chhāiñ* (spirit) of such deceased relative has been re-born in the child; and this is why in many cases a second name is given and this name is kept secret, as otherwise sorcerers and other malicious persons may harm the child through this name. The washing of the baby's feet is by some said to amount to washing the feet of the deceased relative who is re-born in the child. Among the Ḍhelkis of Jāshpur this washing is done by some one who is related to the family by marriage. Among the Gāngpur Khāṛiās, if the baby cries too often, its feet are on such occasions washed with rice-beer by some *kūṭūmb* relatives, saying-"*Abui iāmnām musātāe*" ("Don't cry from this day"); and it is said that generally the child becomes quieter from after that. It is interesting to note that of this purification ceremony the Khāṛiās say, "So long the baby was an 'untouchable', like a *Lohrā* or a *Ghāsi* or a *Ḍōm*; but now by this *Kōnsong* ceremony it has been assimilated into the tribe".

4. Ear-Boring Ceremony, or *Lutur-tābki* or *Lutur-to'onā* **(Dūdh)**; *Lūtūr Tō'oṭeki* **(Jashpur Ḍhelki)**; *Lūtūr-Ṭipiey* **(Gangpur Ḍhelki)**

It is considered essential that every Khāṛiā child of either sex should have his or her ears bored before he or she attains the age of about five or six years. Among the Gāngpūr Khāṛiās this is in many cases done at the age of from one to three years. Col. Dalton [67] says, "From the Hindus they have adopted the custom of solemnizing the boring of the ears of the children". But this inference is not free from doubt. Dalton is certainly mistaken in supposing that probably "among the Khāṛiās on the Koel" alone this custom is found. As a matter of fact, we meet with this custom all over the Khāṛiā country in the Rāñchi District (on the Koel and also on the Sankh) and also in the Ōṛissā State of Gāngpur and the Central Provinces State of Jāshpur. In fact, it is now regarded as an important and indispensable part of the ceremonial life of the tribe. It is an article of faith with these Khāṛiās that a child, whose ears are not bored, will not, when dead, be incorporated by the deceased ancestor-spirits amongst them. This is why children dying before ear-boring are buried outside the village burial-ground. In fact, according to Khāṛiā ideas, the boring of the ears is a mark placed upon the child by social custom to signify its affiliation to the Khāṛiā community. This ear-boring ceremony takes place on the morning of the day followiug either the *Bandāi* or the *Nawākhiā* (*ñyoḍem ñyeonā*) festival.

Early in the morning of the day appointed for the ceremony, the child must be given a bath and dressed in new clothes. Among the Hill Khāṛiās, as we have seen, the ear is bored by any two tribe-fellows: among the Dūdhs by the *bũñim* or *mitā* of the child, while among the Ḍhelkis this is done by two men of the *Muru*

67 *Ethnology of Bengal*, pp. 159-160

clan or, at any rate, by two tribe-fellows belonging to totemic clans different from the child's.

The child sits before the assembled guests with his face turned any way. The babe's ears at the points where they will be bored are marked with powdered *āruā* rice. Some powdered *ārua* rice (as among the Ḍhelkis of Gangpur) or raw *urid* pulse (*Phaseolus Roxburghii*) in a leaf-cup is placed before the child. He is allowed to eat it in order to divert his attention. When the child is thus engaged, the man (among the Dūdh) or two men (among the Ḍhelkis) sitting by the child's side, pierce the ear-lobes each with a copper-needle obtained by melting a copper pice. In the absence of copper-needles brass needles are also used. The needles are finally bent into the shape of rings and left on the ears. Some powdered rice or chewed *urid* pulse is applied over the wound. When the child grows up, these improvised ear-rings are replaced by regular brass rings in the case of a boy and rolled palm-leaves in the case of girls.

The guests are ordinarily treated only to a drink; but sometimes if a goat is available, it is sacrificed for a first-born child, and fowls are sacrificed for other children, and the guests are treated to a feast.

4. Ului-tōlnā, or Rolui-tōlnā, or Solui sōsō (Hair-tying).

The Khāṛiās of either sex, as a rule, formerly used to wear long hair on the head. But at present owing to contact with civilization and the spread of Christianity, Dūdh Khāṛiā males have begun to cut their hair short. Hill Khāṛiās and Ḍhelki Khāṛiās of either sex still generally wear their hair long.

Khāṛiās of either sex, at about the age of twelve, but seldom beyond that, have their hair ceremonially tied for the first time. This is done on the morning of the *Bandāi* or *Nawākhāni* festival day. As a preliminary to this ceremonial hair-tying, the boy or girl concerned takes a cold water bath. A sack or bundle of *lōṭni* (a variety of mustard) or rice grains is placed in the centre of the court-yard adjoining the house, where invited relatives and tribe-fellows are gathered. The grand-father (mother's father) and, in his absence, some other old relatives belonging to a clan different from the child's (preferably a man of the *Muru* clan), takes his seat over the grain-bundle and presides over the ceremony. Among the Dūdh Khāṛiās, the *Mitā*, [68] if available, is the most suitable person to preside over the ceremony. The child is then seated on a mat before him. A pot of rice-beer, a cup generally of brass, a new piece of cotton cloth, and a string made of the *sābāi* grass, are placed before him.

The officiant of the ceremony rubs oil over the child's head and combs the hair with a new bamboo comb, which is allowed to hang down on the back of the child. The officiant fills the cup with rice-beer, dips the string into it, and holding the child's hair in his left hand and the *sabai*-string in his right encircles the hair just below the head with the string. He then unfastens the string and repeats this process of binding the hair seven times as before. At the seventh or last

68 See *ante*, p 212.

time, the hair is finally gathered up and tied into a knot. The Ḍhelki binds the knot on the left. If the child is a boy, he binds the new cloth round the boy's head in the shape of a turban, and in the case of a girl wraps it round her body. The officiant now leads the child round the assembled guests and both make ceremonial salutation to everybody present. Then all sit down to dinner and the officiant and the child are first served with meat of the fowl killed for the occasion and with rice-beer left over in the pot out of which some beer was used for the ceremonial immersion of the *sabai*-string.

It is interesting to note that among the Ḍhelki Khāṛiās of Jāshpur the parents of the child are not permitted to partake of this meat and drink; for, should they do so, the child's life, it is believed, will be in danger. But Dūdh Khāṛiā parents do partake of it, as we found in the Gāngpur State and the Rāñchi District. Strict observance of all the items of the hair-tying ceremony is now gradually falling into neglect. This is due, partly to the influence of their more civilized neighbours and their fellow-converts to Christianity and partly also to poverty. The orthodox ritual is generally observed in its entirety by the Ḍhelkis and very rarely observed by the Hill Khāṛiās. Since their first hair-tying, girls observe certain taboos: They will not eat cooked food nor drink water touched by persons of other castes or tribes. The Ḍhelki Khāṛiās of the Gāngpur State generally perform the hair-tying ceremony when the child is four or five years old. Among them the ceremony consists simply in a man of the *Muru* clan rubbing oil (without turmeric) on the hair and combing the hair seven times and tying up the hair in a knot.

No sacrifice or feast marks the occasion; but only two pots of rice-beer brewed for the occasion are distributed to all present, after the child has taken a few drops of beer and made *Jōhār* or obeisance to all. The child's hair is not tied up with *sabai* grass but with a cotton string. This ceremony marks the first stage in the child's entry into membership of the community.

5. **Cicatrization, or Sikā** :—Khāṛiā boys at about the age of ten or twelve get usually nine cicatrices or scars raised on the dorsal aspect of the radial side of their fore-arms, usually left fore-arms. Some have also a *sikā* mark or cicatrice made at the base of the thumb to acquire skill in archary. Generally these are made by the boys themselves burning scalds on each oher's hands with lighted wicks. Now-a-days cicatrization is not compulsery but is looked upon only as a test of the power of manly endurance; and many do not undergo the test. But old Khāṛiās still claim that these marks distinguish their tribe-fellows from other tribes and castes. There is a tradition that the nine *sikā* marks and the nine original clan-names were adopted in memory of the nine men or families whom the Dūdh Khāṛiās left behind them in the Gangetic valley when their ancestors migrated to their present home.

6. **Tattooing, (or Khōḍā-ḍōmnā, or Khōḍorḍōmnā [Ḍh])-** In the matter of tattooing, we again find the Ḍhelki section of the Khāṛiās having more detailed observances than the other sections. Dūdh Khāṛia women of the Rāñchi District are tattooed only with three short vertical lines on the forehead, the outer line on each side terminating at the top with a crook thus:- , and two vertical lines on each temple. This pattern is

the forehead like ⊓⊓, and that on each temple as \//. The small female population of Dūdh Khāṛiās in the Jāsh-pur State, in addition to the above tattoo-marks, get also tattoo-marks made on other parts of the body, particularly on the wrists and upper arms, presumably in imitation of their Ḍhelki and Ōrāoñ neighbours. Ḍhelki Khāṛiā women of Jāshpur tattoo their arms, chest, and the neck below the collar bone, and the legs just above the ankles. Those who like it get also their feet tattooed. But it is said that not long ago Ḍhelki women of the Jāshpur State also used to get their forehead and temples tattoo-ed, but they have since abandoned this practice in order to distinguish Ḍhelki women from their Ōrāoñ sisters.

The Ḍhelki women of Gāngpur still, however, contin-ue to have their forehead and temples tatooed. When a Khāṛiā girl is old enough to walk, she is tatooed. In some cases tattooing is delayed till about the tenth or eleventh year, but, in any case, it must be completed before the girl is married. An omisssion to do so is regarded as a social and religious offence, and has to be atoned for by the offender sacrificing a white fowl to Pōnōmōsōr or God and drinking a few drops of this sacrificial blood. The services of a woman of the Mālār (tinker) tribe or of the wandering Ḍhokar community are requisitioned for the purpose. She uses for puncturing the skin a three-pronged iron instrument, and the dyeing stuff is made of soot formed of the smoke, preferably, of burning *Bheloā* (*Semicarpus anacardium*) wood, but sometimes also obtained by burning common fuel-wood. In former times human milk, either the mother's or some other woman's, went to the composition of this dye which is called "*mōkōe*". After the operation, the operator smears the tattooed parts of the body with turmeric paste diluted in water. Some Ḍhelki Khāṛiās first apply a mixture of cowdung and water, then wash it and apply turmeric paste diluted in water. The tattooing is performed outside the house, and after the operation, the tattooed girl is not permitted to enter the house until she has been anointed with turmeric and oil all over the body and has taken a bath. The touch of a Ḍhōkar woman or of a Mālār woman, in the estimation of the Khāṛiā, causes ceremonial pollution and requires lustration by turmeric and water. Should tattooing happen, for some reason or other, to have been omitted at the proper time, it must be gone through prior to marriage.

As for the origin of the practice of tattooing some old Khāṛiās of the Rāñchi District recount the following tradition: In the course of their migrations, before they had reached their present habitat, the Khāṛiās had encamped at the junction of two rivers and hoisted their flags there. While they were crossing the river in canoes or boats, an alien enemy (whom the tradition describes as "*Tūrkō Sipāhis*" or '*Tūrūk soldiers*') took some of their men, who still remained behind, as captives, but could not capture the Khāṛiā flag. It was in memory of that sad event in their chequered tribal history that their women took to making tattoo marks on their foreheads in the form of flags . They still sing a song in Hindi which is said to be reminiscent of that sad event. It runs as follows:—

Orē Gangā, pārē Jumnā, bichmē lāli jhāṇḍā;
Bhāi mōr chōri gelaiñ, rē!
Gangā upar ḍōngā, ḍōngā upar mānoā;
Mānōāke lōr pāṇi kasāe, rē!

[Translation]

This side [was] the Ganges, and that side the Jumnā,
Our brethren—they were robbed from us, Oh !
On the Ganges the canoes; on the canoes the men ;
Tears rolled down the men's cheeks, oh !

It is interesting to note that not long ago, at a meeting of an advanced section of the Dūdh Khāṛiās of the Rāñchi District who are interested in social reform, the question of abolishing the practice of tattooing came up for discussion; but on the strength of this tradition the older men succesefully pleaded that as these tattoo marks on the forehead of their women are made in commemoration of the valour of their women-folk who had thrice repulsed the enemy in ancient days, the practice should not be abolished. So the practice is still kept up, at least by the non-Christian Dūdh Khāṛiās of the Rānchi District.

Such are the rites, ceremonies and precautions by which a Khāṛiā child is received into the world, sought to be protected against evil influences and supernatural dangers attendant on birth and childhood, given a name, and recognised as a reincarnation of some departed ancestor or, at any rate, as a new member of the clan or kin. Thus started in social life with the good wishes of the community and the blessings of the ancestor-spirits and gods, the child is, in time, admitted into the wider circle of the tribe by admission into the dormitories for the unmarried, and finally by marriage which makes the Khāṛiā a full-fledged member of the tribe possessing all the rights and privileges and charged with all the duties and functions of an adult tribesman, and fully sharing in the common life of the community. In the case of girls this admission is specially symbolised at an early age by the peculiar tattoo-marks of the tribe. In this progress from birth to manhood, every turning-point on the road is marked by religious and magico-religious rites and ceremonies designed to avert unforeseen risks and dangers and to ensure safety and prosperity to the individual, the family, and the community.

The Bachelors' Dormitory (pp. 77-78 *ante*) is now in a moribund condition and will probably be as extinct as the Dodo in another generation or two. The authority of the village elders and of tribal traditions and custom and of public opinion are now the only disciplinary forces that help to mould the character of Khāṛiā youth in conformity with the tribal ideals, such as they are, of manliness and virtue, self-restraint and good conduct. Khāṛiās of all sections avoid close personal contact with Ghāsis, Ḍōms, Chamārs, Lohārs, and even Muhammadans. All these communities they regard as "untouchables". From the day of their first hair-tying, as we have seen, Khāṛiā girls may, on no account, eat cooked food or drink water touched by anyone of a caste or tribe other than their own. Boys begin to observe this taboo strictly from the date of their marriage, when they are regarded as having reached social maturity. By such taboos Khāṛiā society seeks to maintain intact their **tribal "mana"** and, with it, **tribal 'luck'**. Life is not, however, merely a round of taboos and fears to the Khāṛiā. In connection with the rites here described we have occasional glimpses of wit and jollity, a zest in life, warm hospitality, parental affection, and other sentiments that relieve the pathos and sorrow of the Khāṛiā's existence and make life worth living.

CHAPTER IX.

Marriage, Pregnancy and Divorce.

Marriage is regarded by Khāṛiā society as essential for every adult member of the tribe. It is only after marriage that a Khāṛiā is considered to be a full-fledged member of the tribe. As among other Mūṇḍā-speaking tribes, marriage is regulated by the rule of clan-exogamy among the Dūdh and Ḍhelki sections of the Khāṛiās and also among the Hill Khāṛiās of Mānbhum and Singbhūm, but not now among those of Mayurbhañj. None of the three sections of the Khāṛiās may intermarry, one with the other. They are strictly endogamous in so far as their own sub-tribe is concerned. There can now be no valid marriage of a Khāṛiā, following his tribal religion, with a non-Khāṛiā, and any such union deprives such a Khāṛiā of his tribal rights. The violation of the rule of endogamy within the tribe and sub-tribe is regarded as a heinous social offence.

All sections of the Khāṛiās practise cross-cousin marriage. As we have seen in a previous chapter, this custom is reflected in their kinship terminology. We were told by a few Khāṛiās that there was no bar against marriage with a woman distantly related either as mother's cousin-sister or as grand-aunt by the mother's side, but we have not been able to find any living instance of such union nor any trace of it in the geneologies we collected. A man may not marry his wife's elder sister, nor may a widow marry her deceased husband's elder brother. But a widow may marry her husband's younger brother.

For purposes of marriage relations, a Khāṛiā's kin and those of his wife may be classed under three groups:-

(1) Agnates.

(2) A woman and her husband's elder brothers or elder cousins, or husband's father and uncles; and a man and his wife's elder sisters or elder cousin-sisters, and wife's mother and aunts.

(3) Non-agnates including cross-cousins but excluding (2) above.

Roughly speaking, a Khāṛiā may marry into group (3), but not into groups (1) and (2). Khāṛiās generally do not marry in the same village or settlement, though it is not now forbidden, as such, by customary law. The probable reason for this village-exogamy is that originally members of one and the same clan (*gotra* or *gotar*) lived together, as the traditions of the Dūdh and Ḍhelki sections definitely testify, and as is still the case in many Hill Khāṛiā settlements.

Adult marriage is the rule among all sections of the tribe. Marriage is not thought of before a boy is old enough to earn his own livelihood and a girl is old enough to fetch water from the village spring or tank and perform other household duties. Under the influence of Hinduism, a few well-to-do Khāṛiās now marry their children before they have attained puberty. But this is an exception and not the rule. As a general rule, boys are married at the age of about twenty or twenty-one, and Khāṛiā girls at the age of from fifteen to eighteen years. The bride is, as a rule, younger than the bridegroom. This is generally the case even when the bride is a widow.

In the form of marriage which they call *Āsli* or 'real' or regular marriage, neither the boy nor the girl has any direct voice in the selection of a partner in life. Their parents conduct all negotiations for the marriage. But there are other recognised forms of marriage (though now regarded as somewhat irregular) in which the parties choose their own partners. In fact, the modern *āsli* marriage with its customs, as the Hindu name implies, would appear to be an adaptation and elaboration, through contact with neighbouring Hindu castes and Hinduised aboriginal tribes, of an indigenous tribal custom of marriage by *purchase* or payment of bride-price which appears to have been long prevalent in the tribe. 'Buying a wife' is a common expression for 'marriage'.

We shall begin with a separate account of the Hill Khāṛiā marriage customs and then give a joint account of the marriage customs of the other two sections of the tribe, noting such differences as exist between the two.

Marriage Customs among the Hill Khāṛiās.

(i) General.

Hill Khāṛiā girls are, as a rule, married after they have attained puberty. The Hill Khāṛiās of the Mayurbhañj State do not, at the present day, possess any regular clan-system and therefore marriages between families owning the same clan-name are not infrequent, although marriage between near kin is interdicted. The Hill Khāṛiās or, as they are locally called, Kheṛiāhs or Kheṛeys, of the Mānbhūm and Singbhūm districts of

Chōṭā Nāgpur, however, possess a regular clan (*gotra*, *gotar*, or *gosṭhi*) organisation, and observe clan-exogamy. Among Khāṛiās of all sections, cross-cousin marriage is in vogue, but marriage between agnatic cousins is tabooed. In some Hinduised Hill Khāṛiā families, before a young man is married, a Hindu Vaiṣṇava preceptor (Gosāin̐) ceremonially intiates him by whispering into his ears the name of some Hindu God who is to be regarded as his tutelary deity.

Although "elopment marriage", "intrusion marriage", and "marriage by forcible application of vermilion" are not unknown to the Hill Khāṛiās, these forms of union are, it is curious to note, even less frequent among them at this day than among the more advanced Ḍhelki and Dūdh sections of the tribe. But in these forms of union as well as in the more orthodox and now common form of 'marriage by purchase', the rituals observed by the Hill Khāṛiās are less elaborate than amongst the other and more go-ahead sections of the tribe.

(ii) Love Marriages.

Although love-marriages, as we have said, are not unknown among present-day Hill Khāṛiās, matches are ordinarily arranged by the parents or guardians of the parties. In the few cases in which a young man and a maiden, not within the prohibited degrees of relationship, have developed a mutual attachment but cannot marry on account of the opposition of the parents of one or both of them, either the young lovers elope, or the young man, as if by force (but generally by pre-concert), all on a sudden, smears vermilion on the forehead of the maiden at a market or in some other crowded public place. This smearing of vermilion is, in the tribe's estimation, tantamount to actual marriage. This is known as *Jhikā* or *Ṭānilā* marriage. Later, the guardians of the parties generally come to terms and formal marriage rites are arranged on payment of something more than, often double, the usual bride-price. The tribe-fellows are given a feast and the marriage is formally recognised. But if the couple are within prohibited degrees of relationship or if there be any other social bar to their union they are excommunicated and later, if expiation is permissible, a tribal assembly has to be called to restore them to caste (see pp. 178–182 *ante*).

(iii) Orthodox Marriage among the Hill Khāṛiās.

Marriage Negotiations.—Marriage negotiations among all sections of the Khāṛiās, as among most other Mūṇḍā tribes, are now generally carried on through intermediaries. But before this is done, the boy's parents generally manage to see the girl without the knowledge of her people. If the girl is to their liking, the parents send a go-between called *Dāṇḍia* with their proposal to the guardian of the maiden whose hand is desired. If the girl's guardian has no objection, he appoints a day when he and his people will go to the boy's place to see him for themselves. On the appointed day the girl's parents with four or five relatives, male as well as female, start for the boy's place. On the way they mark any omens that may cross their path. If they come across an elephant or a bear, the journey is considered propitious. The sight of a serpent or a tiger or a barking-deer (*Kuṭrā*) is regarded as an evil omen;

and, if any of these is met with, the party return home. The Khāṛiās in and about Gurguṛiā in Mayurbhañj may proceed further with the negotiations even after meeting any such inauspicious omen; but in some places either an attempt is made to kill the snake or other animal, if possible, or the journey is again undertaken on a subsequet day of which notice is sent beforehand. On the party's arrival, the boy's people accord them a cordial reception, wash their legs and feet with water mixed with turmeric, spread out mats for them to sit upon, and serve them with tobacco-powder and lime. If after seeing the boy, his people, and his house, the girl's people approve of the proposed match they signify their provisional approval; but the final answer is communicated later through their own *Ḍānḍiā* who further informs them of the date on which the boy's people in their turn will go to the girl's place to see her.

On the appointed day, the parents and two or more relatives of the boy go to the girl's place with presents of flattened rice and sweets (*chiṛā-miṭhāi*), a bead-necklace and a new cloth dyed yellow with turmeric-juice. In some places (as in Gurguṛiā) no *chiṛā-miṭhāi* is presented but only *mūṛi* or fried rice. On their arrival their legs and feet are anointed with turmeric paste and washed with water. Then they are seated on mats in the *āngan* or courtyard and given powdered tobacco and lime to chew. Relatives and friends of the girl's family are also called in. The lady of the house distributes the *chiṛā-miṭhāi* to the children present. The girl is conducted to the *āngan*. Among the Hill Khāṛiās of Dhalbhūm and Mānbhum the boy's father puts on the necklace round the girl's neck and hands over the new cloth to her to wear. Among the Hill Khāṛiās of Mayurbhañj the boy's father hands the presents over to some female relative of the girl; and she dresses the girl in the new cloth and places the necklace round her neck. Thereupon the girl makes her salutations to all. Then the boy's father declares, "From to-day she becomes my daughter-in-law". After being duly entertained with drink and dinner the boy's people take leave. In Dhalbhūm and Mānbhūm, the bride-price is settled and, if possible, paid on this occasion, but among the Hill Khāṛiās of the Mayurbhañj State, as among the Dūdh and Ḍhelki Khāṛiās, another date is appointed for payment of the bride-price (*pan-dewā*) and for fixing the date (*lagan*) of the marriage. The amount of bride-price is actually, though informally, settled beforehand by negotiation through the respective Ḍānḍiās of the two parties.

Payment of Bride-price (Pan-dewā).— Among the Hill Khāṛias of Mayurbhañj, as we said, the payment of the bride-price constitutes a ceremony by itself. On the appointed day, the boy's parents with about half-a-dozen relatives and friends go to the girl's house with the bride-price, their Dāṇḍiā accompanying them with an earthen-ware pot painted white with rice-flour and marked red with vermilion marks and filled with flattened rice (*chiṛā*) and sweets. On arrival at the bride's house, their legs and feet are anointed with turmeric paste and washed; mats are spread out for them to sit upon, and they are given powdered tobacco and lime to refresh themselves with.

Relatives and friends of the bride's parents assemble. Then a mimic bargaining for the bride-price is enacted.

A relative of the bride asks the bride-groom's people,-"Where have you come from? What brings you here? Why are you loitering in our settlement ?" They reply,-"We have come to purchase something". The spokesman of the girl's relatives says,—"We have the thing here. If you agree to pay the proper price, you may stay here". The boy's people reply, "Then name your price". Upon this a man of the girl's side hands over some (eleven, thirteen or fifteen) cracked *cowrie-shells* to a man of the boy's side who shows these to others of his side. The boy's relatives then take out a few of the *cowrie*-shells and return the rest to the spokesman of the girl's side. The girl's people, in their turn, add a few more *cowrie*-shells and hand the *cowries* back. This process of symbolical indication of demand and offer is repeated for the third time when the boy's people reduce the *cowries* to the actual number of rupees at which the bride-price has already been settled by negotiation between the Ḍānḍiās of the two parties, and declare,-"We are not in a position to pay more". And the bride's people say,-"Well then, we have to accept what you can pay". After this mimicry of bargaining, enlivened by sallies of wit and fun, the bride-price is paid. The bride-price is usually fixed now-a-days at three, five, seven or nine rupees, according to circumstances. But in no case may the figure be an even number. Besides this money and a *sāṛī* cloth and ornaments for the bride, the boy's parents have also to present a *sāṛī* cloth to the bride's mother.

A date for the wedding is either fixed on this occasion, or the boy's people are asked to come on some other date which is appointed for the purpose. No particular ceremonies or formalities are required for the fixing of the date. When the boy's people come for the fixing of the date they are welcomed with the usual fẹet-washing, *etc.*, and entertained with food and drink. The month of *Māgh* (January-February) is the orthodox season for a Hill Khāṛiā marriage, but a marriage is also permissible in the month of Phālgūn (February-March). Any day of the week except a Sunday or a Saturday or a Thursday may be conveniently chosen to celebrate a marriage. Should it, however, be found convenient to fix a Thursday for a wedding, the bride may on no account leave her parents' house on a Thursday. This ban on Thursday is obviously due to the influence of Hindu ideas. The Hindus regard that day as sacred to the Goddess of Fortune (*Lakshmī*), and the departure of a daughter from the house on that day may amount to the departure of "Fortune" or 'Luck' from the house. Similarly a Tuesday or *Mangal-bār* is regarded as a particularly auspicious day for marriage as the word "Mangal" in Saṁskrit and its derivative languages (Bengali, Ōṛiyā, Hindi, *etc*) signifies 'auspiciousness'. It may be noted that in a Hill Khāṛiā wedding, a Mangal-hāñṛi" or "auspicious cooking-pot", and a "Mangal-ghaṭ" or "auspicious jug", are used for ceremonial purposes.

Place of Wedding.—Among the Hill Khāṛiās in and about Gūrgūriā in the Mayurbhañj State (as among the Dūdh and Ḍhelki Khāṛiās) the wedding is celebrated at the bridegroom's place whither the bride is conducted by the Ḍāṇḍiā and four or five relatives (not the parents) of the boy; and almost all the fellow-villagers of the bride's parents escort the girl and attend the wedding. Among the Hill Khāṛiās of Mānbhūm and Dhalbhūm, contrary to the custom among the other sections of the tribe, the marriage is celebrated in the house of the bride's parents. The bride-groom's party consisting of both men and women start for the bride's place after break-fast on the day before that fixed for the wedding so as to reach there by evening. Before the party starts, five, seven or nine married women whose husbands are living, go with the village-priest (Kālo or Dehuri) to the *Bāsūki-thān* or seat of the village-goddess Bāsuki where the priest offers rice, milk and molasses to the deity. Then the women jointly hold a spade, and dig seven spadefuls of earth which they carry to the house of the bridegroom, and construct with it a small mud-pulpit called '*Vedi*' (a Saṁskrit word which is wrongly pronounced as 'Badhi' by the Khāṛiās). While the women dig the earth for the purpose, the Kālo or priest places his hand upon the handle of the spade so as to remain touching it all the time. This "Badhi" or "Vedi" is the sacred pulpit on or near which the essential ceremonies connected with a wedding must be performed. The same day a similar 'Badhi' or "Vedi" is also erected with the same ceremonies at the bride's house.

The Bridal procession.—The bridegroom wears new clothes dyed yellow with turmeric for the occasion, and his relatives who form the procession also have their clothes similarly dyed yellow, if possible. If available, the bride-groom puts on a new *dhoti* and *chādar* (wrapper), both dyed yellow, and winds a yellow cloth round his head in the form of a turban. Before the procession starts from the bridegroom's place women lift up the bridegroom on a wooden plank and dance about carrying him seven times round the marriage-pulpit. Then the procession starts, accompanied, if possible, by music. Throughout the journey, mirth and jollity, jests and jokes, enliven the party. The bridegroom's Ḍānḍiā goes in advance to the bride's house to apprise the bride's people of the approach of the bridegroom and his party. A bit of earth from the "badhi" or marriage-pulpit of the bridegroom's place, and a small earthen pot called by the Hindu name of "mangal-ghaṭ" or auspicious waterpot, besides rice-beer and some sweets are taken to the bride's.

When the bridegroom's party reaches the boundary of the bride's settlement, they are given a cordial welcome and conducted to the quarters (*Chhāmṛā*) arranged for them, where they are provided with rice-beer, water, *etc.*

A party from the bride's house comprising young men and women (married and unmarried), with the bride in the middle, go in procession with music to meet the guests and, on meeting, they all dance and sing. The whole night is spent in dancing and merry-making except that after some time the bride and bridegroom are allowed to go to sleep, the former in her father's home, and the latter in his party's quarters.

The Wedding.—In the morning the bride and the bridegroom are conducted to the *māṛoā* or marriage-booth in the centre of which the *Badhi* or marriage-pulpit has been erected. The bride and bridegroom are seated side by side upon a mat, with their faces to the east. It is interesting to note that the Hill Khāṛiās of the Simlipal hills of Mayurbhañj do not use vermilion at the actual wedding, but it is after the actual marriage that one or more married girls mark the foreheads of bride and bridegroom with vermilion. Anointing with vermilion, they say, is a new practice adopted in imitation of the Hindus. In place of the *Kārsā-bhāṇḍā* of the other sections, most Hill Khāṛiās use the auspicious *mangal-ghaṭ* to which we have referred. This, too, as the name implies, is a feature borrowed from their Hindu neighbours. Thus the Hill Khāṛiās have not escaped the influence of contact with the Hindus even in their marriage ritual. Even the raising of a *māṛoā* or pulpit is a Hindu custom and the mound of earth which they place at the centre of it and call 'Badhi' is, as we have seen, an imitation of the Hindu 'Vedi' or altar, of which the word 'Badhi' is obviously a corruption. It may also be noted that in some Hill Khāṛiā families of Mayurbhañj (e. g. in Kusumbandi), the bride and bridegroom are given *Vaisṇav* initiation (*Guru-karṇa*) by a *Vaisbaṇ gūru* muttering into their ears some name of the Deity meant to be reverentially repeated everyday by the initiate. But, as a matter of fact, this attempt at Vaisṇav proselytism has had little success. Thus Keshari Khāṛiā of Gurguriā told us that some forty years ago, when he was a little boy, he was initiated by a Vaisṇav whom his father paid a few pice and one *seer* of rice for his ministration, but that he has now altogether forgotten what was the divine name that he was asked to repeat daily and what it was meant for. Since then there has been, as we were told, no other initiation in that village.

A Hill Khāṛiā couple are not made to stand, like the Ḍhelki and Dūdh Khāṛiā bridegroom and bride, on the yoke, *ōlōng* (straw), or *silōṭ* (-stone); but both are seated face to face on a mat on the platform of the *māṛoā* near the *Badhi* placed in the centre. In some places, a small earthenware plate with oil in it and lighted wicks jutting out of it is placed on the 'Badhi' or marriage pulpit. A cloth-screen is put up between the couple so that the one may not see the face of the other. The presiding officiant of the ceremony is the maternal uncle of the boy. He puts on a ring of silver, if possible, or otherwise of brass, on the ring-finger of the bridegroom's right hand by way of ceremonial acceptance (*varan*) and reception; and it is he who brings out the bride and seats her on a mat in front of the bridegroom, but with a screen in between the two. In some places a pith-crown is placed on the head of each. The bridegroom first pelts a few grains of rice across the screen on the head of the bride, and she, in her turn, similarly pelts back rice grains on the bridegroom's head. This is generally repeated seven times. Then they exchange their grass finger-rings. Their right hands are next joined palm to palm by a tribal elder, the bride's upturned palm below the bridegroom's palm, and placed, from below the screen, over a pot (*mangal-ghaṭ*) full of water with a mango twig jutting out of its mouth. Some grains of rice, a conch-shell and some *kusa* grass are placed over the joined palms. Then the officiant drops water on the joined palms in the name of the deceased ancestors of the bridegroom and the bride. All assembled then shout "Haribōl" (Glory to Hari or God), in the manner of the Hindus.

In the marriage rites of the Hill Khāṛiās of Dhalbhūm and Mānbhūm, however, a pot full of water is not used, and the couple simply join the palms of their hands together standing on the mat. In some cases vermilion is also applied in the same manner as among the Ḍhelki and the Dūdh Khāṛiās. Then the screen is taken off. The bride is then conducted by her father or other guardian round the bridegroom, from left to right, and seated to the left of the bridegroom. Then the ends of their clothes are tied together as among most Hindu castes. The mother and then other near female relatives of the bride wave with a circular motion a lighted lamp in front of the couple and give some cash presents of a few pice each to the bridegroom. The couple are then taken outside the *māṛōā*,—the bride on the hip of a maiden and the bridegroom on the hip of a stalwart young man; and these with their happy burdens dance round the marriage-booth (*māṛōā*) along with other young men and women. When the dance is finished, the father of the bride addresses the bridegroom before the assembled guests in these words:—"So long she was mine, now she becomes yours. Divide with her what you get. Do ye both live together in amity". Among the Hill Khāṛiās of Gūṛgūriā, before the *Chāngu-nāṭ* or bridal dance, the bride takes up the *mangal-ghaṭ* with water and mango-twig and all and, accompanied by a few other girls, goes to bathe in a neighbouring stream or spring and comes back with a pot filled with water. If there is no stream or spring near by, the bride is bathed in the open space (*āngan*) in front of the house. She stands with the water-filled pot on her head. The bridegroom takes up a bow and seven arrows and, placing his hands on the pot of water on the bride's head, shoots each arrow one after another. A younger brother of the bride picks up each arrow as it is shot, and it becomes his. This ceremony is called the *Kumbha-bindhā* (hitting the pot).[69]

Now all sit down to a feast; and then dancing and singing go on throughout the rest of the day and the whole night. The next morning at cock-crow the bridegroom's party return home with the bride accompanied by her brother and a few of her male relatives. She goes walking, but is carried in arms across streams or waterways. On reaching the bridegroom's house the bride's people take leave of the bride and go back to their own village. The bride laments loudly at parting from her people. This wailing and lamentation, though the outcome primarily of natural affection, has now assumed something of a ritual complexion.

It is worth noting that among the Hill Khāṛiās of Gūṛgūriā and its neighbourhood in the Mayurbhañj State, the bridal *Chāngu-nāṭ* is the last dance which a woman may dance in her life; for, among them, though a man may dance at any age, a woman may never dance after her marriage.

Kādo Māṭi.—On the day after the bridegroom has led the bride home after marriage, the couple have to take a ceremonial bath in the village spring or tank where they go escorted by a bevy of girls. The "badhi" pulpit is broken up, and the couple are anointed with its clay. The girls break up into two parties, one party siding with the bridegroom and the other with the bride in finding out a small earthen or metal jug which the bride and

---

69. For an analogous custom among other Mūṇḍā tribes, see *The Mūṇḍās and Their Country*, pp. 449-450, and *The Birhōrs*, p. 240.

bridegroom by turns secrete in the mud of the spring or tank for the other to find out. [70] Then, with their wet clothes on, the couple make offerings of rice to the bridegroom's ancestor-spirits. They then put on new clothes. The bride fetches water in the jug, and with it cooks food which is served by her for the first time to her husband and his relatives. After marriage the new couple generally occupy a separate hut which has been already erected for them to live in.

A couple of months or so after the wedding, the bride and bridegroom are invited to the bride's father's house and entertained there for two days and a half, and presented each with a new cloth. This is known as *Bahuriā.* Then they return home.

IV. Sāgāi or Widow-marriage.

A widow may again marry either a widower or a bachelor. Ordinarily no bride-price has to be paid in cattle or money. But the bridegroom has to give a new cloth to the bride and provide a pot of liquor to her people. Some female relative of the bride marks her forehead with vermilion (*sindūr*) diluted in oil. This vermilion is brought by the bridegroom but not applied by him with his own hands. Among the Dūdh and Ḍhelki Khāṛiās, as we shall see, a more elaborate procedure is generally followed.

70. In connection with the concealing of the jug and seeking for it, it may be noted that an analogous custom is not only found among some other Mūṇḍā tribes (vide S. C. Roy's *Mūṇḍās and their Country*, pp. 450-1, 454) but is common among most Hindu castes who generally substitute a ring or some such object for the jug and substitute a small spot drenched in water for a spring or tank. It is sometimes said that this is a test to divine which of the two will, in life, dominate over the other.

II. Marriage among the Dūdh and Ḍhelki Khāṛiās.

The different forms of marriage still in vogue amongst the Dūdh Khāṛiās and the Ḍhelki Khāṛiās are the following:—

1. Regular Marriage (*Ōlol ḍāe*, or *Āsli Bihā*, or *Māngni Bihā*)
2. Elopement Marriage (*Ūḍhrā-ūḍhrī Cholki*, or *Kōlḍūm Yāro*)
3. Marriage by forcible application of vermilion (*Sūnarūm T'ā'p'ā*, or *Sūndrum Lā'ki*)
4. Intrusion Marriage (*Ḍhūkū Cholki*, or *Ḍhūkū Ḍiārki*)
5. Widow-Marriage (*Sāgāi*, or *Bandāi Ḍōmki*)

1. Orthodox Marriage, or *Āsli* Marriage, or Māngni Bihā, or Ōlol ḍāe.

Though not universal, this is now regarded as the orthodox or regular form of marriage, because under Hindu influence this is considered more respectable than the other forms. The very name 'bihā' indicates Hindu influence in this form of marriage. In the '*āsli*' marriage, the programme of formalities, rites and ceremonies is a fairly heavy and protracted one. The successive ceremonial stages in this form of marriage are:— (i) the selection of a bride (*Kānḍāe bāinā* or *Yo-Yo-ḍāe*) (ii) Omen-reading (*Gōjhūng-sangōḍnā* or *Gōjhūng-ḍechhō*), (iii) Betrothal (*Jūng-jūng-ḍāe*), (iv) Present of cloth (*Chhinṛhā obsūinā*), (v) Fixing the Bride-price (*Gining tāng*), and (vi) The wedding (*bihā*).

(i) Selection of a Bride (Kāṇḍāe bāinā)

When the parents of a Khāṛiā boy knows or hears of a suitable girl with whom they should like to marry their son, they send a friend or relative to sound the views of the parents of the girl. Formerly it was considered proper for the parents of the boy to propose directly and without the help of an intermediary (*dāṇḍiā* or *ānjōr*). And even to this day, sometimes Ḍhelki parents themselves go to other villages in search of brides for their sons, though the first proposal is made through some intermediary. Thus Lākho Hāṅsdā (Ḍūng-ḍūng) and his wife, of village Padā (in Rāj-Gāngpur *thānā*), who were looking out for a suitable bride for their son Bāhādur reached village Kāṭi-āmbā (in the Bargāoṅ *thānā* of Gāngpur), and they asked some relative of theirs whether they might secure a suitable bride there for their son. They were informed that Kubā of the *Muru* clan had a marriageable daughter; and so they sent a relative named Mākṛa Surin to sound Kubā's views. Kubā having favourably received the proposal, Lākhō and his wife went to Kubā's house and were duly received and entertained. On their approving of the girl, the match was arranged. Later, each party selected their *ḍāṇḍiā* or messenger to carry messages to the other party. Thus, whether a *ḍāṇḍiā* starts the negotiations or not, the subsequent negotiations must be carried on through such an intermediary. When, however, the Khāṛiā father has only one or more daughters and no son and wishes to secure, for his daughter, a husband who will remain in the house of his parents-in-law as their "Ghar-dāmād" or "domesticated son-in-law" and heir, it is the girl's father who makes the proposal personally and in some cases through a friend or a relative. As among the Mūṇḍās, the proposal of the marriage of a Khāṛiā must emanate in the first instance from the boy's side and not from the girl's side. If the parents of the girl do not feel favourably inclined to the proposed match, they avoid giving a blunt refusal, but politely excuse themselves under some such plausibe pretext as that they need time for consulting relatives and friends.

(ii) Omen-reading (Gōjhung-ḍechhō or Gojhūng-Sangōḍnā)

If the proposal is to their liking, the girl's parents convey a hint of their approval. When the boy's parents thus come to know of this approval either through an intermediary or directly, the boy's father, accompanied by two or three relatives on a convenient day of which previous notice has been sent, goes to the girl's parents' house taking a pot of rice-beer with him. On their way they go on marking any omen that may cross their path. Among good omens [71] are a bear, a leopard, a corpse, a deer, a tiger, a pot full of water, a cow or a bullock, *etc.* Among evil omens are a sheep, an empty pot, a *Nilgāi* (*portex pictus*), or a jackal running across the path in front of the party, an animal being killed or quartered, sweepings of the house being thrown away, a dry branch falling from a tree, *etc.* If any bad omen crosses their path the journey is forthwith postponed, but the negotiations are not abandoned, as is the case

71. For other omens, *vide* chapter XV *post.*

with some other allied tribes such as the Mūṇḍās. [72] Information is sent to the bride's people, and some other day is fixed for the purpose. Bad omens, according to the Khāṛiās, only portend some quarrel during the negotiations, or the absence of the girl's guardians from the house during the intended visit. It may be noted that Sunday, Monday, and Friday are considered auspicious days for the journey.

(iii) Betrothal (Jūng-jūngḍāe).

On the appointed day, the girl's people, who have been expecting the visit, receive the visitors with the customary salutation as honoured guests, spread out mats for them to sit upon and offer them powdered tobacco and lime to chew. After a little formal conversation about the journey and the omens, if any, that they might have seen on the way, the crops and the like, the boy's father makes the proposal formally.

Dūdh Khāṛiā Custom.

Here it is interesting to note that the two sub-tribes, the Dūdh and the Ḍhelki, make the proposal in two different ways. Dūdh Khāṛiās make the proposal in a round-about way and are answered in the same fashion, as will be presently seen. The Ḍhelkis, on the other hand, make the proposal directly and receive a direct answer. Thus, the Ḍhelki boy's father declares, "I have come to seek the hand of your girl for my son. I am a man of little means. But if need be, I shall work as a labourer to maintain her". Unless the girl's parents, as a result of further enquiries, have changed their mind, the girl's father accepts the proposal

72. *See The Mūṇḍās and their Country* pp. 438-39

with some such words as the following:- "If I do not marry my girl into *Kuṭūmb* [73] families to whom else shall I marry her ?" Among the Dūdh Khāṛiās, the girl's father or other relative asks the boy's relative :—"From where are you coming ? Where had you been last night ? What are you seeking here ?" The boy's father or one of his companions makes the proposal in the following figurative form:- "We came from such-and-such village (names their own village) on a hunting expedition to such-and-such forest (names). We saw a bear and shot at it with our arrow (meaning, aimed at securing a bride). The deer fled and we ran in its pursuit till evening and, quite exhausted, reached the jungle of such-and-such a village. There we put up for the night, cooked our meal, ate and slept. At dawn, again, we went out in search of our missing game. We lighted upon its blood-traces and followed them. Then we reached the jungle of this village (names the bride's father's village). The keeper of the jungle (meaning the *Ḍānḍiā*) asked the reason for our trespass. We told him the reason (repeats the whole account). He told us,—'The deer has indeed come to our jungle. But we won't let you have it without a permit and proper price. Come to the village. We shall discuss and decide about it'. Thus, sir, he has brought us here before your Pañches to decide what money we have to pay for our game. The keeper told us that it had entered your jungle. Is it here ? What price do you demand for it ?" The bride's people name in reply a certain number of plough-cattle.

73. '*Kuṭumb*' in this connection means a tribe-fellow who is not an agnate and with whom marriage-relations may be contracted.

Then the bargaining goes on with many a jest and joke and merry laughter till the bride's people come down to five heads of cattle or so. Then the bridegroom's people say:– "Very well, we agree, bring out your deer (girl)". This is not, however, the actual fixing of the bride-price, as we shall see presently.

In the meanwhile, while their conversation is going on, a few relatives and friends of the girl's parents are called in. Water is brought out in an earthen pitcher or in a brass jug, if available, and oil in a cup, by young men or elderly women. They honour the visitors by besmearing their legs from the knees downwards to the feet with oil, and by washing the legs and feet with cold water. Thus honoured, the visitors go round and salute everyone present.

Now the girl is conducted to the place; and she makes obeisance (*jōhār*) to the new-comers. Among the Ḍhelkis, she stands by the side of her father or guardian; whereas among the Dūdhs she is seated on the lap of her future father-in-law or the elder brother or mother's brother of the future husband. If she is seated on the lap of her future husband's elder brother, young boys and girls of the bride's side also establish themselves, some on the shoulders of the girl's future '*bāo*' or '*bhāisūr*' (husband's elder brother) and some on the lap of the bride, and sing a few songs (generally, five marriage songs).

Then even in the day-time a lighted lamp is brought and placed before the girl. Then the father of the girl addresses the boy's relatives, saying,–"Here is my 'article' (merchandise). Look well and see whether she is blind or lame or decrepit or has any defect in her hands or legs or feet or any other limb or is a witch or a thief. If you regard her as a treasure worth having, well and good; if not, tell us frankly".

The boy's father examines the girl closely to see if she is strong and healthy. When he expresses his approval, the sticks and umbrellas and *chādars* or wrappers of the party are taken inside the house.

Then, among the Ḍhelkis, a day is fixed for the final performance of the betrothal ceremony (*jūng-jūng-ḍāe*). Finally, the future relatives are entertained at dinner that night. They take leave the following morning.

But among the Dūdhs, as soon as the approval of the match is expressed and the guests are taken inside the house, two small vessels of rice-beer are brought to the future bride, who hands them over to her future father-in-law or other guardian of the boy. He drinks the same saying, "Now we have found what we have been seeking for. Our girl has given us water and we have drunk it." The rice-beer is then passed on to others. The future father-in-law of the girl gives her some money, one or two *annas* up to a rupee, according to means. This is called *Māngni*; and the marriage thus arranged is called "*Māngni Bihā*". The girl once more salutes the guests and then returns inside the house. The guests are then treated to a drink, but not, as amongst the Ḍhelkis, to dinner as well. They take leave the same evening after paying an even number of copper coins to the bride's people. This present of coin is called *Durā Paisā* (door-money or gate-money). In return, the guests' clothes are dyed with oil and turmeric and they are given three or four seers of rice, one leaf of tobacco besides some powdered tobacco and lime. They now leave the girl's house after *Bheṭ-ghāṭ* or ceremonial salutations. On their return home, the female relatives of the boy's family fry the rice brought from the girl's parents' house. Fellow-villagers are invited and are given fried rice and rice-beer. All rejoice and sing songs till the liquor is finished. In some cases the bride-price is settled and half of it paid down on this day.

Dhelki Khaṛiā Custom. The procedure with regard to the Betrothal ceremony among the Ḍhelkis is somewhat more elaborate. It is as follows:- On a day appointed beforehand the boy's father or other guardian, in company with two or three relatives who have been invited to accompany him for the purpose and have been treated to rice-beer brewed for the occasion, starts for the girl's house. The boy's father takes with him a pot of rice-beer for his future relatives. Their departure is so timed as to enable them to reach their destination by evening.

On their arrival they are received at the courtyard where a mat is spread out for them to sit upon. Powdered tobacco with lime is given to them and a pot of rice-beer to regale themselves with, after the journey. When they have finished this pot of beer, the beer brought by the boy's father is served to the girl's relatives, old and young, present, even to children. Then a vessel filled with cold water, a winnowing basket with a small quantity of paddy in it, a pot of tepid water, a little oil in a cup and a low wooden stool or a plank of wood to sit upon, are brought out and placed in a central position in the *āngan* or courtyard. The boy's father or other guardian now puts out his legs over the wooden stool or plank and a man from the girl's side besmears oil over his legs and feet from the knees down to the toes. Another man of the girl's side begins to rub the legs with a handful of unhusked rice while a third goes on slowly pouring tepid water on the legs. Then the legs of the companions of the bridegroom's father are similarly oiled, rubbed and washed. The boy's father pays an *anna* (four copper coins) or so to the person who washes his feet. Then he and his companions go round the assembled guests to make their salutations to each one individually.

Then the girl's father and two other elderly men among the girl's relatives have their feet oiled, rubbed and washed by the boy's father's companions. The girl's father and his companions, thus honoured, salute every one present. Then the girl's father stands up and declares, "Listen ye (bear witness), from this day I have made over my daughter to *Kūṭūmb bandhūs* (these relatives). What her lot may turn out to be, neither does she know nor do I. Now she is hale and hearty, later she may become blind, lame or halt; who knows? Listen ye all present, I have made over my girl to him." All present reply in chorus, " We Pañches have heard it (i. e. ,we stand witness to it)."

More pots of rice-beer and meat of the fowl supposed to have been purchased with the copper coins paid by the boy's father to the man who washed his legs are brought out and distributed to all parents.

The next morning the boy's father and his companions and the girl's father with one or two companions of his start together for the boy's village. While about to start, some boys and girls of the bride's side manage to besmear the clothes of the bridegroom's father or guardian and his companions with turmeric powder as a token of their having been duly entertained by the bride's people.

On their arrival at the boy's house, the girl's father and his companions are received with the usual ceremony of feet-washing, *etc*. Then they take their seats on mats spread out for them in the *āngan* or court-yard. The bride's father brings with him the *jūng-jūng-ḍāe ḍhebūā* or *durāng paisā* as also the stick left at his place by the boy's father on the day of *Māngni*. He now returns the money and the stick. This is known as '*Ḍāṇḍā-oyeng*' (returning the stick). Then they are treated to a feast. They spend that night in the girl's village. The betrothal ceremony is thus completed.

Among the Ḍhelki Khāṛiās, it may take some more time,—even a year or more,—before the actual wedding is celebrated. Among the Dūdh Khāṛiās it is usually celebrated much sooner.

(iv) Ceremonial Presents of cloth (Chhīṛā obsūinā).

Ḍhelki Khāṛia Custom.

Among the Ḍhelki Khāṛiās in particular the betrothal, in some cases, takes place when the boy and the girl are quite young, and in such cases the actual marriage takes place several years afterwards. But in such a case, the boy's people take care to see that the incipient relationship between the families grow more and more intimate as time passes, and may not flag for want of nursing during the intervening years. So, every year, on the day before the annual ceremonial eating of the new rice (*ñyōḍem ñyōnā*) at the boy's house, the boy's mother with a female companion goes to the girl's father's house to bring the girl to her place. On their arrival at the girl's father's house, the boy's mother and her companions are honoured with the customary anointing and washing of their feet, and after the customary salutations they are seated on mats spread out for them. Then the girl's mother enquires what gives them the pleasure of their visit. The boy's mother replies,– "We have come to take our future daughter-in-law to our place. To-morrow we shall celebrate the *ñyōḍem ñyōnā* (eating of the new rice)". Unless the girl's people have changed their minds, consent is given as a matter of course. If, however, they have changed their minds (which rarely happens) the consent is withheld on the pretext of heavy work at home. If consent is obtained, on the following morning the girl with another girl as her companion accompanies the boy's mother to her future husband's house. On arrival, the boy's mother affectionately rubs oil over the girl's leg and washes them. When all are seated to dinner, the boy's mother places a new *sāṛi*-cloth over the girl's shoulders. The girl stays in the house of her future husband for a week or so. But she is not allowed to mix with her future husband. The omission of the annual present of cloth in any year is regarded as a legitimate ground for breaking off the marriage negotiations.

Now-a-days, in most places, as we found particularly among the Ḍhelkis of the Gangpur State, this custom is falling into disuse, for marriages now generally take place within one year or so and in some cases even within a couple of months, after betrothal.

Dūdh Khāṛiā Custom. Among the Dūdh Khāṛiās, the returning of the stick (*Ḍānḍā oyeng*) is treated as a separate ceremony which is held a little later. After about a month or so, the bride's father with three or four companions starts for the bridegroom's house. They take with them as presents for the boy's people twenty-four pots (but now-a-days often only twelve pots) of rice-beer. They also carry a gourd filled with rice-beer which they themselves drink on reaching the boundary of the village, reserving a little for the boy's parents. When they reach the boy's house, they are welcomed as honoured guests and their feet are washed and they are given powdered tobacco and lime to chew and rice-beer to drink. Before cock-crow another party of ten or twelve men (called *mojhimki* or *mojhituriā*) start from the bride's house. Some of them carry axes in their hands. As they proceed towards the boy's house singing songs, they cut with their axes small notches on prominent trees on the way. This is said to be done in order that the girl after marriage may, if need be, find out the way by which to return to her father's house by following these marks. They also go on marking omens. When they reach the boy's house they are welcomed with the customary ceremonial rules of hospitality (oiling and washing the feet, *etc*.)

Later on the same day, a third party consisting of four, five or more men (who are called "*Lōḍhōālebu*") also start from the bride's house for the bridegroom's place on what is called *Baṛkā-gōtiā* (the big relationship) visit. When they reach the house of the boy's father they, too, are received and honoured according to the customary rules. A castrated goat is slain for them and they are entertained with plenty of rice-beer. They are not treated to dinner but are given sufficient uncooked rice, pulse, vegetables, *etc.*, besides cooking vessels and all other requisites for peparing their own meals. They cook their food for themselves and eat. In some villages, however, now-a-days, meals are prepared for them and they are treated to a feast. The whole night is spent in drinking, singing and merry-making.

(v) **Settling the Bride-price** (*Gining tāng*).

Dūdh Khāṛiā Custom.

Among the Dūdh Khāṛiās, as soon as the *Baṛkā gōtiā* party arrive and before they are given provisions for cooking their meals, the bride-price is settled after a pretended show of bargaining, although the bride-price has been already actually settled through negotiations between the *dānḍiās* or intermediaries of the two sides. The mock bargaining is conducted in the following manner. Five or six men of the boy's party form one group and a similar number of men of the girl's party form another group. The former go to some open field (*ānkāl*) outside the compound and the latter remain inside the boy's house. The former presonate "he-goats" and the latter "she-goats" and bleat in the fashion of goats,—the former imitating the cry "bā'-bā", the latter "mā'-mā"!

Then two of the she-goats' party take a leaf-cup containing twelve pairs of clods of earth (to represent cows) to the other party thereby implying that twelve yokes of cattle are demanded as bride-price. To make the semblance of goats more complete, one of the two men personates a goat-herd and carries a goad with which he pokes his companion walking in front of him representing a 'she-goat'. Then a member of the other party takes out all the clods except two and hands back the leaf-cup to the she-goats. This implies that they are willing to give only one yoke of cattle. The "she-goats"-party now again bring up the leaf-cup with six pairs of clods in it.

The "he-goats" now take out all the clods except two pairs and return the leaf-cup to the "she-goats" Then, on the third occasion, the "he-goats" must indicate the actual number of cattle (already settled) by returning an equivalent number of clods.

Then the bride-groom's party bring out a number of pots of rice-beer and all drink and rejoice.

The orthodox customary bride-price is five heads of cattle. But now-a-days there are very few who can afford to give so much. Therefore a rupee in cash is now regarded as equivalent to one head of cattle. But generally, in practice, few guardians of Khāṛiā maidens would agree to accept a bride-price of anything less than two heads of cattle and three rupees in cash. In addition to this, a *sāṛi* cloth (10 to 14 cubits long) called *māi-sāṛi* is given to the girl's mother.

Next morning, pots of rice-beer and a hind-leg of the castrated goat are given to the guests as provision for their journey; their clothes are besmeared with turmeric diluted in water, and they are given a hearty send-off.

A date is fixed, not later than one month from this settlement of the *Gining-tāng* or bride-price, for payment of the same.

Ḍhelki Khāṛiā Custom.

Among the Ḍhelki Khāṛiās, the ceremony of settling the bride-price (*gining tāng*) is not carried on by bargaining with a mock show of goats. When the boy and girl are considered to have attained marriageable age, and there has in the meanwhile been no hitch in the relations between the two families, the amount of the bride-price is formally settled. With the Ḍhelki Khāṛias, too, the orthodox customary bride-price is five heads of bullocks. But, as among the Dūdh section, one silver rupee is now regarded by convention among the Ḍhelkis, too, to be equivalent to one head of bullock. In actual practice few guardians of Ḍhelki Khāṛiā maids would agree to accept a lower bride-price than two heads of bullock and three rupees. For the payment of the bride-price, a day, generally not later than a month, is appointed according to mutual convenience.

(vi) Payment of the bride-price and Fixing the date of Marriage.

On the appointed day, a few relatives and tribe-fellows come to the boy's house, drink rice-beer and then accompany the boy's father or other guardian to the girl's father's house with the bride-price (*gining tāng*, called in local Hindi, *sūk mūl* or *sūkmūṛ*) as settled before.

On arrival at the girl's house the party enter the house carrying the cash and cloth but leaving the bullocks outside in charge of one of themselves. After the party have been duly received with the customary salutations and formalities, and served with powdered tobacco and lime, the boy's father or other guardian notifies that the bride-price has been brought, and invites the bride's people to inspect and accept the same. The girl's father or guardian and relatives go out to inspect the bullocks, and their approval is signified by the girl's father placing his hand on the back and tail of each of the cattle.

Among the Ḍhelki Khāṛias of Gangpur it is the *Mūṛū* (man of the *Mūṛū* clan who presides over the ceremonies as the social head) of the bride's side who expresses the approval or disapproval of the bride's people. Should any of the cattle happen to be not to the liking of the girl's father, the boy's father promises to replace it before the wedding ; and this must be done.

Then both parties take their seats and the boy's father hands over the stipulated money to his *ḍāṇḍiā* who, in his turn, hands it over to the *ḍāṇḍiā* of the other party, and the latter makes it over to the girl's father. Similarly, the *sāṛi*-cloth is given, and the women of the bride's family inspect it and finally accept it. Among the Ḍhelki Khāṛiās of Gangpur, however, the *māi sāṛi* is not always given.

When the bride-price has been accepted, the guests' feet are rubbed, oiled and washed as usual. The man who does this receives one *anna* in cash which is supposed to cover the price of a fowl. Then they are regaled with rice-beer and fowl's meat. Finally, a date is fixed for the marriage. This date must be sometime in the month of Māgh, but now-a-days the month of Phālgūn may also be chosen; and the day fixed must be ordinarily either a Monday or a Friday or a Wednesday.

The next morning, the boy's party depart and return to the boy's house where a jar of rice-beer is brought out for them and, after a hearty dinner, the relatives who accompanied the boy's father return to their respective homes, and the parents of the bridegroom set about making preparations for the forthcoming wedding.

(vii) Preliminaries of the Wedding Ceremony

The Khāṛiās have no word for marriage in their own language but they have words for husband (*Kenḍōr*) and wife (*Kāñṛāe or Sauṛāe*), as they have for other relations by marriage.

The month of Māgh (January-February), after harvesting is over, is the orthodox season for a Khāṛiā wedding. But, as noticed above, now-a-days many marriages are celebrated in the first half of Phālgūn (February-March). Unlike the present practice among most other Mūṇḍā-speaking tribes, a wedding amongst the Khāṛiās, as a rule, takes place in the bridegroom's house in his own village, where the bride is brought on the eve of the wedding day. But among the Hill-Khāṛiās of Mānbhūm and Dhalbhūm, as we have seen, the wedding takes place (as among most Hindu castes) in the bride's house in her village; and the bridegroom with his party goes there on the evening of the marriage.

The Wedding Booth:— For the wedding, the court-yards of the houses of both the bridegroom and the bride are cleaned with cowdung and water. A marriage booth or mud platform with four posts at the four corners supporting a thatch made of either tree-leaves or thatching-grass is set up in the middle of the courtyard.

At the bridegroom's place this 'Māṛoā', as the marriage booth is called, is further provided with a "*chhāmṛā khūñṭō*" or decorated central post of *mahūa* or *muṛūn* timber plastered over with mud and cowdung and decorated with "*kāyār ulā kēkē*" which is a string to which mango leaves are fastened at intervals of about one foot or more. This string of auspicious mango leaves passes round the four posts, encircling the *māṛoā* like a garland. The mango tree, it may be noted, is an emblem of fertility and its leaves are used by the Hindus in all auspicious ceremonies. Among the Ḍhelki Khāṛiās of Gāngpur, the *maṛoā* is supported on eight posts besides the *chhamṛā khūñṭō* or central post which is of *murun* (*bassia latifolia*). Of the other eight posts one must be of *beeja* wood and the other seven of *śāl* (*shorea robusta*) wood. The posts are arranged in three rows of three in each row, including the central post.

By about mid-day, when the invited tribe-fellows and relatives have arrived at the bridegroom's place, one of the party, who knows the art, is requested to draw the customary symbolical wedding designs round the *chhāmṛā khūñṭō* with rice flower and red earth. The designs are in the form of zigzag cross-lines in red and white, forming a square round the *chhāmṛā-khūñṭō*. This man receives for his pains a small pot of rice-beer to which he does justice in company with some friends. The Ḍhelkis of Gāngpur generally omit these drawings. Among the Hill Khāṛiās, as we have

49. Dūdh Khāṛiā youth (Prem Prakāsh Kerkeṭṭa) at College.

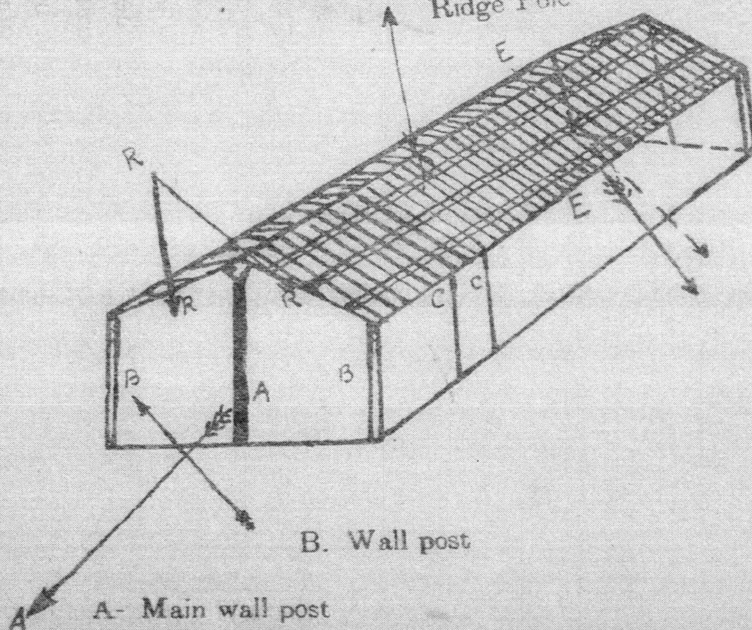

50. Framework of a respectable Khāṛiā Hut.

(To face p. 257)

seen, neither is a *Chhāmḍā-khūnṭō* or *Chawrā-khuñṭā* erected, nor any designs drawn.

Among the Dūdh and Ḍhelki sections, before the bridal party starts, bride and bridegroom are each made to sit in their respective houses on a low wooden stool or plank (*sōkṛōm* or *soṛkōm*) by the side of the *māṛōā*, but not over it, and a few women besmear their limbs with oil and pounded turmeric. In the bride's house, a few young women lift up the *sōṛkōm* (wooden seat) with the bride sitting on it, and dance about carrying the bride seven times (in Gāngpur either five or seven times) round the *māṛōā*, just as the Hill Khāṛiās do with the bridegroom before he is carried in procession to the bride's house for the wedding.

The *Ḍāṇḍīā* of the boy's side comes to the girl's house to invite the girl's people to their village with the bride. Before the bride's party (consisting of both men and women) start, the *dāṇḍiās* of both sides are sent in advance to convey the news of their approach to the bridegroom's place. The bride's *ḍāṇḍiā* takes with him two pots of rice-beer for the bridegroom's parents and relatives. He is received with the customary ceremony of smearing oil on his legs and feet and washing them. The rice-beer brought by the *Ḍāṇḍiā* is now drunk by some elders (*siāns*) of the bridegroom's party and by the two *Ḍāṇḍiās* themselves. Among the Ḍhelkis of the Gāngpur State, no rice-beer is brought from the bride's house. The *Dāṇḍiā* is also called *Āguā* or *Ānjorkāṛ*.

(viii) The Bridal Procession and its Reception.

In the meanwhile, the bride's party (consisting of

men and women) start for the bridegroom's village with music and dance. The bride decked with ornaments and in new clothes is carried weeping in the arms of other women up to the boundary of her village. Then she goes on foot, but is carried in arms again when crossing a stream or pool, so that she may avoid any harm from the *Dārhā* spirit of the place.

When, by evening, the bridal party reach the boundary of the bridegroom's village, they are met by their own *ḍāṇḍiā* or *āguā* and that of the boy's side. The Dāṇḍiās conduct them to the place assigned for their residence, generally underneath a *pōrā-māchā* or raised wooden platform for keeping straw (*pōrā*) or under some shady tree. They are given powdered tobacco and lime to chew and plenty of rice-beer to drink, and their legs and feet are ceremonially anointed and washed. The bride's party are not treated to ready-made meals that night but they are provided with provisions and utensils, fuel and other requisites to cook their own meals and one or more jars of rice-beer and one or more jars of drinking-water, according to the number of the party. By the time that the bride's party have prepared their meals, the bridegroom's party with the bridegroom in the middle go in procession with drums and other music to escort them to the bride-groom's place. The respective fathers of the bride and bridegroom embrace (*mergherāi*) each other, and all the other men and women of each party salute those of the other party. They all go in procession to the bridegroom's house, dancing and singing, and two women, one of each party, carrying each on her head a benedictory earthen jug (*kāñṛsā bhāṇḍā*) [74] filled with water and painted on the outside with white rice-flour and adorned with plaited wreaths of ears of paddy wound round its neck and covered up at its mouth with a hollow saucer containing a quantity of *māsō* (*Phaseolus Roxburghii*) and a little oil and having lighted wicks sticking out of it. The two women carrying these earthenware jugs (*Kāñṛsā-bhāṇḍā*) dance with the rest. Indeed theirs is the most important function in the procession as the *Kāñṛsā-bhāṇḍā* with the ears of paddy are calculated to bring luck to the couple. A few old women also carry little leafy twigs of the fruitful mango, also regarded as auspicious. Arrived at the house, the bride and bridegroom are conducted inside the house for certain ceremonies, and the others are seated on mats in the *Kinbhār* (*āngan*) and treated to two pots of rice-beer. Among the Dūdh Khāṛāis, in some places, the girl's mother, too, carries on her head a new bamboo-basket containing some paddy and other grains, and a jug of water with mango-twigs jutting out of it and covered up with an earthen-ware saucer with oil in it and lighted wicks.

(ix) The Oil-Test.

The bride and bridegroom who have been conducted inside the house are seated side by side on a palm-leaf mat. Among the Ḍhelki Khāṛiās, The *Muru* of the bridegroom's party now rubs sesame (*til*) oil on the boy's head and combs his hair, and with one

74. The use of the benedictory *Kāñṛsā-bhāṇḍā* (*Mangal-ghaṭ*) or luck-giving earthen pot appears to be a Hindu custom borrowed by many agricultural tribes such as the Mūṇḍās, the Orāons, the Santāls, the Hōs, the Khāṛiās, etc. from the Hindus.

hand holds a tuft of his long hair in the front and places it across his face and along his nose so as to reach down below the tip of the nose, and with the other hand holds a mango-leaf curved in the form of a small cup with some sesame oil in it, and pours the oil down this tuft of hair to see whether the oil flows almost in a straight line along the hair downwards or gets spilled or scattered. If the oil flows straight down, it is believed to augur well for the future happiness and prosperity of the couple, but if the oil gets scattered and spilt it is believed to bode ill ; and the test is repeated till the oil flows in the desired direction. The *Muru* of the girl's party similarly oils and combs the girl's hair, and holding a tuft of her front hair along her nose downwards pours sesame oil on it for a similar prognostication. Then the *Muru* of the bride's side takes hold of the bridegroom's right little finger and dips it into a *Sindūr kiā* or wooden receptacle for holding vermilion, and with the finger thus besmeared with *sindūr* makes the groom put a *sindūr* mark on the bride's forehead. Then the boy's *Muru* similarly holds the bride's right little finger, dips it in *sindūr* and makes the bride put *sindūr* marks on the bridegroom's chest. Then the bride's *Muru* makes the bridegroom drink from a leaf-cup a little rice-beer (taken out of one of the pots of rice-beer brought by the bridegroom's party) and makes the bride drink the residue of the rice-beer left in the cup after the bridegroom has drunk out of it. In some places, the bridegroom's mother or elder brother's wife, and not the "*Muru*", oils and combs the hair of both bride and bridegroom and makes the oil-test described above. When the tuft of hiar is drawn over the nose, the bride or bridegroom, as the case may be, has just to touch the ends of the tuft with the teeth. Then they are taken to the *āngan* or open space where the young men and women of both the parties are dancing and singing and playing music; and bride and bridegroom join the dancers of their respective parties. Dancing and singing and drinking go on till a very late hour, often till the smaller hours of the morning. That night the bride sleeps in the quarters of her party and the bridegroom in his own house.

Among the Dūdh Khāṛiās, the oil test is applied on the following morning during the wedding proper.

X. Circum-ambulation of the Māṛoā.

On the following morning at cock-crow, the bride and the bridegroom duly dressed and decorated, are carried on the arms and seated, side by side, on a mat by the side of the māṛōā. By this time two maidens, one of each party and not belonging to the same clan (*gotra*) as that of either the bride or the bridegroom, (but who, among the Ḍhelkis, must be of the *Muru* clan) bring each a ceremonial *Kāñṛsā-bhāṇḍā* or benedictory water-jar described above. Then the *Ḍheṇḍā* or boy selected to be the bridegroom's companion or 'best man', takes up the bridegoom on his hip, and the *Ḍheṇḍī* or girl-companion of the bride similarly takes up the bride on her hip, and all dance round the *māṛōā* seven times. The girls carrying the *Kāñṛsā-bhāṇḍā* also join the dance.

XI. The Wedding.

After the dance is over, the bride and bridegroom are again conducted to the *Chhāmḍā Khuṇṭō* or central post of the marriage-booth and seated side by side upon a mat with their faces to the east, just as the Hill Khāṛiā couple are seated near the *badhi* at the centre of the māṛōā. Among both the Dūdh and the Ḍhelki Khāṛiās, the *māṛōā*, with the bride and bridegroom and the two officiants inside it, is surrounded with a cloth screen held up by the hands by a few men. A few others then whirl swords and axes round the *māṛōā* out-side the screen. The object of brandishing weapons is to ward off evil spirits and the evil eye.

Now, among the Dūdh Khāṛiās, one of the officiants first parts the hair over the forehead of the bride and that of the bridegroom with a mango leaf. The other officiant pours sesame oil from a cup over the parted hair on the line of the parting, and all mark the direction in which the oil trickles down. Should it trickle down towards the middle of the chest, then it is believed to portend happiness and prosperity to the couple; but if it takes any other direction then the marriage, it is apprehended, may prove unhappy: either of the two may die or there may be a separation. So the test is repeated till the oil trickles down to the chest. The oil used must be extracted from sesamum seeds by unmarried young men and maidens. Then two maidens, one from the bridegroom's party and another from the bride's side, go each with a new earthen pitcher (*rō'ḍā bhāṇḍā*) to a neighbouring stream or spring along with other girls, and fill them with water, and, carrying the pitchers on their heads, stand by the side of the *māṛōā*.

A curry-stone (*pāṭ-sōr*), a bundle of thatching grass (*ōlōng*) and a yoke (*rōdkōng*) are arranged in a row on the *māṛōā*, one beside the other and touching each other.

Then the bride stands, facing the rising sun (east), over the curry-stone and touching the grass bundles (*ōlōng*) with her heels; and the bridegroom stands over the yoke behind her, also facing east, and touching the bride's heels with his toes. The officiants presiding over the marriage must be of clans other than those of either the bride or the bridegroom ; and the maternal uncle (mother's brother) of the bride and that of the bridegroom should preferably be the officiants. Among the Ḍhelkis they should preferably belong to the *Muru* clan and in no case should they be of either the *Tōpnō* or of the *Mail* clan. One of the officiants holds the bridegroom's left little finger, dips it in vermilion taken from the boy's house, and with it makes the bridegroom mark the bride's forehead with a red dot, and mark the parting of her hair with a red line. The other officiant similarly makes the bride, with her left little finger, put a round red mark on the bridegroom's chest, with vermilion brought from her parents' house.

Then among the Dhelki Khāṛiās, each of the officiants holds in his arm one of the water-filled new pitchers (*rō'ḍā-bhāṇḍā*) but among some Jāshpur Ḍhelkis, holds the Kāñṛsā-bhāṇḍā of his party. Then the officiant of the bridegroom's side first empties the water of his pitcher (*bhāṇḍā*) over the couple's head, and then the other officiant pours the water of the pitcher of his side over the couple's head. Among the Dūdh Khāṛiās, it is the Pañches who sprinkle with mango-twigs the *ro-ḍā* or water from the two pitchers all around with shouts of "*Hari-bōl*" (Glory to Hari or God).

Finally all present shout "Hari-bōl" in chorus. In many instances this devout Hindu exclamation is mispronounced by the Khāṛiās, particularly by many Ḍhelki Khāṛiās, as "*Hāl-bair,*" perhaps on the supposition that it stands for 'Hār-bail' or 'plough and plough-cattle'! In fact, among the Dūdh Khāṛiās, after the anointing of vermilion, this sanctifying water (*ro-ḍā*) from the two pitchers is sprinkled all around with mango-twigs dipped in the water, when the Pañches shout "Hari-bōl". This shout of "Haribōl", like the Khāṛiā's use of the *Kāñṛsā-bhāṇḍā* and certain other marriage-rites of the Khāṛiās and other agricultural Mūṇḍā tribes, must have been borrowed long ago from Hindu Vaiṣnavs. The allied tribe of Birhōṛs also give lusty shouts of 'Haribōl' while bride and bridegroom put vermilion marks on each other's head.

The bridegroom now holds the bride by the waist and lifts her off the '*ōlōng*' (straw) and '*silouṭ*' (grind-stone) over which she was standing, and puts her down on the ground, and himself gets down from the yoke. Then the bridegroom retires, leaving the bride with her companions. After a short time he returns and takes out the string of mango leaves from the *māṛōā* and thows it into a tank or stream while bathing. But among the Gāngpur Ḍhelkis one of the officiants and not the groom removes it and throws it away in a stream. The couple with a party of young men and women go to a tank or stream to bathe. There the boys take their bath in one part of the tank or the stream and the girls in another.

When they return after bath, the couple are made to stand on a mat near the *māṛōā.* Then the village headman sacrifices a male white cock to Pōnomōsor or Dharam, and, taking a few drops of the sacrificial fowl on a leaf-cup containing powdered turmeric diluted in water, makes the couple drink this sanctifying mixture. This is believed to absolve them from all past 'sins', and incorporate the bride into the bridegroom's clan. This is the orthodox custom, but it is in some cases omitted, particularly among the Dūdh section and among the Ḍhelkis of Gāngpur.

Then some near female relative of the boy (usually the *āji* or elder brother's wife) steps forward with a little vermilion and oil and, standing behind the couple, oils and combs first the bride-groom's hair and then the bride's. She goes round each of the other young men and women present and besmears a little oil on the forehead of each. She then goes back to the newly-married couple, anoints them with vermilion in the same way as the *siān* did. Finally with a reed, besmeared with vermilion at one end, she marks the bride's forehead at the parting of her hair and then the forehead of all the young married women present.

One of the village-elders or *siāns* of the bride's party now addresses the bridegroom thus:—"We make over this girl to thee. She now belongs to thee and not to us. Examine her now and see if she is lame or blind. Do not turn up later and accuse us of having thrust her upon thee. Should any harm come to her by accident, do not give her up or neglect her, but do thou ever support and look after her. Share with her whatever thou gettest. Live in love and peace."

He next addresses the bride with exhortations like the following:—"Live in peace with thy wedded husband. Work with a will and eat with relish. When guests come to thy house, accord to them due honour and offer them water and tobacco".

Then the couple go round and salute every one present.

The guests are then invited to dinner. One or more goats are killed for the feast. At the dinner the bride and bridegroom are seated side by side in the middle, their respective *Ḍhenḍiās* sitting by their side. The bridegroom is made to put some rice from his own plate on the bride's, and the bride does not begin to eat unless some suitable present is promised. The bride's desire for presents is expressed by her *Ḍhenḍiā* and the bridegroom's promise is conveyed by the bridegroom through his *Ḍhenḍiā*. Jests and jokes go round galore and enliven the dinner party.

Taking some rest after dinner, the bridal party take leave in the afternoon. Before their departure the bride's father or other guardian formally makes over the bride to the bridegroom's parents, saying—"Should you ever feel that our child is not wanted in your house, do, please, bring her back to us".

When the bridal party takes leave, the bride laments is some such words as the following "Oh, my father! Oh, my mother! take me with you. Where do you leave me?" The parents of the bridegroom console her, saying, "It is to your own house that you have come;- do not cry, child, you will live here quite happily". That night the couple do not sleep together. The bride sleeps with her mother-in-law and other female relatives.

As we have seen, some of the above ceremonies are not observed by the Hill Khāṛiās, and, even in the Dūdh and Ḍhelki sections, except in the essential rites, there are local variations and differences and additions or omissions in the minor rites. It is interesting to note that the Ḍhelki section has a more elaborate ritual and appears to retain more of the ancient customs than the more progressive Dūdh section.

XII. Lauri or Kādomāṭi.

On the second day following the marriage, the couple go to take their bath in the village tank or spring accompanied by a number of girls, just as the Hill Khāṛiā couple do on the morning following the arrival of the bride at the bridegroom's place. There the girls break up in two groups, one forming the bride's group and the other the bridegroom's group; and then a small earthenware or brass jug is concealed in the tank or spring by the bridegroom and this is sought out by the girls of the bride's party. Similarly, the bride next conceals it and the girls of the groom's party try to find it out. The process is repeated seven times, and jest and jokes go on all the time, particularly at each failure [75].

Then the bride fills a new pitcher with water and carries it on her head to her husband's house, and the bridegroom follows her with his party. She then cooks rice in an earthen vessel with the water she has brought. The bridegroom then offers the food thus cooked by her newly-wedded wife, together with rice-beer, to his ancestor-spirits.

Then relatives and follow-tribesman are treated to a dinner. This completes the festivities. The *ḍāṇḍiās* get each a new cloth from the party which each repre-

75. Compare the similar practice among the Mūṇḍās. *Vide "The Mūṇḍās and their Country"*, p. 450.

sents. Except in well-to-do Khāṛia families who own commodious houses, a new hut is generally erected for the newly-married couple to live in.

From the day of their marriage, Khāṛiās of both sexes have to observe certain taboos with regard to food and drink. They will no more eat cooked food touched by persons of other castes and tribes.

A Khāṛiā girl after her marriage must no more enter her parents' cattle-shed.

Eight or nine days after the wedding, the bride's people come to take the bride and bridegroom for a visit to their place. The bride-groom goes with one or two companions and the bride. They take with them as presents for the bride's people some cakes made of rice-flour fried in oil. On their arrival their feet and legs are washed, and the mother-in-law of the boy takes him inside the house and enquires about the health of his people and so forth. When meals are served, the son-in-law sits still and does not begin eating. This is an indication that until some presents of value are promised he will not touch the food. This affords an occasion for the younger sisters and cousins of the bride to make fun of their new brother-in-law. They chaff him and crack many a joke, and at length one of his younger sisters-in-law brings either a little cow-dung or a little buffalo-dung, as if to serve it on his plate. Then he begins eating his meal, as the offer of the dung signifies that either a cow or a buffalo will be presented to him. It is only after the bridegroom takes the first morsel of food that his companions begin eating. After a stay of about a week, the couple with their companions return home.

2. Ūḍrā-Ūḍri Chōlki, or Kolḍung Yārō.

The 'Āsli Bihā' or regular marriage described above bears on the face of it unmistakable marks of several elements having been borrowed from the Hindus with such modifications as suited the lower culture of the Khāṛiās. The very name 'Bihā' or 'Asli Bihā' has been borrowed. Besides this, there are other forms of Khāṛiā marriage. These forms of union, at least three in number, are, however, now gradually falling into disuse. These are known respectively as—(1) *Ūḍrā Ūḍri Chōlki*, which is an elopment marriage; (2) *Sūndrom Tāppā* or *Sūndrom Lāhki* which is a faint echo of Capture marriage, being a marriage by forcible application of vermilion to the forehead of a desired bride; and (3) *Ḍhūkū Chōlki*, which is an 'intrusion-marriage' the reverse of a 'capture marriage'.

In the '*Ūḍrā Ūḍri*' form of marriage, when a young man and young woman fall in love with each other, and apprehend any difficulty to their union, the boy gets hold of the girl at a market or a dancing-meet (*kūḍhing*), generally by preconcert. A show of resistance is made by the girl, and the boy's friends are at hand to help him, in case there should be any resistance from the girl's people. They elope, and live in hiding as husband and wife for a few days. Their relatives generally make a search for them. When they are found and brought home, if the parents of the boy are fairly well-off, a bride-price of five or six bullocks or their price estimated according to customary convention has to be paid. Vermilion is then formally applied to each by the other, and a feast given to tribe-fellows according to the means of the boy's family. The Khāṛiās call this form of marriage by the name of *Kolḍūng yārō*.

3. Sūndrōm Tāppā, or Sūndrom Lāhki.

Another form of marriage is by forcible, or rather unauthorised, application of vermilion by a young man on the forehead of the girl of her choice. The girl is generally a consenting party. This form of taking a wife is ordinarily resorted to when the guardians of the boy or of the girl or of both, and even in rare instances the girl herself, are not agreeable to the union. The application of vermilion is regarded as tantamount to marriage, and if for any reason the boy cannot secure possession of the girl, the girl cannot take another husband except by an union in the *Bandāi* or *Sāgāi* form prescribed for the remarriage of a widow. On such forcible application of vermilion, the boy is generally severely beaten. A Pañch or council of village-elders is convened on a date notified beforehead, and the Pañch generally authorise the father or guardian of the girl to bring from the boy's house five or six head of cattle by way of bride-price. The boy's people are also required to give a feast or rather two feasts (generally on two successive days) to the girl's people and to the Pañches and others. The Ḍhelki Khāṛiās call this form of union *Sūndrōm Lāhki*, and the Dūdh Khāṛiās *Sūndrōm Tāppā*.

4. Ḍhuku Cholki (*Dūdh*) or Ḍhukụ Ḍiārki (*Ḍhelki*).

In this form of marriage, which may be called 'Intrusion marriage', it is the woman and not the man who takes the initiative. And it may be resorted to by a widow as well as by a maiden. In fact, more often it is a widow rather than a maiden who has recourse to this method of securing a husband. The woman takes a pot of rice-beer or a basket of the corolla of the *mūrūn* or *mahuā* (*Bassia latifolia*) flowers on her head and enters the house of the man she loves and establishes herself there, unmindful of all remonstrance and even sometimes persecution. After a day or two, often from the very beginning, the man and his people are reconciled to the intrusion and she is kindly treated. If she is a widow, the question of bride-price does not arise. If she is a maiden, although her people are not by custom entitled to bride-price, the people of her chosen husband generally pay it in order to establish friendly terms between themselves and the people of the bride. It is popularly believed that the woman is attracted to the man by some secret spell or some drug indirectly administered. The bridegroom and his people arrange a feast where the bride's people and the village Pañches and other tribe-fellows are invited, and vermilion is anointed on the bride's forehead, and the couple are then formally recognised as lawful husband and wife. The Dūdh's term for this form of marriage is *Ḍhūkū Chōlki*, and the Ḍhelkis call it *Ḍhūkū Ḍiārki*. For a valid marriage the parties must belong to different clans.

5. Sāgāi or Widow-Marriage.

The Khāṛiās, like other Mūṇḍā tribes, permit the re-marriage of widows. Generally it is a widower who marries a widow. But even a bachelor sometimes, though comparatively rarely, takes a widow for his wife. In such a marriage the wishes of the woman are consulted. A widow desiring to remarry, generally goes after her husband's death, to live with her parents if they are alive.

When the widowed bridegroom secures, generally through a go-between, the widow's consent to the marriage, he goes to the widow's place with one or two relatives to propose. After they are received with the customary formalities of washing the legs and feet, and given tobacco and lime to chew, the '*siāns*' or elders of the settlement assemble and the woman is called before them. She stands in front of the men, but a little apart. The *Siāns* then address the man, saying,-"Look at her, and say whether you would have her for your *Sāgāhi* wife." He replies in the affirmative, saying, "I would not have come here to-day if I did not desire to take her to wife and was encouraged in the preliminary negotiations". Then the *siāns* enquire of the woman what her wishes are. If she declines to marry, the visitors forthwith withdraw. If, however, she signifies her consent, a jar of rice-beer, if available, is brought out; and all drink, and a date is fixed for the marriage. Although the marriage in such a case is celebrated in the bride's place, the expenses of a feast are borne by the bridegroom. On the appointed day, the bridegroom accompanied by a few relatives and tribe-fellows arrive at the bride's house before sunset. They bring with them a jar of rice-beer, a he-goat, some rice, pulses, turmeric and other condiments, a *sāṛi* cloth, and either a bullock, or if the man cannot afford it, a rupee in cash as bride-price. The bride-price is paid only if the woman has been dependent upon her parents or brothers or some other relatives.

Arrived at the bride's house, and after the customary formalities of welcome, a *siān* or village elder of the man's side makes over to the bride's people the bullock, if any, or the rupee meant for bride-price, and the rice and other things brought by the bridegroom. A dinner, prepared with the articles brought by the bridegroom, concludes the proceedings for that night. Early next morning, the man hands over the *sāṛi* cloth to the bride who takes it inside, puts it on and then comes out again for the *sāgāi* ceremony. The couple sit down on one and the same mat, the bride to the right of the bridegroom, and both with their faces towards the Sun. The man's mother or elder brother's wife smears oil over his head and combs his hair. She next smears oil over the bride's head and combs her hair, and then sprinkles a little oil on the head of every woman present. She finally smears the parting of the bride's hair with vermilion. Then a *Siān* belonging to a totemic clan different from that of either of the couple, takes hold of the man's right little finger and lightly dips it in a small receptacle containing vermilion, guides the finger so smeared to the bride's forehead which is thus marked with vermilion. The bride is similarly made to put a vermilion mark on the bridegroom's chest.

Finally, the *Siān* addresses the couple as follows. To the bridegroom he says,—"From this day this woman is your *sāgāhi* wife. Take proper care of her, maintain her with your earnings, do not neglect her or abandon her".

To the bride he says,—"From to-day he is your *Sāgāhi* husband. Even if he should abuse you or beat you, do not run away. From this day regard his house as yours". After a drink of rice-beer, the bridegroom's party with the newly married couple start for the bridegroom's place. One or two relatives of the bride accompany them.

Arrived at their destination, the newly married couple undergo a ceremonial purification, by each drinking a sanctifying potion made of a few drops of blood of a white cock sacrificed to *Giṛing* or the Sun-God, mixed with pounded turmeric and water.

Monogamy is the rule among the Khāṛiās of all sections. The marrying of a second wife during the life-time of the first, though permitted, is rare and is looked down upon. The same ceremonies as in a regular marriage are gone through if the second wife is a maiden, and the same ceremonies as in '*sāgāi*' if she is a widow.

Such are the different forms of marriage sanctioned by Khāṛiā tribal custom. As we said above, the *Āsli Bihā* or "real marriage" which is now the regular form of marriage bears evidence of extensive borrowing from the Hindus. But, as already noticed, it is not entirely a borrowed form. In fact, it is the Khāṛiā's tribal custom of "marriage by purchase" overlaid with features borrowed from Hindus with whom the Khāṛiās have been in contact for long centuries. The simple marriage by payment of a customary bride-price appears to have been the most popular form of marriage with the average Khāṛiā as far back as can be traced. But the other forms of marriage,—those by a simultation of capture or by the forcible application of vermilion or by "intrusion" on the part of the woman,–have always been recognised and sanctioned by tribal custom, though not now regarded with as much favour nor considered as decent and honourable as *Āsli Bihā*. But such marriages, too, have their counterparts in the forms of marriage in vogue among most of the Mūṇḍā tribes. [76]

III. Pregnancy Rites (Dōrhō-jo-ḍōm).

When a woman is in the family way for the first time and also when a woman gets still-born children or loses successive children in infancy, the *Dōrhō-jō-ḍōm* ceremony has to be performed. The term *Dōrhō-jō-ḍōm* means expelling the Dōrhō or Dārhā spirit, from the woman. This must be done at the first pregnancy.

When a Khāṛiā woman shows signs of pregnancy for the first time, information is sent to her parents, and two men come from the woman's parents' house to take her there in company with her husband and one or more male and female relatives of the latter. When they reach the woman's parents' house they are provided with a jar of rice-beer. Then the exorciser (*māti*) of the wife's side winds round the neck of the pregnant woman and also of her husband wreaths made of bits of *putri* root stringed together on unbleached thread, and also a worn-out broom and a *binḍā* or head-pad used for carrying a water-vessel.

The Māti exorciser of the wife's side and that of the husband's side, each holding in his hand a peacock's feather and a winnowing fan filled with ashes, dance a

76. Compare the different kinds of marriage among the Birhōṛs (*The Birhōṛs*, pp. 144 ff), among the Santāls (*District Gazetteer of the Santāl Parganās*, pp. 134 ff), and among the Hill Bhūiyās (*The Hill Bhūiyās of Orissa*, pp. 149 ff.)

weird dance, different from the usual tribal dances. They go on dancing by turns round the pregnant woman and also round her husband, and finally throw the ashes over them. Each *māti* also fastens round his own waist a cord made of straw from which are suspended a worn-out broom, a piece of half-burnt wood, a broken winnowing pan, an old straw pad used in carrying jars on the head, and various sorts of other refuse. They dance the whole night through, swinging their heads as in a trance. Others may join the dance. The dancers tear off by bits the *pūtri* roots from the wreaths round the necks of the couple. The *mātis* and others now and then throw ashes in handfuls over the couple, and some one or other present fans them with a broom and peacocks' feathers, so as to fan away and expel the *Dārhā* spirit from their bodies. Below is given a specimen of the incantations the magicians sing :—

"Hāe Giṛing Lerāng ! Hāe Pōnōmōsōr !
Bārōnā beṭā, Bārōnā beṭi.
Hāthī-pātā keḍnom; ṭh'ūnṭhi jōnō nūnūnōm;
Gāmnā-bhērē gāmōm; tũinā-bhēṛē tũiỹōm.
Bārōnā-beṭā, bārōna beṭi,
Āmgā Dōrhō-ḍāe, āmgā Simbhō-ḍāe" .

[Translation]

"Oh Sun-Moon (God) ! Oh Pōnōmōsōr (God) !
May [this woman get] twelve sons and twelve daughters.
Like elephant's tails [are her] waist-belts ; like worn-out brooms [are her full] breasts.
You (the woman and her husband) spoke to each other like man and wife ;

Like man and wife did you behave.
May you have twelve sons and daughters.
O Thou Simbhu-Ḍāe! O Thou Dōrhō-Ḍāe!
[Do ye spare her further trouble!]"

Incantations, like this, are chanted *ad infinitum.* This process of exorcism goes on till day-break. In the morning, the *Mātis* take off from the necks of the couple any remnants that may be left of the *pūtri* garlands.

Then they take a white hen, a black cock, a red cock, and a spotted cock, and some sun-dried (*āruā*) rice and go towards the village-spring or pool or tank. On their way they slay the fowls with a *balūā*-axe and pour a little of their blood over five small heaps of *āruā* rice arranged in a row on a spot selected by the road-side.

The entrails of the fowls are taken out on a *sūp* or winnowing-basket; and these together with the *pūtri* roots and other remnants of the two garlands, and the bride's comb and hair-strings, *etc*, are put down on the road leading to the village-spring, pool or tank, and are covered over with the winnowing-fan; and over all is placed a stone. The meat of the sacrificed fowls is eaten and rice-beer drunk by the *mātis* near this spot.

Then the party return to the woman's father's house, which has, in the meanwhile, been swept and cleaned with cow-dung and water. Here relatives and friends are given rice-beer to drink and are provided with a feast. The night is spent in dancing and singing. The couple remain in the bride's father's village that night, and take leave the following morning.

IV. Divorce (Sauṛaidōm Melaynā).

Among the Khāṛiās both the husband and the wife

may, on certain grounds, obtain divorce. The following are the principal recognised grounds for divorce :—

(1) Sexual unchastity of either partner, after marriage.

(2) Sterility of the wife.

(3) Confirmed laziness of the wife and her neglect of her household duties.

(4) Refusal of the wife to live in her husband's house.

(5) Thievish propensities of the wife.

(6) The adjudication by the village Pañch that the wife is a witch.

The village Pañchāyat is the recognised tribunal to adjudicate on the validity of the claim for divorce. After due deliberation they give their verdict, and, if the alleged grounds are proved and deemed adequate, the marriage is formally dissolved.

If divorce is granted on the ground of the wife's adultery, the wife's people are required to return the bride-price.

Conclusion.—From the rough account of Khāṛiā marriage-customs given above—both the simpler rites of the Hill Khāṛiā section and the more elaborate rites of the comparatively more advanced Dūdh and Ḍhelki sections,—it will be seen that Khāṛiā marriage, like marriage among peoples of a higher culture, besides serving the common biological function of the propagation of the species and adding to the strength of the tribe, and the economic function of securing, on payment of compensation, a domestic helper for the bridegroom's family, constitutes the basis of the natural grouping of the family. The family and higher forms of social organisation, composed of an aggregation of families, are the nurseries of parental, filial and brotherly love and other social affections. At every stage of his marriage negotiations and ceremonies we get glimpses of the social virtues of the Khāṛiā,—the exuberance of his heart on meeting relatives or in contracting new relationships, his expansive and hearty hospitality to relatives and tribe-fellows, his respect for elders and his sense of self-respect, and—running through all,—his sense of humour and his geniality and warmth of heart. In the marriage customs of all the three sections of the Khāṛiās, we further meet with rites such as the joining of the couple's hands, tying together of their garments, and their eating and drinking out of the same vessel,—all symbolising union not only of the body but also of souls between husband and wife. Such rites as the first cooking of food by the bride in new vessels, and both bride and bridegroom first offering this food to the groom's ancestor-spirits and then serving food to his clan-fellows and other invited tribe-fellows, symbolise not only the mystic spiritual union of the couple but also the communion of the bride with the husband's clan and community and her incorporation into it. The curry-stone on which the Khāṛiā bride has to stand with her face to the Sun (the symbol of the All-Seeing God) is symbolic of a vow to remain steadfast in her attachment and faithful to her husband and her clan; the yoke (symbolising agriculture) and thatching-grass (symbolising the house) placed in contact with the curry-stone while the bride stands upon it symbolise the bride's vow to prove a worthy help-meet to her husband and the couple's vow to be loyal to their mutual obligations.

Indeed, although barring the inconsiderable number of cases of love-marriages, premarital romance among the Khāṛiās does not always end in actual marriage, and the average Khāṛiā youth dutifully submits to social regulations and restrictions, and marries only socially eligible girls selected by their parents,—the married life of the Khāṛiā is, in general, fairly happy, though uneventful; and connubial infidelity is rare.

The change of social status of the wedded couple is, as we have seen, symbolised by their putting on pith crowns at marriage and wearing new clothes, and abstaining, since after marriage, from taking cooked food and drink at the hands of other castes and tribes.

Ceremonial bathing and anointing of the body with turmeric paste and drinking of sacrificial blood are among the means adopted to cleanse the couple from past 'sins', and to neutralise the mutual dangers apprehended from sexual contact. Magical methods, also, as we have seen, have their place in the ceremonies. To ward off external evil influences such as those of the evil-eye of malicious persons and the evil attentions of mischievous spirits, swords and axes are brandished round the screens within which the wedding is solemnised. Lamps are lighted during the ceremonies even in the day-time obviously with a view to repel and banish evil influences and to attract the good influences of fire and light. The beneficent 'luck'-conferring virtue or "*mana*" of such objects as mango-leaves induces fertility; paddy and water-filled pitchers (*Kā̃rsā-bhāndā* or *managal-ghat*) symbolise plenty and prosperity; and particularly the ministrations, at certain rites, of women living in wedded bliss, are utilised to secure good luck and "*mana*" for the couple. Above all, Religion plays the most important role: By sacrifices and prayers to the gods and the ancestor-spirits, the wedding is sacralised, and divine blessings and help secured for the couple in the new life into which they have just entered. In all this, Khāṛiā marriage customs hardly differ in pattern and essence (though differences occur in details) from certain more refined marriage customs of their civilised Hindu neighbours and, in fact, from those of many other old civilised societies.

It is particularly in the folk-ritual of a Hindu marriage that we find analogues of some of the salient marriage-rites of the present-day Khāṛiās. The participation, in certain rites, of married women whose husbands are alive; the ceremonial use of cetain 'luck'-bringing articles; the ceremonial circumambulation round the sacred *Māṛoā* (corresponding to the circumambulation of the Hindu couple round the sacred *Hōma*-fire); the knotting together of the ends of the couple's clothes and joining their hands to symbolise union; and bride and bridegroom concealing by turns a tiny jug (ring, in the case of the Hindu couple) for the other to find out and the party failing to discover it acknowledging defeat,—a magical rite to divine which of the two may have mastery over the other;—these and certain other customs have their analogues among folk-rites practised by Hindu females in Bengal and elsewhere. Of course, the similarities may not in all cases indicate borrowing. Nor does the Khāṛiā consciously formulate to himself the inner significance of these rites enjoined by tribal custom.

CHAPTER X.

Death and its Attendant Ceremonies.

The Khāṛiā's Conception of Death and After-life.—Khāṛiās of all sections, like most other communities of the lower culture, generally attribute death and disease not to natural causes but either to the displeasure or malignancy of supernatural beings or to witchcraft.

Ideas of the Soul and After-life.

In the Khāṛiā language, the soul or spirit is called *Jiōm*; and when a person dies the Dūdh Khāṛiā says, "*Jiōm Chōlki*", i. e., "the spirit is gone". The Khāṛiā has no conception of a heaven or hell. He believes that spirits of the dead live underground where they are united to their fathers and live in the same way as men do on earth. He makes no distinction between the souls of good men and bad men, except that it is believed that persons killed by tigers or snakes or by fall from a tree are debarred from joining the company of their deceased relatives and friends, and so, too, are Khāṛiās of either sex who have had sexual commerce with persons of other castes and tribes. A person who died in debt is believed to be reborn as a dog in the house of his creditor; but a good man dying in debt is reborn as a cow or a bullock in the house of his creditor. When a child is born to a Khāṛiā within a year of the death of a former child, the new-born child is believed to be the dead child reborn. Wicked people, it is said, are reborn as insects, dogs and pigs. Good people, if not reborn as human beings, are said to be reborn as cows.

The soul of a child whose ears have not been bored in life cannot, at death, go to the abode of its deceased ancestors. This is why such a child is buried outside the village burial ground which is called *marā ghāṭṭō* by the Ḍhelkis and *marghā'ṭi* by the Dūdh Khāṛiā.

When a pregnant woman dies, her womb is opened and the unborn child is taken out and given a special burial outside the village. This is because a pregnant woman after death is believed to become a ghost called "Churil" or "Chūngūṛi", and cannot go to the abode of either her own or her husband's deceased ancestors. Similarly, corpses of Dūdhs and Ḍhelkis dying of cholera or small-pox are thrown away and not even buried, and they cannot go to the abode of their deceased ancestors.

Married women at death go to the abode of the deceased ancestors of their respective husbands. The Khāṛiās believe that all the deceased ancestors of the Khāṛiās of whatever clan go to the same place, except those of the unhallowed dead mentioned above.

The Shades.

Besides the *jiōm* or the immaterial soul, every man or woman is believed to have a *lōngōe* or *chhāīn̄*, (literally, 'shade') which keeps company with the soul during the person's life-time. When the man dies, it is the *lōngōe* or shade which is ceremonially called back and accommodated in the cooking room, whereas the *jiōm* or spirit is ultimately joined to the fathers. The *soul* is in time re-incarnated and re-born, but the *shade* of a dead Khāṛiā, ceremonially conducted back to the house and accommodated and propitiated there, remains in the house watching over the inmates and protecting them from harm so long as libations and sacrifices or offerings to them are not neglected. But the shades of persons dying an unhallowed death and therefore not accommodated in the house, wander about hankering for nutriment, and are known by the generic name of *Ḍāñṛ Masān*.

Treatment of the Corpse.—No devices appear to be employed to prevent the escape of the soul from the body, nor is the dying person removed from the house or from his bed, nor are doors and windows opened to make the passage of the departed soul easy. As with tribes on the same or even a somewhat higher level of culture, wailing and lamentations at a death, though orginating in natural love and affection, appear to have assumed something of a ritual character. But the Khā-ṛiā has no idea, at any rate at the present day, of scaring away foreign spirits, or placating the spirit of the departed, or effecting any other definite object by wailings and death-dirges. No section of the Khāṛiās pay any attention to the toilet of the corpse.

The main object of the Khāṛiā's funeral rites appears to be to rid the survivors of the death-pollution and of the evil attentions of the spirit of the deceased which is believed to haunt them until it is united to the company of the ancestor-spirits. Khāṛiās of all sections believe that by death a person leaves the body and, unless the person has died an evil death, goes to the abode of his deceased ancestors. A child whose ears have not been bored in life cannot, at death, go to the abode of its deceased ancestors. Nor is a woman dying in pregnancy or childbirth admitted there. This is why corpses of such persons are buried outside the village burial-ground and the ordinary rites of burial are denied to them. When a pregnant woman dies, her husband rubs her face with oil and turmeric. She is then given a special burial outside the village burial-place (*Rāṅābrāb*). For the dead body of such a woman and also of a woman dying in childbirth, the ordinary ceremonies of a Khāṛiā burial are omitted and special rites are performed by the *Deoñṛā* or *Māti* (spirit-doctor) to prevent the malignant spirit of the unholy dead from haunting its old home or harming the survivors. Such a corpse is carried beyond the boundary of the village and, if there be any river or stream within easy distance, across such river or stream or, at any rate, beyond a long stretch of low-lying paddy-fields. There, in the case of a dead pregnant woman, the womb is ripped open and the fœtus taken out and buried separately from the mother. These rites will be described in a subsequent section.

As may be expected, the funeral ceremonies of the Hill Khāṛiā section is much simpler than those of the other sections of the tribe.

Hill Khāṛiā Funeral Customs.

Disposal of the Dead:—The dead of the average Hill Khāṛiā generally receive an earth-burial. Only a few families who are either more or less Hinduised, or are better off than their average tribe-fellows, practise cremation. But the corpses of Hill Khāṛiās dying of such malignant diseases as leprosy, small-pox and cholera are burnt, and so, too, those of persons dying of snake-bite, fall from a tree or hill, or other forms of violent death. A Hill Khāṛiā dying of leprosy is generally burnt by setting fire to the *kūmbā* or hut of leaf or straw in which a leper is generally segregated. A Khāṛiā corpse is carried to the grave or cremation ground, as the case may be, on a pier made of branches of trees. In the Mayurbhañj State, the more well-to-do Hill Khāṛiās of the Kusumbandhi area, if they can afford it, carry the corpse on a string-bed with the corpse's head to the north; but those of the Gūrgūṛia area in the same State generally use a bier made of tree-branches, and the head of the corpse may point to any direction. Arrived at the boundary of the village, the bier is placed on the ground, and all rest for a while. At this spot, for the next nine days or until the final funeral ceremony, the eldest son or, in the case of a sonless man, the deceased's widow puts down a little husked rice and a little fried rice (*khai*) and a tooth-brush and water in a leaf cup, every day at sunrise and sun-set. In the case of a burial, the Hill Khāṛiās of the Kusumbandhi area put down the corpse side-ways in the grave with the head to the north and face to the east; but those of the Guṛgūṛiā area bury the corpse with face turned either upwards or sideways and with the head in any direction. All the clothes of the deceased, both those that the deceased had on at death and those not worn, are buried or burnt, as the case may be, along with the corpse.

The eldest son first throws a clod of earth into the grave; then the pall-bearers do so; and then others. When the grave is filled with earth, stones and twigs are spread over it by all to prevent the ravages of wild animals. In a case of cremation, the corpse is laid on a pile of fire-wood, with its head to the north. The eldest son of the deceased with his head turned in a direction away from the corpse and with his hands to his back throws fire towards the mouth of the corpse. An old winnowing basket and an old empty earthen-ware jar are taken by the Kusumbandhi Khāṛiās to the cremation-ground or grave-yard. In cases of cremation, water is brought in the jar to put out the funeral fire.

Purification.—When the burial or cremation is finished, all who attend it purify themselves by a bath and go to the house of the deceased with their wet clothes on. There they sit down for a while, and inhale the smoke of frankincense burnt in a new earthen-ware plate. Among the Kusumbandhi Khāṛiās the sons of the deceased, and other members of the family observe a fast that day; but among the Gūrgūriā Khāṛiās, the sons and other members of the family eat what is called "*Pitā-bhāt*" or bitter rice consisting of leaves of the margosa or *Nim* (*Melia Azadirachta*) tree boiled together with rice by a male relative in a new earthenware pot. Among the Kusumbandhi Khāṛiās, "Pitā-bhāt" is eaten on the following day by the members of the deceased's family who must all observe death-pollution.

Removal of the Death-pollution and Death-taboos.—For the adult dead, death-pollution and consequent taboos on surviving relatives last for ten days as among the Brāhmaṇs. The purification and funeral feast in the case of the death of young people may be held on the fifth or sixth day after death. Members of the deceased's family may not, during the period of pollution, rub oil on their bodies nor eat fish or flesh, nor shave, nor pare their nails. On the tenth day, all the members of the family, male as well as female, get themselves shaved, their hair clipped and their nails pared by a fellow-tribesman not of the deceased's family. And all anoint themselves with oil and turmeric and take a bath. The pall-bearers, even if not belonging to the family, also get themselves shaved and their hair clipped and nails pared. They too anoint themselves with oil and turmeric, and purify themselves with a bath.

After a purificatory bath, the eldest son of the deceased, who has remained fasting since morning, puts on new clothes. A funeral feast is provided to relatives and tribe-fellows. This communal meal is known as "*Shūdhā-bhāt*" or "purifying-meal". Some male members of the family sit down to dinner with the guests. After a hearty meal, all give lusty shouts of "Hari-bōl" in the manner of all neighbouring Hindu castes. The eldest son of the deceased cooks his own food by boiling rice and pulses (*ḍāl*) and a little sugar or molasses (but no salt) together, in a new earthen-ware vessel. When this "Khichṛī", as it is called, is ready, he tells his relatives,—"Go and bring my father [to take his meal]". Three relatives go to the boundary-line of the village where the bier on its way to the grave first halted. There they call out the deceased by name and shout,- "Do thou come home. Thy obsequies are finished. Curds, vegetable-curry and rice have been prepared. Come and help yourself." ("*Tumi ghar āsha; tōmar kāj karma haila. Dahi tūn bhāt haichhē, khai jā*"). The three men return and report,—"Your father has come". Then the son offers part of the *khichṛī* in the names of such of his deceased ancestors as he can name. He then throws away the offerings into water and sits down to eat himself.

Thus are the members of a deceased Hill Khāṛiā family reunited with the community of their living tribe-fellows as also with their dead relatives. And their sense of a common life is thus renewed and reinforced.

(II) Death-customs of the Dūdh and Ḍhelki Khāṛiās.

Cremation is now falling into disuse. It is expensive, not so much because wood for burning is not as cheap or easily available now as before, but because for a cremation two feasts have to be provided to tribe-fellows,—one at the deceased's village another at the Bhūiṅhāri or ancestral village of the deceased where the bones have to be ceremonially carried for interment in the clan ossuary. Formerly menhirs or upright slabs of stone used to be erected by the side of the graves of old and important persons, besides flat stone-slabs or dolmens in the cases of all. But now this practice, too, has fallen into disuse among the Khāṛiās on account of the labour and expense involved.

(1) At Death-bed.

When a person is on death-bed, a *deoṅṛā* (spirit-doctor) is generally called in. The *deoṅṛā* is given a handful of *āruā* rice and a little oil in a small earthen lamp. A wick is placed on the lamp and is lighted. He takes up in his right hand a winnowing-basket (*sāmu*) with some *āruā* rice on it. He goes on chanting incantations to the spirits. Sometimes the sick man gets cured and the *ḍeoṅṛā* or *māti* gets the credit. But in most cases death ensues.

(2) The Funeral.

When a person dies, the relatives are informed. The relatives and other Khāṛiās of the village or settlement come to the deceased's house to make arrangements for the burial or cremation, as the case may be. Four men are told off to carry the corpse.

The Khāṛiā does not bathe a corpse nor dress it in new clothes, but takes it out with the mat or cloth in which it lay at death, and carries it on a wooden bier (*ṭhaṭra*) to the *marghā'ṭi* or burning place. If available, a new cloth may be used in covering up the corpse. A *deoñṛā* (spirit-doctor) and a number of men, but (except among the Dūdh Khāṛiās) no women, accompany the corpse. Among Dūdh Khāṛiās men fetch to the cremation-ground water to pour over the embers after cremation.

In the case of a cremation, the bones of the deceased are collected and placed in a small eathen pot (*chūkā*) which is, in most cases, hung up on some tree and, later, either carried to the Bhūiñhāri or ancestral village of the deceased to be deposited in the clan ossuary there, or thrown into a stream or pool. Thus is the union of the soul of the deceased with those of his predeceased ancestors and relatives finally effected.

Every Khāṛiā village (though not always among the Hill Khāṛiās) has its own graveyard. Where there is a river or stream within easy distance, the graveyard is invariably situated by its side. Generally it is under the shade of a few large trees such as *sāl* (*Shorea robusta*), *murun* (*Bassia latifolia*), or mango. Like the Mūṇḍās, a few Khāṛiās also, if means allow, take the corpses of their dead for burial in the grave-yard of their ancestral village, when it is not too far off.

One or two of the relatives of the deceased carry

a winnowing basket containing some paddy and, among the Dūdh Khāṛiās, also some *māso* or *urid* (*Phaseolus Roxburghii*), a small earthen pot containing oil, and some unbleached cotton. Another man carries an empty pitcher. The corpse-bearers on their way to the *Marghā'ṭi* halt for a while at every trijunction, where the man with the winnowing basket drops some cotton and a few paddy grains and *māso* grains, if any. This is done till they reach the grave. If the *Marghā'ṭī* is at a distance, and the procession has to halt on the way, these are dropped on the ground at every halting-place. If the corpse is carried on a *khāṭiā* (stringed bed with four legs), these are dropped at the spot on which each leg of the *khāṭiā* rests.

As soon as the corpse is taken out of the deceased's house, a man closes the door of the room. He puts down some ashes in a winnowing-fan upon the floor, and remains inside the room. Ashes are also strewn on the spot where the corpse was first laid on the floor.

By the time the corpse reaches the *Marghā'ṭi*, a pit is dug, lengthwise from north to south. The pit is about six feet in length, three feet in breadth and three feet in depth. The pall-bearers take the corpse five times round the pit, keeping the pit to their left. The corpse is then laid to the east of the pit, the head of the corpse pointing north. They then lower the corpse, and two robust men swing it across the pit seven times so as to touch the earth heaped up on the two sides of the pit. Then if there are any ornaments on the person of the deceased they are taken off the corpse by some relatives. Then the son or brother in the case of a man, or the husband or son in the case of a woman, or the father in the case of a child, anoints oil mixed with powdered turmeric on the face of the corpse and washes it with water. And he and others lament saying,—"Alas! We shall see thy face no more!"

Then the bed-sheet or other cloth on which the deceased lay at death is spread inside the grave-pit, and the corpse is laid down in the grave with its head to north and face to the east. Before the earth is thrown into the grave, a bit (three fingers' span long) of the deceased's cloth is torn off and kept for ceremonial use. The *Deoñṛā* hands over a lighted bundle of thatching grass (*ōlōng*) to the man who anointed the corpse. This man stands at the head of the grave with his back turned towards the grave, and drops the lighted *ōlōng* into the grave. He next throws five handfuls of earth into the grave. Then every one else present throws earth into the grave. Ornaments or other things to which the deceased was particularly attached during life, along with an earthen pot, are thrown into the grave, which is then closed up.

Before earth is thrown into the grave-pit, a long reed of the species known in the country as '*mandra*' grass is planted by the Dūdh Khāṛiās at the head of the corpse. As the pit is being filled in, the reed is gradually pulled up so as to leave a very narrow hole on the grave. Instead of a grass reed the Ḍhelki Khāṛiās employ a long native tooth-stick called *anārgi*. This is intended to leave the way to the other world open for the soul of the deceased. Some Khāṛiās say that this is done to allow free egress and ingress to the soul. Some say that this opening is left for the soul to visit the body when it likes. In case a wide hole or opening appears on the surface of the grave, some Khāṛiās take it to be a sign that the soul has left the grave for good to join the ancestor-spirits in the other world. But all are not definite as to where this other world is—whether it is under-ground or up in the sky or in the *āding*. The more well-informed Khāṛiā, however, makes a clear distinction between the two souls,–one conducted to the *āding* and the other joining the ancestors in the nether regions.

When the grave has been filled in, one of the village-elders (*Siāns*) among the Ḍhelki, and a female relative among the Dūdhs, fetch water in an earthen pitcher and places the jar of water and a small earthen-ware pot of oil and a tooth-pick (*ānārgi* or *dāñtan*) at the head of the grave. Before putting down the water-pot and the oil-pot, a perforation is made at the bottom of each so that their contents may trickle down. Finally, the grave is covered up with blocks of stones or, where these are not available, with twigs and branches of trees, in order to prevent wild animals from digging out or damaging it.

Before leaving the burial ground, one of the elders (*Siāns*) strikes at a tree close by with a stick. While striking at the tree the man addresses the tree, saying,—"So long he or she (the deceased) was ours; now we make him or her over to you. Do thou look after him or her". The funeral party proceeds to a tank or stream to bathe, and thence to the deceased's house. There a female member of the family hands over to a male member of the family, preferably a young bachelor, a small cup containing a little powdered turmeric diluted in water. The young man drinks a portion of the mixture himself and distributes a little to each one present. Then the female members of the family go to some tank or stream and bathe themselves, and, on return home, each drinks a little mixture of turmeric and water by way of ceremonial lustration.

(3) The First Purification (Jibsōng [*Dūdh*], Jipsōng [*Ḍhelki.*])

The *Jibsōng* has to be performed in all cases of death except in the cases of persons dying of cholera or small-pox and women dying in child-birth or during pregnancy.

This ceremony is intended to remove, from the deceased's family, the taboo on the use of fish. It may be performed either immediately after the burial or one or two days later, or on the day of the *Kāmu Bainā* or *Tiljāng* ceremony which takes place eight to ten days after the death. The orthodox *Jibsōng* ceremony is as follows:—All the members of the family and relatives, including those who carried the corpse, go to a stream or tank and take their bath. One of the *Siāns* takes with him a little oil from the oil-pot left by the side of the grave. At the stream or pond, one of the elders catches a crab or fish or both and takes them to the deceased's house along with the bit of cloth, torn off the deceased's wearing cloth at the time of burial, which is now soaked in water. All go to the deceased's house with these. The crab and fish are powdered and mixed with water, cow-dung, and either a little *Birni* (*Andropogon muricatus*) root or some tender grass shoots. Two tiny pits in the shape of miniature tanks are dug in the courtyard of the deceased's house and filled with water. The bit of rag torn off the deceased's wearing cloth is rolled up into a wick.

This wick is lighted and put in the earthen cup filled with oil from the pot left beside the grave. This is placed by the side of one of the pits, and the leaf-cup containing the mixture of pounded crab, fish, cow-dung, *etc.*, is also placed by the side of this lighted earthen cup. Then this sanctified mixture is sprinkled on all present. The *Siān*, who officiated at the burial, stands in front of the lighted earthen-ware lamp, crosses his arms first over his chest and then over his back and on his legs close to the heels, and then anoints his arm with the turmeric and oil in the leaf-cup. After this, he washes his hands in the other pit and warms them over the lighted lamp and again washes his hands and moves away. Then, one by one, all present come up to the light, takes up a pinch of the mixture, crosses his arms over his chest, and warms and then washes his hands as the *Siāñ* has done. When all have washed their hands, a hen's egg is put into the pit in which the hands have been washed, and a *pipar* (*Ficus religiosa*) twig is planted above it in the pit so as to crush the egg. If the twig takes root, it is left to grow.

Then all drink turmeric-water; and all are freed from the death-pollution except the deceased's sons and other near relatives belonging to the same clan. In most Dūdh Khāṛiā families, the *Jibsōṅg* ceremony is now-a-days gone through in a simplified form immediately after the burial or cremation. It is as follows:—The funeral party while taking their purificatory bath in a tank or stream catch a fish or crab or both. Fish is regarded as a 'purifier'. These are taken in a leafcup or on an earthen plate, filled with water. With these and with the bit of cloth torn, as described above, from the deceased's garment and soaked in water, they return to the house of the deceased, and, on their arrival there, sprinkle the fish-water and some turmeric-water all over the house to remove death pollution. Water squeezed out of this bit of cloth is also sprinkled on the floor of the house where ashes had been strewn. This water is called "*Jiu pāni*" (*lit*, "water of life", but meaning, water for the departed soul), and is supposed to be offered to the departed spirit to drink. Two pits are dug in the courtyard (*kinbhār* or *āngan*) of the house, and, one by one, all who took part in the funeral take up each a bit of cow-dung and touch their own feet, knees, chest and forehead with it, and wash their hands in the other pit. Then they anoint oil mixed with turmeric, on their chest, forehead and shoulder-joints. Then a fowl's egg is placed in the pit in which the men washed their hands, and the *Pipar* or *Irjōḍ* twig is stuck through the egg, breaking it. The twig is planted there and left to take root and grow, if it will.

They then all enter the room in which the death took place and look for any marks, resembling foot-prints of man or animal or reptile, on the ashes strewn on the floor. If any such marks are found, the deceased is believed to have come by his death through witch-craft, but if straight lines are found on the ashes, the death is believed to have been a natural one. Water pressed out of the wet clothes is dropped on the ashes. All the old earthen cooking-pots in the house are thrown away.

(VI.) Rice-offering to the Dead (*Pejo-ȳōnā or Pe-obȳonā*).

This is performed in all cases where the Jibsōng has been or has yet to be performed. The Khāṛiās believe that until the **Tiljāng** or the final purification ceremony, the deceased's spirit haunts his or her house, the grave-yard and the village. So it is necessary that the deceased should till then be given his or her usual share of the daily meals. Otherwise the deceased would do harm to the family. So until the Tiljāng ceremony, the family of the deceased offer food twice every day to their dead relative. A part of the food cooked for their own mid-day and evening meals is first set apart and deposited in leaf-cups at about hundred yards from the house, on the path leading to the grave. The mid-day meal also includes a cup of water with an *ānārgi* (a country tooth-brush) made by splitting up one end of a small thin twig about six inches long.

The death pollution in the case of the whole family lasts for nine days during which dance and music are forbidden and the family members may not eat meat but may take fish.

(v) Calling Back the Shade (Longoe Sim, or Longoe ḍibhārnā).

This ceremony is performed either on the night following the burial, or a little later, but in any case before the *Tiljāng* ceremony.

On the night of the *Lōngoe-Sim* ceremony the female members and the children of the family leave the house after spreading ashes or rice-flour on the floor of the room which is assigned for the abode of the spirits of the deceased's ancestors and of other deceased members of the family. The adult male members of the family together with the few relatives or tribe-fellows who have been invited for the occasion take part in the ceremony of calling back the shade of the deceased.

Two of the relatives are left in the house, and the others proceed in the direction of the burial-ground, carrying with them four branches either of the *Lambḍūm* or *Pipar* (*Ficus Religiosa*) or of the *Keoñd* (*Diospyros Melonoxylon*) tree besides a leaf-plate, an egg, and a new earthenware pitcher or cooking vessel and an earthen-ware lamp. Among some Dūdh Khāṛiās, an elderly female member of the family accompanies the party. In such a case she carries the empty earthen vessel covered up at the mouth with a leaf-plate over which is placed the lighted earthen-ware lamp. The party stops about a hundred yards from the deceased's house, and there the shade is called out by name. There the earthen vessel is placed over a tripod of *Keoñd* or of *Pipar* twigs. Then an elderly relative (Kūṭūmb) calls the spirit of the deceased by crying aloud,-"O ! Thou so-and-so (names the deceased),-come back to thy home quickly. It is going to rain: Where art thou? Art thou resting on some tree or in a ditch or in an ant-hill?" This invitation is repeated until the flame of the lamp inclines in the direction of the deceased's house. As soon as this is noticed the woman throws the hem of her cloth forward and folding it on her breast turns towards the house and one of the men breaks the pot and the egg. Then all come back home in procession. At the head of this party a man comes beating one sickle against another. He is followed first by the man who broke the earthen vessel and the egg, next by the woman, and next by the corpse-bearers, and last of all by the others. The whole party return in silence to the house of the deceased.

On approaching the deceased's house the man who heads the party notifies their arrival by kicking at the door of the house and shouting :—"Who is inside the room? Are you a *Rākshas* or what?" The man inside the room replies. "It is myself". Then the man who broke the egg kicks at the door of the room which is now opened. A lamp is lighted and everybody looks for any mark of foot-prints of either a man or a beast or a bird or a reptile on the ashes. As soon as they notice anything resembling a foot-mark they conclude that the shade of the deceased has returned to the house. Then the ashes are scraped up and thrown away into a tank or a stream.

Should they fail to find any trace of such foot-prints they do not, as the Mūṇḍās do, repeat the ceremony over and over again. They content themselves with merely observing that the spirit has strayed to some place or other but will find its way back to its old home some day.

If the *Tiljāng* ceremony is performed on the same day, then the guests are given only rice-beer to drink. This is not prepared in the deceased's house, because the death-pollution of the family has not yet been removed.

(VI) The Final Purification Ceremony (Tiljang).

Generally nine days after death, the *Tiljāng* ceremony is performed. But in some cases, for some reason or other, the date of this final purification is postponed to some date from fifteen to thirty days after death. In the early morning, the house and court-yard are cleansed with cow-dung diluted in water. Used earthenware cooking-pots are thrown away, but metal or stone utensils are only cleansed. Then all the family members wash their clothes. In cases where the *Longōe-Sim* ceremony has not yet been performed, that ceremony is first gone through. Then the *Deoñṛā* with the members of the family and invited guests go to an ant-hill towards the eastern end of the village. He takes with him his magic winnowing basket, some *āruā* rice and his magic lamp. Some of his assistants carry fowls and an axe. On arriving near the ant-hill, but a little way off it, the members of the family shave one another or clip one another's hair short. In the meanwhile, the *Deoñṛā* with his assistants proceed to break up the ant-hill, while the relatives of the deceased are engaged in shaving. The *Deoñṛā* sits down before the broken ant-hill facing east and begins to rub his left hand over the rice placed upon his magic winnowing-basket in accompaniment to the rapid chanting of spells in a sing-song tone. He places five small heaps of rice before the broken ant-hill. Then holding a white cock in his hand makes it peck at the first heap of rice; and while the cock is thus engaged, he cuts off its head with an axe as a sacrifice to Dharam and addresses Him in some such words as the following :—

"*Dharam Rājā! Chāñd-Sūruj! Ugat hāi būṛat hāi. Saik Rājā! Dharam Rājā! Dekhbē hō Pōnōmōsōr!*" "O King Dharam! Thou Sun-Moon! Thou risest, Thou settest (i. e., Thou seest all that we do from sunrise to sunset). O Supreme King! King Dharam! Do Thou look [after us], O Pōnōmōsōr!"

Then the *Deoñṛā* [77] puts down the severed head of the sacrificed cock on the rice-heap from which the cock was made to eat and throws the cock's trunk aside. Then a

77 It is to be noted that these *Mātis*, or *Deoñṛās* or sorcerers generally or almost invaribly use some Āryan language (Hindi or Bengali

red fowl (cock, if the deceased was a male, and hen, if female) is similarly sacrificed to the spirit of the deceased. Its blood is taken in a leaf-cup and poured into the ant-hill, while the *Deoñrā* prays:—

"*Ho* (names)! *Tōkē dethi. Pelā pāṭi nā karbē.*"

"Thou so-and-so (names the deceased), here is offering for thee. Do not trouble the family"

Then a third fowl is sacrificed to the spirit of the companions of the deceased in the other world.

Then a fourth cock—a spotted one—is similarly sacrificed to the Deoñṛā's familiar spirit who is implored to prevent the spirit of the deceased and other spirits from causing trouble to the family.

Last of all, a black cock is sacrificed to the *Khūñṭ-Bhūts*, who are the leaders of the minor spirits of the village. The *Deoñṛā* now leaves the lighted lamp and moves a little apart. The assembled relatives come up one by one to the opened out ant-hill. Each one takes up a little rice from the magic basket of the *Deoñṛā* and puts it into the hollow of the broken ant-hill, warms his hands over the flame of the lamp and washes them over the hole. Finally the *Deoñṛā* does the same, collects the rice-grains left over in the five small heaps, together with the sacrificed blood on the ground and puts them all into the hollow of the ant-hill, which is then covered up with stone. Some of the blood of the second fowl is kept in a leaf-cup, and rice-beer is now poured over the broken ant-hill. Then the *Deoñṛā* places his left heel on the stone and mutters some incantation three times.

Then all go to the tank or stream to take their bath. after which thev assemble at the court-vard of the deceased's house. The *Deoñṛā* cooks the heads of the sacrificed fowls and eat them alone or shares them with a few village-elders.

Before taking his dinner, the *Deoñṛā* takes some rice-beer in a leaf-cup, goes into the room where the death took place and pours the rice-beer on the floor in the name of the deceased, addressing the spirit as follows:—"Do thou, so-and-so (names the deceased), stay in the house from to-day, and partake of the offerings that will be made to thee. Do not leave the house."

Then the *Deoñṛā* distributes the cooked meat of the sacrificed fowls to each member of the deceased's family who all sit down in a row in the court-yard. The *Deoñṛā*, as the spokesman of the community, addresses them as follows: "We Kūṭūmbs give you this sacrificed meat; you may from this day eat flesh again". The rice-beer and cooked meat of the sacrificed fowls are served to all present. Then a he-goat, if available, is killed and the funeral feast takes place. After dinner all depart and the death-pollution is removed.

(VII). Funeral Rites for Women dying in Child-bed or in Pregnancy.

As stated before, a special funeral ceremony is observed in the case of a woman dying during pregnancy or in child-birth, for the soul of such a woman is believed to turn into an evil spirit known as *Churil* or *Chũngũṛi* or *Chũngũni*.. The degree of its malignant power as a spirit is believed to be foreshadowed by the trouble she gave to her people in her last days in life, the degree of deformity and fearfulness that her features assume on death and the trouble that her corpse, by the voilent contortions of its limbs on its way to the grave gives to the pall-bearers. With a view to reducing to a minimum the powers for evil of such a spirit the following measures are adopted, particularly among the Ḍhelki Khāṛiās. Before the corpse is taken out of the house, the dead woman's husband besmears its face with powdered turmeric diluted in oil. Arrived at the spot selected for the burial, the spirit-doctor (*Māti*) fashions four rings and a string out of a wild creeper known as *benḍo* (*Spatholobus, Roxburghii ?*). Muttering his *mantrams* or magic incantations, the Māti puts on the rings one on each wrist and ankle of the corpse and fastens the string round the waist of the corpse. Then, without further ceremony, the corpse is laid down in the grave, and earth piled over it. The spirit-doctor then circum-ambulates the grave three times, muttering his magic spells.

The funeral party now move a little away from the grave, and the *Māti* calls out to the deceased :—"O so-and-so (names the deceased) ! Do thou come back. They want thee back at home". They generally fancy that they hear the deceased making some such reply as the following:—"Wait ye,—I shall accompany you home. Who has tied me down?" The *Māti* forthwith returns to the grave-side and again circumambulates the grave three times, muttering *mantrams*. The rest of the party in the mean-while move a little further away. The *Māti* returns to them, and again addresses the deceased as before, asking her to return home with them. Should they fancy hearing a response again, the *Māti* again returns to the grave-side and repeats the same magic process while the rest of the party move a little further off still. This process is repeated until no response is heard or rather imagined to have been heard. Then all go to some river or stream or pool, take a purificatory bath, and return to the house of the dead woman. There they undergo further purification by drinking a little water mixed with pounded turmeric, and, in some cases, with leaves of the sacred basil plant and a bit of copper steeped in the water, and thus rid themselves of the contaminating effects of contact with the unholy dead. The ceremonies of *Jibsŏng*, *Pe-yŏnā*, *Longoe-sim* and *Tiljāng*, described above, are not gone through in the case of such a death. For a day or two after the death and burial, one or two relatives of the deceased visit the grave to see if it has been disturbed by jackals or other wild animals. If the grave is found to have been opened, or the earth over it disturbed, it is filled up or levelled again. No offerings are made nor food deposited on the grave; and, indeed, no further attention is paid to it. Generally it is arranged that the services of the spirit-doctor (*Māti*) should be easily available, if required within the next two or three days after burial, to protect the survivors from any harm that might be attempted on them by the spirit of the dead woman.

Such, in brief, are the funeral rites that Khāṛia society has, through long centuries, developed and adopted. Besides precautions and devices against the natural tendency of the departed spirit to haunt the survivors, the funeral rites of the Khāṛiās include measures designed to give rest to the departed soul and to secure the union of the departed soul with its fathers in the other world. The death rites, as we have seen, are followed by ceremonial purification of the survivors and of the house, and the termination of the death-taboos and the re-assimilation of the survivors into the tribe by a common meal with their tribe-fellows.

General View of the Khāṛiā's Socio-religious Rites.

In this and two previous chapters, we have given a rough account of the principal socio-religious rites and ceremonies that Khāṛiā society has developed in its age-long organised effort to face the important crises in an individual's life in society. An overpowering sense of absolute dependence on the power and protection of society, on the one hand, and on that of certain mysterious spiritual powers and beings behind and beyond Nature, on the other,-would appear to give us the **key-note** to most of these rites and observances. In these rites and ceremonies, as will be noticed, methods of both religion proper and of what is known as 'magic' have been utilised and intermingled. These Khāṛiā rites and ceremonies, as we have seen, include prayers and sacrifices, spells and adjurations, besides special observances and taboos, and rites of purification and of social integration. The Khāṛiā's present organised relations between the individual and society, on the one hand, and between man and the invisible powers whether in Nature or in the supersensuous world, on the other, are the product of the joint acting and slow thinking of innumerable generations of the tribe itself. But not a little has also been borrowed and assimilated from their neighbours of a somewhat higher culture. The influence of some ideas and practices of their Hindu neighbours is obvious. Such rites and practices as have been borrowed, have, however, been, in most cases, altered and, in some cases, considerably transformed to suit their own level of culture. This is how culture develops in all communities, and this is how it has developed in Khāriā Society, as well.

Two master motives or rather ruling sentiments, as we have seen, dominate the Khāṛiā's life in society, and run through and shape his social customs and socio-religious rites. These are, first, his hankering for **social solidarity** and union among his own tribe, class and community, as a bulwark against the manifold risks and dangers of individual and tribal life, particularly against the hostile influences or activities of alien communities and the anti-social activities of individuals of his own or some other community; and, secondly, the equally supreme need and yearning for security and protection against the incalculable and invisible hostile forces of Nature and of the spirit-world. The former he seeks to satisfy through suitable social organisation and customs and institutions calculated to produce a real fusion or communion of souls,—and the latter through an organised ritual of sacrifices and supplications, offerings and libations, calculated to establish communion with and win the grace of the invisible beneficent spiritual Powers. Many of his social as well as religious rites are further designed to secure, preserve and augment individual and tribal **Luck** through close contact with objects and beings, persons and situations instinct with **good mana**, and through avoidance and **taboo** of objects and beings, persons and situations believed to possess uncanny **evil mana.**